The Liguori Guide to Catholic U.S.A.

THE
Liguori Guide
TO

CATHOLIC
U·S·A

A TREASURY OF
Churches ✳ Schools
Monuments ✳ Shrines
and Monasteries

JAY COPP

Liguori
LIGUORI, MISSOURI

Published by Liguori Publications
Liguori, Missouri
http://www.liguori.org

Library of Congress Cataloging-in-Publication Data

Copp, Jay.
    The Liguori guide to Catholic U.S.A. : a treasury of churches,
schools, monuments, shrines, and monasteries / Jay Copp. —1st ed.
        p. cm.
    Includes bibliographical references and index.
    ISBN 0-7648-0371-9
    1. Catholic Church buildings—United States—Guidebooks. 2. Chris-
tian shrines—United States—Guidebooks. 3. United States—Guidebooks. I. Title. II. Title: Liguori guide to Catholic USA.
BX2320.5.U6C66   1999
282'.73—dc21   98–43555

Printed in the United States of America
03 02 01 00 99 5 4 3 2

CONTENTS

ACKNOWLEDGMENTS

Many kind people with a deep appreciation of Catholic landmarks contributed to this book. Space does not permit the listing of all, but your generosity was most gracious. Thanks especially to Adrienne Alston of the Diocese of Fresno; Ann Augherton, managing editor of the *Arlington Herald;* the Rev. Steven Avella of Marquette University; Roy Barkley of the Texas State Historical Association; Bill Bruns, communications director of the Archdiocese of Indianapolis; Bud Bunce, director of communications of the Archdiocese of Portland; Bernadeane Carr, editor of the *Southern Cross* in San Diego; the Rev. Robert Dale Cieslik, chancellor/ archivist of the Archdiocese of Louisville; the Rev. Michael Coleman of the Diocese of Kansas City-St. Joseph; James Divita, history professor at Marian College in Indianapolis; J. Norman Dizon, archives assistant of the Archdiocese of Seattle; Julie Downs, special projects manager of the Diocese of Charleston; Mary Dunn, assistant archivist of the Diocese of Alexandria; the Rev. William Barnaby Faherty, S.J., director of the Midwest Jesuit Archives in St. Louis; Roman Godzak, archivist of the Archdiocese of Detroit; Chuck Hrncir of the Diocese of Austin Historical Commission; Chris Krosel, director of archival research of the Diocese of Cleveland; Veronica Lima of the Diocese of Providence; the Rev. Thomas Merson, administrative assistant to the archbishop of San Francisco; the Rev. Robert O'Grady, assistant to the editor of the *Pilot* in Boston; Kris Beisser Olson, assistant archivist of the Diocese of Green Bay; Sister Therese Pelletier, archivist of the Diocese of Portland; Msgr. Jacques Plante of the Diocese of Providence; Jane Quinn, archivist of the Diocese of Orlando; David Schroeder, archivist of the Diocese of Covington; the Rev. Wendell Searles, vicar general of the Diocese of Burlington; the Rev. James White, historian of the Diocese of Tulsa; Ed Wilkinson, editor of the *Tablet* in Brooklyn; and Jennifer Willems of the *Catholic Voice* in Omaha, Nebraska.

DEDICATION

To Laura, Kevin and Andrew,
the wind at my back

INTRODUCTION

In the 1920s members of St. Hugh Parish near Chicago donned their work clothes and dug out with shovels from the rocky soil the foundation of an addition to the parish school. The parish was short on cash but long on loyalty. I received my first holy Communion at the church in the mid-1960s, graduated from the parish school, and formalized my relationship with God through Sunday Mass. The church is a simple structure that had a complex effect on me. First-time visitors may find the nearly bare walls and modest appointments uninspiring, but for me the church has always inspired a deeper connection with God and God's people. The piety of the priests struck me at an early age, too. Worshiping beside neighbors and friends gave me a sense of belonging. Each time I return to the church, I am sure I've come home again.

I am not an anomaly. Catholics cherish deep ties with their churches. They treasure familiar retreat houses, Marian shrines, and devotional sites. It would have been impractical, but certainly not absurd, to list in this book every U.S. church, retreat house, and so on. As it is, my goal was to include Catholic sites that carry a powerful resonance among those without a personal history attached to the site. The sites are extraordinary because of their architectural brilliance, association with a saint, or connection with a historical event. The sites are testaments to faith, brick-and-mortar representations of spiritual beliefs.

Collectively, the sites tell the story of Catholicism in the United States. Immigrant pioneers, settling in plains and cities, carried with them their faith, a precious family heirloom passed down from generation to generation. They survived the perils of the wilderness, the dangers of cities, wrenching poverty, and virulent anti-Catholicism. Today, Catholics are surviving contemporary secularistic culture. Despite all the talk about the unbelief of modernity, holy sites continue to draw deep devotion. Faith enabled Catholics to make their home in the New World, and faith remains triumphant over modern materialism.

The sites, too, are where the giants in U.S. Catholicism walked. Here are the holy haunts of Elizabeth Seton, John Neumann, and Dorothy Day. Their lives were a gift to us from God. The places they labored and prayed are God's vineyards, accessible to us. They are gone, but their stories of faith and piety amaze and inspire.

All the sites are sacred spaces, made holy by spiritual longings. Immigrants built city churches that transformed alien territory into familiar ground. The broken in spirit came to Marian shrines to find their way to peace. The weary and dismayed paused at roadside shrines to pray and rediscover God. If there are a thousand stories in the naked city, there are millions of stories connected with these holy places.

The majestic cathedrals of the Middle Ages awed ordinary Catholics, unaccustomed to wealth and splendor. Today, amid the economic and technological wonders of the twentieth century, we are not so easily impressed. Wealth and splendor is all around us. Yet, though we no longer build cathedrals on a massive scale, our holy sites continue to give us a sense of the Divine. The spirit within us responds to the Spirit, whether suggested by Notre Dame in Paris or St. Mary's down the street. God is infinitely larger and more glorious than stone and concrete. The marvelous sites held dear by Catholics reveal the more marvelous cathedrals of the heart, where God truly resides.

NORTHEAST

CONNECTICUT

Central Connecticut

Hartford

St. Joseph Cathedral (150 Farmington, 860-249-8431) is a brownstone edifice featuring 26 huge stained-glass windows. The Stations of the Cross are cut into the piers that form the side aisle. Over the three bronze entrance doors is a statue of Christ reaching out his arms to the world. The cathedral replaced an earlier church that burned in 1956.

Sts. Cyril and Methodius Church (55 Charter Oak Ave., 860-522-9157) is a neo-Gothic structure with traditional Polish iconography. Two white eagles are visible at the roof of the presbytery, signifying the Polish roots of the church. The building, dedicated in 1917, includes a chapel to the Black Madonna.

A notable church in Hartford is **St. Justin** (230 Blue Hills Ave., 860-246-6897), completed in 1931. The structure has a crossing tower, perpendicular windows, and a Romanesque basilica interior. The light and shade that engulf the altar area offer a sense of warmth and tranquillity.

Near Hartford

New Britain

Polish immigrants streamed into New Britain in the 1880s to find manufacturing jobs. The influential but sometimes autocratic

Msgr. Lucyan Bojnowski helped Poles establish themselves in America. He erected two churches. Also begun under his leadership were a school, a religious order, a cemetery, an orphanage, a home for the aged, a Polish-language weekly, two dozen parish societies, and several businesses. **Sacred Heart of Jesus Church** (163 Broad St., 860-229-0081) was dedicated in 1904. The church has gray-blue granite stone on the outside; white sand marble decorates the inside.

Discontent with Bojnowski led to the founding of **Holy Cross Church** (Farmington Ave. and Biruta St., 860-229-2011) in 1927. The church, completed in 1942, was built in Norman Gothic style in the form of a cross, with a 175-foot tower. Stained-glass windows show scenes from the life of Christ and Polish saints and patrons. In the vestibule is an icon of the Black Madonna and stained-glass windows of St. Maximilian Kolbe and Pope John Paul II.

Northern Connecticut

Enfield

Poles who came to the area as part of a scheme to break up a strike for higher wages at the Bigelow-Hartford Carxx Company began **St. Adalbert Church** (90 Alden Ave., 860-745-4837) in 1915. The brick Romanesque church has a 90-foot bell tower that begins as a square and ends at the top with an eight-sided roof.

Western Connecticut

Darien

On a road that passes a land of tennis courts and horses, plush homes and luxury cars, is the **Convent of St. Birgitta's** (Tokeneke Trail, 203-655-1068), also known as the Vikingsborg Guest House. The semicloistered Brigittine Sisters, who live in an adjoining convent, run this rustic, 12-room retreat house. The nuns observe "the great silence" from 9:00 P.M. to 8:15 A.M. Guests can enjoy the walking trails and the St. Francis Hermitage cottage, a small brick-and-stone prayer room with a window overlooking Long Island Sound.

The guest house was established in 1957 when a wealthy woman, who was a Catholic convert, donated her turn-of-the-century mansion and wooded property to the order. The house has antique furniture, a grand piano, a library with books in a half dozen languages, and sun porches with a stunning view of Long Island Sound.

New Haven

In 1881, a small group of men met in the basement of **St. Mary's Church** in New Haven (5 Hillhouse Ave., 203-562-6193) at the request of twenty-nine-year-old Fr. Michael J. McGivney. Local Catholics suffered from virulent prejudice. When the church was founded, residents objected to the "aristocratic avenue being blemished by a Roman Catholic edifice." McGivney, one of thirteen children born to Irish immigrants, wanted to counter anti-Catholics and to increase solidarity among Catholics.

The meeting was the genesis of a mutual aid society of Catholic laymen pledged to the ideals of charity, fraternity, and patriotism. The group would assist widows and orphans of deceased members through its life insurance program and boost their pride in their frequently attacked faith. Four months later, the group adopted the name "Knights of Columbus." Columbus was chosen to demonstrate pride in America's Catholic heritage and to evoke allegiance to the Church.

The Knights today are the world's largest Catholic family fraternal service group. The Knights donate millions of dollars to charity, volunteer their time to service, and demonstrate a strong allegiance to the pope. They are particularly active in the pro-life movement. The Knights are also known for their civic political power. They used their influence to help make Columbus Day a national holiday and led the effort in 1954 to amend the Pledge of Allegiance to include "under God" after the phrase "one nation."

McGivney lived only eight years after he founded the group,

dying of pneumonia. He was interred in the family plot. In 1982, on the one hundredth anniversary of the Knights, he was reinterred in a granite tomb at the rear of the nave of St. Mary's. The daily 7:30 A.M Mass is offered for deceased members. McGivney's cause for sainthood is under way.

The **Knights' international headquarters** are located in New Haven (1 Columbus Plaza, 203-772-2130). The 23-story, glass-faced building has four 320-foot towers that symbolize the order's four ideals of charity, unity, fraternity, and patriotism. Tours include a museum and Holy Family Chapel.

Meriden

Poles settled in Meriden in the 1880s to work at its cutlery firms, and in 1891 they founded **St. Stanislaus Church** (Olive and Akron Streets, 203-235-6341), the state's first Polish parish. The church itself was dedicated on Labor Day in 1908. Near one of the altars is an impressive painting of Our Lady of Czestochowa.

Stamford

Downtown Stamford has a trio of historic churches: the recently restored, one thousand-seat **St. John Church** (279 Atlantic St., 203-324-1553), the elegant French Gothic **St. Mary's Church** (566 Elm St., 203-324-7321), and the ornate **Holy Name of Jesus Church** (4 Pulaski St., 203-323-4967). Holy Name is the most intriguing. The prized possession of the Polish parish, founded in 1903, is a bell cast for the World's Fair in New York in 1939. Depicted on the 14-foot bell are Polish saints, statesmen, and generals, as well as the coat of arms of major Polish cities. Also shown is a figure of the Madonna of Czestochowa, who gazes with mercy on a mother and child.

Waterbury

The founder of the Knights of Columbus is honored in his hometown by the **Father McGivney Statue**, a ten-foot bronze monument located at Grand and Meadow Streets.

The **Church of the Immaculate Conception** (74 W. Main St., 203-574-0017) is a paean to God. Dedicated in 1927, the Italian Renaissance-style structure was inspired by St. Mary Major in Rome. In the apse is a mosaic of textured gold that depicts the Blessed Mother flanked by two angels and Saint Catherine and Saint Augustine. The white vaulted ceiling shimmers with 23-carat gold leaf.

Father McGivney, the founder of the Knights of Columbus, was baptized in the parish and said his first Mass here. Two presidential candidates have visited the parish. In 1960 John F. Kennedy attended Mass here. In 1982 Ronald Reagan made a campaign speech near the church. He paused during his remarks and commented, "Never have I seen a more beautiful church."

MAINE

Northern Maine

Van Buren

Maine's Acadians are descendants of the seventeenth-century French settlers of Nova Scotia. The British forced them out of Canada, and they made their way to Maine (others went to Louisiana and became known as Cajuns) in the late eighteenth century. **Acadian Village** (US Rte. 1, 207-868-5042) is a dozen or so replica buildings, including **Notre Dame de L'Assumption**, an unpretentious log-cabin chapel.

Southern Maine

Bath

The cheerful red-brick exterior of **St. Mary's Church** (144 Lincoln, 207-443-3423) gives no hint of the violent persecution that parishioners once faced. In the 1850s, Catholics in Bath leased the

St. Mary's Church.

Old South Church, located on a hill on High Street. At this time in a number of states, the anti-Catholic American Party, consisting of Americans hostile to immigrants, gained adherents. They met in secret. Asked about their activities, they replied that they "did not know anything"—hence they were called the "Know-Nothings."

In Bath, Catholic families, faced with threats, sometimes spent the nights in the forests. On July 6, 1854, a street preacher railed against "popery" and whipped a crowd into a frenzy. Waving the American flag, the mob broke into the Old South Church and burned it down.

A prominent non-Catholic, Oliver Moses, allowed Catholics to worship in his home until they could find another building. His stately brick home is at 1024 Washington Street.

The town's library owns a set of paintings by a local artist of the time showing Old South Church before the fire and during the disaster. The National Gallery of Art in Washington also has a set of the paintings.

Catholics built St. Mary's Church in 1856. During the construction two attempts were made to set in on fire, only to be thwarted by the church custodian. The church, creaky and outdated, was torn down in the 1960s, and a new church was built. The steeple was moved to Thomas Point Beach.

Eastport

In the 1840s Catholics in Eastport were persecuted by the "Know-Nothings." The pastor of **St. Joseph Church** (51 Washington St., 207-853-2825), who spoke out about allowing Catholic students the right to read their own Bible, was tarred and feathered and ridden out of town on a rail.

Kennebunkport

St. Anthony Monastery and Shrines (near junction of Rte. 9 and Rte. 35, 207-967-2011) began in 1947 when Lithuanian Franciscans purchased the William Rogers estate on the Kennebunk River and converted it into a friary and shrine. Notable are the Lithuanian Wayside Cross and the Infant of Prague Chapel.

Lewiston

St. Peter and St. Paul Church (Ash and Bartlett Streets, 207-777-1200) was founded in 1870 to serve French Catholics. The present church was constructed of Maine granite in 1906. The impressive, French Gothic structure has two pinnacled towers, reminiscent of thirteenth-century church architecture in France. The pews and interior woodwork are oak.

Newcastle

A lovely, small brick building crowned with a spire, **St. Patrick Church** (on State Rte. 215, 207-563-3240) is the oldest Catholic church in New England. Irish immigrants founded the parish in 1796, and it was the first U.S. church dedicated to Saint Patrick. The thick-walled church was dedicated in 1808 by Fr. Jean de Cheverus, who became the first bishop of New England that same year. Cheverus's ordination in France in 1790 was the last public ordination before the French Revolution. He came to Boston in 1806 and as bishop sometimes said Mass at St. Patrick's. Among Cheverus's personal items owned by the church are his mahogany walking stick, ancient straight-back chair, breviary, and chalice. Also from Cheverus was a remarkable nativity set, genuine French antiques in excellent condition.

The church has several paintings that were taken from a Mexican convent during the Mexican War. The steeple houses a Paul Revere bell, cast in 1818, the year the famous patriot died. The bell is one of 93 Revere bells that remain of the original 400 and the only one in a Catholic church in New England.

Buried in the church cemetery is Edward Kavanagh, who decided in the early 1800s not to become a priest and instead became the first Irish Catholic from New England to be elected to a state legislature, Congress, and governor's office.

Norridgewock

The **Monument to Father Sebastian Rasle** (near Rte. 8) honors the pioneer priest who in 1724 gave his life in defense of Native Americans attacked by British soldiers. The handsome granite obelisk was erected by the Knights of Columbus.

Portland

The Franz Mayer Studio in Munich made the brilliant stained-glass windows of the **Cathedral of the Immaculate Conception** (307 Congress St., 207-773-7746). Work on the cathedral began in 1866, but a disastrous fire swept through the city on July 4 that year destroyed its nearly completed walls. On the day of the cathedral's dedication in 1869, the skies grew suddenly dark, and a gale wind toppled its steeple, which was quickly repaired.

South Portland

In 1604 Catholics built a crude church near Eastport. A memorial window at the **Church of the Holy Cross** (30 Emery St., 207-799-4611) honors the pioneering missionaries. The exterior of the church, built in 1963, has an exquisite tower of mosaics, formed of an incredible 350 thousand pieces of Venetian glass, that depict the life of Christ.

MASSACHUSETTS

Eastern Massachusetts

Attleboro

The **Shrine of Our Lady of La Salette** (947 Park St., 508-222-5410) is famous for its Festival of Lights during the Christmas season, its Festival of Flowers in the summer, and various ethnic pilgrimages. The shrine was constructed in 1953 to commemorate the nineteenth-century apparition of the Blessed Mother to two shepherd children in the French Alps.

Boston

The **Ann Glover Memorial** at Our Lady of Victories Shrine (27 Isabella St., 617-426-4448) honors the first Catholic martyr in Massachusetts. Glover was an Irishwoman hanged as a witch near the site of this church in 1688. The Puritans' rabid anti-Catholicism most likely contributed to her death.

Workers and shoppers frequent **Saint Anthony Shrine** (100 Arch St., 617-542-6440), also known as the Workers' Chapel. The shrine is located on the lower floors of a ten-story Franciscan monastery whose facade has an eighteen-foot crucifix.

The **Cardinal Cushing Memorial** (in the small park opposite the Saltonstall Building in Old Bowdoin Square) pays tribute to the son of an Irish blacksmith who became a prince of the church and a friend of a president. Richard Cushing, archbishop of Boston from 1944 to 1970, defended presidential candidate John F. Kennedy from critics who charged he would be swayed by the Vatican. Cushing gave the invocation at Kennedy's inauguration and said his funeral at St. Matthew's Cathedral in Washington.

The immense **Cathedral of the Holy Cross** in Boston (Washington and Malden Streets, 617-542-5682) is the largest church in Boston and one of the largest Gothic cathedrals in the world, comparable in size with Westminster Abbey. Dedicated in 1875, the church was designed by Patrick Keeley, a Brooklyn architect responsible for many other celebrated churches. The driving force behind the church was Bishop Fitzpatrick, of whom Keeley said he "never met a man who had such a grand vision of what a church should be."

The structure is 364 feet long and 170 feet wide. The entire interior is open space, broken only by two rows of columns along the nave. The ceiling is a carnival of carved wood. The arch separating the front vestibule from the church is made of bricks taken from the ruins of the Ursuline convent in Charlestown (now Somerville), burned during anti-Catholic riots in 1834. The site of the church was under water as late as the 1820s until the city began reclaiming the land from the sea.

The superb **Church of the Immaculate Conception** (775 Harrison St., 617-536-8440), one of Boston's handsomest structures, was designed by Patrick Keeley in 1861.

Boston is awash in JFK sites, like the **John F. Kennedy Library** (on Columbia Point, 617-929-4523), which overlooks the ocean. The library is the official repository of all Kennedy's presidential papers and many of his personal belongings. Not to be missed are a stunning recreation of the Oval Office, a 17-minute film chronicling JFK's prepresidential years, a film on the Cuban Missile Crisis, a gallery of photos, personal items like the coconut shell in which he carved a plea for help after his PT boat was sunk, a tribute to his brother Robert, and an exhibit devoted to his wife, Jackie.

A bronze **John F. Kennedy Statue** on the south side of the State House (Beacon and Park Streets) catches the president in purposeful stride, with his right hand casually tucked in his coat pocket.

Erected in 1823, **St. Joseph Church** (68 Cardinal O'Connell Way, 617-523-4342) became a Catholic house of worship in 1862.

Members of the Twelfth Congregational Church had second thoughts about selling to Catholics. They first tried to reestablish the congregation and then attempted to raise money to turn the site into a park. The church is close to the site of the first Mass celebrated in Boston. In October 1788 a small group gathered in a private home; the celebrant was the chaplain of a French warship anchored in the harbor.

Founded in 1872, **St. Leonard Church** (Hanover and Prince Streets, 617-523-2110) was the first Italian church in New England. The current church dates from 1891. In front is a cheerful peace garden, created by a Franciscan when the Vietnam War ended. Growing here are two shrubs brought over from the altar on the Boston Common where Pope John Paul II celebrated Mass.

If singing is praying twice, then reflecting on world-class art with religious themes must also be grace-filled. The **Museum of Fine Arts** in Boston (465 Huntington Ave., 617-267-9300) has rooms full of art driven by faith.

The graceful **Old St. Stephen Church** (24 Clark St., 617-523-1230), which dates from 1714, has served members of various denominations, undergone several restorations, and today is an elegant reminder of the sturdy faith of our forebears.

Old St. Stephen's.

The original church served the New North Congregational Society. Paul Revere and his father were members. In 1804, Charles Bulfinch, the nation's first native-born architect, designed a new church, using some of the timbers of the first church. A bell cast by Revere hung in the belfry. The structure is the sole surviving Bulfinch church.

Bulfinch brilliantly patterned

the dramatic towerlike structure that houses the vestibule and supports the belfry on the Renaissance churches he saw in his travels to Italy. The elegant, nearly square interior has a gallery that extends around the sides and the rear of the nave. Most of the woodwork is original, including the columns. The church's pewter chandeliers, each carrying forty-two candles, are copies of the originals.

The Archdiocese of Boston acquired the church in 1862. After a fire in 1929, the great-grandson of Bulfinch restored the church. In 1965 it was restored again to its original Congregational appearance. Rose Kennedy, the mother of John, was christened here. Her funeral was also held here. No longer a parish, St. Stephen's is the international headquarters of The Missionary Society of Saint James the Apostle.

Near Boston

Brookline

The **John F. Kennedy National Historic Site** (83 Beals St., 617-566-1689) is a pleasant, middle-class home restored to its appearance in 1917, when the future president was born. The push-button descriptions of each room are narrated by Rose Kennedy.

Chestnut Hill

Founded in 1863 by a Jesuit priest, **Boston College** (Commonwealth Ave., 617-552-8000) was the first Catholic college in New England.

The school's Burns Library has a vast collection of pre–Vatican II artifacts, books, and miscellany. The Liturgy and Life Collection has more than 25 thousand books, including catechisms, lives of the saints, and biographies of well-known Catholics. The artifacts include richly embroidered vestments, ornate gold chalices, statues, photographs, films, sheet music, relics, paintings and prints of one thousand Last Suppers, a multitude of rosary beads, and cassocks. There are 100 thousand Mass cards, posters, programs, leaflets, and holy pictures. The collection presents a vivid picture of what it was like to grow up Catholic in the pre–Vatican II era. Oddly, the materials were gathered by Jesuit Fr. William Leonard, who took part in the Second Vatican Council and had vigorously campaigned for liturgical reform.

East Boston

The **Madonna, Queen of the Universe National Shrine** (11 Orient Ave., 617-569-2100) has an eye-popping view of the Boston area. The shrine's chief feature is a 32-foot statue of the Madonna, a copy of one that stands at the top of Monte Mario in Rome.

Roxbury

The majestic **Basilica of Our Lady of Perpetual Help** (1545 Tremont St., 617-445-2600) is known as "the mission church": the

Basilica of Our Lady of Perpetual Help.

Redemptorists began the church in 1871 to preach missions. The basilica is also fondly described as "Boston's leaning tower of Pisa." Due to a sloping foundation, the cross on one tower, 215 feet above the ground, is two feet higher than the cross on the second tower. The present church was built of Roxbury stone in 1878. The Romanesque church has a 110-foot dome supported by four clusters of four columns each, all of polished granite.

A silver plaque in the church commemorates the miraculous healing of Grace Hanley, the daughter of a famed Civil War colonel. Her spine was shattered by a fall when she was four. No doctor could help her walk. Her family made countless novenas at the church, and one day in 1883 Grace suddenly gave her crutches to her brother, walked up to the front of the church to offer prayers in gratitude, and marched out the doors.

Above the main altar is a fine statue of Our Mother of Sorrows. Near the altar is a chapel that enshrines the body of Saint Nazarius the Martyr, transported here from Rome in 1873. Nazarius, by the way, is a link to the church's earliest days. The Roman soldier was baptized by Saint Linus, who succeeded Peter as pope.

Somerville

On a cool August night in 1834, a band of fifty wild men dressed in women's clothes stormed the Ursuline convent in Somerville. The Protestant mob ransacked the house and school and burned the complex to the ground. The ten nuns fled into the night; one died two weeks later from tuberculosis.

The burning of the convent was an extreme expression of the hostility directed toward Irish Catholics in Massachusetts. The attack came after rumors that the nuns were held in the convent against their will.

The land lay dormant until 1879, when homes were built. Many Irish Catholics refused to buy a home there. In 1934 **St. Benedict Church** (21 Hathorn, 617-625-0029) was built across the site. Catholics still consider the land anointed ground, and each year a candlelight procession takes place through the nunnery tract.

Watertown

The Gothic-style **St. Patrick Church** (212 Main St., 617-926-9680), dedicated in 1906, is a perfectly proportioned aesthetic wonder. The parish began in 1847 when Catholics bought a Methodist church. The Catholic bishop had to retain a lawyer to complete the sale: the trustees of the Methodist church balked at selling to Catholics.

Weston

Influential Cardinal Francis Spellman, archbishop of New York from 1939 to 1967, was a devotee of stamps. His interest in philately began when he was a student at the North American College in Rome. The **Cardinal Spellman Philatelic Museum** (Regis College, 235 Wellesley St., 617-894-6735) houses his extensive collection. A 37,000-volume philatelic library answers any question one could possibly have on stamps.

Eastern Massachusetts

Fall River

St. Anne's Shrine (818 Middle St., 508-674-5651), part of St. Anne's Church, was established by a grateful priest who fell off the platform on which he was standing to bless the new church. Fr. Adrien de Montaubricq kept his promise to Saint Anne to dedicate a shrine in her honor if he recovered from his injuries. Run by Dominicans, the shrine is the site of frequent novenas. The shrine is located in the basement chapel, completed in 1895.

Notre Dame Church (Eastern Ave. and St. Joseph St., 508-679-1991) contains the Last Judgment of Cremonini painted on the ceiling. It's the largest work of the renowned Italian artist in the United States.

Gloucester

Catholic churches have typically been parochial, built by a specific group with its own special identity. Few churches dramatize this as well as **Our Lady of Good Voyage Church** in Gloucester (142 Prospect St., 508-283-1490). The "Shrine of the Fishermen" was built to minister to Portuguese-Americans who braved the gales of the North Atlantic. A ten-foot statue of Our Lady that faces the sea is perched between the twin towers of the church. In her left arm she holds a full-rigged schooner.

After a fire destroyed the original wooden church, a Romanesque-style stone church was built in 1915. A highly unusual design for New England, the Spanish Mission-type structure was modeled after the Church of the

Our Lady of Good Voyage Church.

Magdalena in Pico, the Azores, Portugal.

Parish leaders had to resort to a clever scheme in 1922 to ensure the arrival of twenty-five bells from London. The U.S. Customs Office impounded the shipment in Boston, demanding a $4,000 tariff applicable to musical instruments. A sympathetic congressman drafted a bill to admit the bells duty-free as works of art. While waiting for the bill to pass, another sympathetic government official designated the church as a bonded warehouse in order to store the bells there.

Each year, the church hosts a blessing of the fleet and holds a memorial service for those lost at sea. The ceremony dates from a celebration in 1902 after a steamer rammed a fishing schooner, whose crew somehow survived.

Lowell

Immaculate Conception Church (144 E. Merrimack St., 508-458-1474) is a Gothic structure made of gray granite. The truncated tower, delicate spires, and great rosette window are reminiscent of a French cathedral.

St. Joseph the Worker Shrine (37 Lee St., 508-458-6346) was built in 1850 to serve Unitarians. In 1866 the Oblates of Mary Immaculate acquired it to serve French Canadians. The stone Gothic structure, located downtown, has no parishioners. In 1956 it was declared a "Worker's Shrine" by Cardinal Cushing of Boston, who grew up in the neighborhood.

Cape Cod

Hyannis

Hyannis is Kennedy country. The **John F. Kennedy Memorial** (Ocean St. on Lewis Bay) consists of a bronze medallion of the president's profile set in a twelve-foot curved wall. The **John F. Kennedy Museum** (Town Hall Building, 397 Main St., 508-790-3077) has five rooms of photographs. The **Kennedy Compound National Historic Landmark** in Hyannisport (on Irving Ave.) features three large frame homes that belonged to the Kennedys. The compound is not open to the public, though local boat tours offer views.

Woods Hole

Founded in 1932, the **Mary Garden** at St. Joseph's Church (33 Millfield St., 508-548-0990) is believed to be the first public Mary garden in the nation. The splendid array of flowers showing their glory amid statues of Mary creates a sense of peace and warmth. The church bell tower was designed by a student at the Marine Biological Laboratory to keep his peers from being too caught up in their studies and neglectful of spiritual concerns.

Western Massachusetts

Petersham

Petersham has been called the most religious town in America. Close to 10 percent of its one thousand residents are members of Catholic religious orders. Oddly, most of the rest of the town's residents are Protestant.

Stockbridge

The **National Shrine of Divine Mercy** (413-298-1184) was inspired by the visions and suffering of Our Lady of Mercy Sister Maria Faustina of Poland. Born in 1905 near Lodz, she began receiving messages of mercy that she was told to spread throughout the world. She was asked to be a model of mercy to others and to graciously accept suffering. Convinced of her own unworthiness, she kept a diary of her divine revelations and mystical experiences. Only her spiritual director and a few of her superiors knew of her visions and physical pains. She died at the age of thirty-three in 1938 from tuberculosis. Blessed Faustina's diary *Divine Mercy in My Soul,* written in plain but moving language, became a popular handbook for devotion to the Divine Mercy.

The shrine is part of a 350-acre religious complex called **Eden Hill**. Also here are the **Marian Helpers' Center**, the provincial headquarters of the **Marians of the Immaculate Conception**, and **Divine Mercy International**.

NEW HAMPSHIRE

Northern New Hampshire

Colebrook

The **Shrine of Our Lady of Grace** (Hwy. 3, 603-237-5511) has a pretty garden with an outdoor altar and a beautifully landscaped Stations of the Cross. The shrine began in 1947 when the Oblates of Mary Immaculate near Colebrook, in gratitude for their twenty-five years as a community, erected a small statue of Mary near the highway. Motorists stopped to pray, and the priests responded to the spontaneous piety by building a flagstone plaza and a granite altar.

Southern New Hampshire

Enfield

Shrine of Our Lady of La Salette. *(Missionary Brothers)*

The wooded property of the **Shrine of Our Lady of La Salette** (NH Rte. 4-A, 603-632-4301) was originally owned by Shakers, who sold it to the La Salette Fathers in 1927. The community began a junior house of studies, and a wealthy benefactor paid for the beautiful Renaissance chapel, with colored marble and glittering artwork in honor of Our Lady of La Salette. The church's stained-glass windows tell the story of La Salette. In 1846 Our Lady appeared to two shepherd children near the little town of La Salette in France, high in the bleak solitude of the French Alps. The "beautiful lady," as the children called her, was seated on a stone, her elbows resting on her knees, weeping bitterly. She told them she cried because of disobedience to God's laws. The centerpiece of the shrine in Enfield is the *Weeping Mother,* a moving stone statue of the Virgin Mary. Founded in 1951, the shrine also includes a Way of the Cross, a Rosary Pond, and a Peace Walk.

Rindge

The grieving parents of a Lieutenant Sanderson, killed during World War II, donated a scenic parcel of land near Rindge that offers a spectacular panoramic view of the Monadnock Mountains and named it **Cathedral of the Pines** (Cathedral Rd., 603-899-3300). The Sandersons struck a nerve. In 1957 Congress, by a unanimous vote, recognized the cathedral's Altar of the Nation as a national memorial to all U.S. war dead. More than fifty different faiths have held services at the nondenominational site. The Hilltop House has flag relics and art objects from around the world. The Memorial Bell Tower is a national memorial to U.S. women war dead.

NEW YORK

Central New York

Auriesville

National Shrine of Our Lady of the Martyrs. *(Joe Connors)*

The Catholic faith was transplanted to U.S. soil at great cost. America's first and only canonized martyrs are commemorated at the **National Shrine of Our Lady of the Martyrs** (Rte. 5S and Noeltner Rd., 518-853-3033).

Frenchmen Jesuit Fr. Isaac Jogues, with Rene Goupil and John LaLande, "donns" or religious laity, evangelized in the 1630s among the Hurons on the north shore of Huron Bay. The Huron hunters, who followed their own deeply ingrained beliefs, were indifferent to Christianity. The missionaries baptized dying infants and sick elderly, but it took three years before they converted a healthy adult.

In 1642 Father Jogues and Goupil were escorting a sick Jesuit back to Montreal when they were ambushed by the fierce Mohawk. The men were beaten and tortured. Though enslaved, the two ministered to fellow Christian captives and even tried to convert the Mohawks. Goupil was tomahawked to death when he was teaching children the Sign of the Cross. The Mohawks thought he was casting a spell on them.

Jogues escaped after a year and returned to France, where he received a hero's welcome. But desperate to return to missionary life, he sailed back to North America, where he was soon again captured by the Mohawks. The Native Americans blamed him for the crop failure that had plagued them since his previous visit. Jogues was beheaded at his mission in 1646. LaLande was killed the next day.

Three years later Jesuit Fr. Jean Brebeuf also died a martyr. Father Brebeuf had enjoyed considerable success among the Hurons. He and his lay helpers learned the Huron language, and the priest published a small French-Huron catechism. He taught the Creed and the commandments to the children and listened respectfully as the Huron elders explained their beliefs.

To help explain Christianity, the priest wrote the first Christmas carol in the New World. "Twas in the Moon of Wintertime" was composed in the Huron language. The priest shrewdly used concepts the Native Americans could understand. Instead of a stable, he described a "lodge of broken bark." The swaddling clothes became a "ragged robe of rabbit skin." The carol was warmly received, and the Native Americans built a small chapel of cedar and fir branches to serve as the manger of baby Jesus.

Father Brebeuf, along with Fr. Gabriel Lalemant, was captured by the Iroquois, who were intent on wiping out the Hurons. Father Brebeuf was strapped to a stake. Mocking baptism, the Iroquois poured scalding water over his head. The priest never screamed. Instead, he preached about Jesus to his captors. Finally, a chief cut his chest and tore out his heart. The braves then drank his blood to take on his courage. Father Lalemant met a similarly ghastly death at sunrise.

Fonda

The Auriesville area is also witness to the success of the missionaries. It is the birthplace of **Blessed Kateri Tekakwitha**, the Lily of the Mohawks. A peaceful shrine (near Fonda, 518-853-3371) honors her.

Kateri was born in 1656, ten years after the death of Father Brebeuf. Her father was a Mohawk warrior and her mother was an Algonquin who had been captured by the Mohawks. When she was four, smallpox ravaged her, leaving her disfigured, impairing her vision, and depriving her of her parents. An uncle raised her. She met Jesuit missionaries and, despite fierce opposition from her uncle and tribe, converted. She was baptized on Easter in 1676.

Her tribe continued to harass her for not marrying and for refusing to work on Sundays. She fled to a Jesuit mission in Quebec. Because of the strength of her faith, she was accepted into a convent and became the first Native American nun. She died in 1680 at the age of twenty-four.

Southern New York

Maryknoll

The **Maryknoll Center** (near Ossining, 914-941-7590) is the seminary and headquarters of the Catholic Foreign Mission Society. A museum is dedicated to the society's founders, Bishop James Walsh and Fr. Thomas Price, who are interred in a crypt on the grounds. Also worth seeing are a sculpture of the Madonna and Child housed in a red kiosk of Chinese design, a bell from a Buddhist monastery, and the Chapel of Mary, Queen of Martyrs.

Middletown

The **National Shrine of Our Lady of Mount Carmel** (Carmelite Dr., 914-344-0876) is situated on sixty beautifully landscaped acres in the scenic lower-Hudson region. During World War II, when the shrine was located at a church in New York City, it supplied scapulars to the armed forces. In 1990 it was moved to its current site, where the magnificent chapel and pastoral setting make it an ideal place for prayer, pilgrimage, and reflection.

West Haverstraw

The **National Shrine of Mary, Help of Christians** (Filors Lane, 914-947-2200) sits on three hundred lush acres of the west bank of the Hudson River. The shrine's main attraction is a 48-foot Rosary Madonna, a nearly seven-ton statue cast in Italy in 1959. Life-sized statues depict the fifteen Mysteries of the Rosary. The shrine also has an outdoor altar and replicas of the grottoes at Lourdes and Fátima.

West Point

Appropriately, all the saints in the stained-glass windows at the **Chapel of the Most Holy Trinity** at West Point are soldiers: Saint Joan of Arc, Saint Barbara, Saint Ignatius, Saint George, Saint Michael, and others. The Norman Gothic-style chapel, built in 1899, seats 550. The most popular Sunday Mass is the 5:15 P.M. "cadet Mass."

New York City

Manhattan-Midtown

Duffy Square, the triangle north of Times Square between 46th and 47th Streets, was named after World War I hero Fr. Francis P. Duffy, a chaplain who accompanied New York's 69th Regiment into World War I. Duffy was awarded the Distinguished Service Cross for his heroism on the battlefield. More than 30 thousand people attended the dedication of the bronze statue of Duffy in 1937.

St. Francis of Assisi Church (135 W. 31st St., 212-736-8500) is home to the **National Shrine of St. Anthony**. The shrine, located in the crypt, has served as a quiet respite since 1930 for those caught in the hustle and bustle of New York. The beautifully adorned shrine features fumed oak, gorgeous mosaics, skillful bronze, and wrought iron.

Guardian Angels Church (193 10th Ave., 212-929-5966), also known as the Shrine Church of the Sea, is a short walk from the Port of New York. Until New York declined as a port in the early 1970s, the parish served dockworkers and seamen who lived in the area. The pastor was port chaplain, responsible for assigning chaplains to ships. The fancy red-brick and limestone Romanesque-style church with a tile roof was built in 1930.

Fr. Francis P. Duffy became pastor of **Holy Cross Church** (333 W. 42nd St., 212-246-4732), whose boundaries included the slums and gangs of Hell's Kitchen. Even though the parish served a poor neighborhood, Louis Comfort Tiffany designed the large circular stained-glass windows of Sts. Peter and Paul, the window of Saint John in the baptistry, and others.

The unborn are memorialized at the **Church of the Holy Innocents** (128 W. 37th St., 212-279-5861). The Book of Life encased at the shrine contains the names of children who died by miscarriage, stillbirth, or abortion. The shrine, whose visitors often carry a nearly unbearable anguish, was dedicated by John Cardinal O'Connor on the feast of the Holy Innocents, December 28, 1993.

The lovely **St. John the Baptist Church** (210 W. 31st St., 212-564-9070) has a gleaming white marble interior, handsome vaulting, and detailed Stations of the Cross. The brownstone church was designed in 1872 by Napoleon LeBrun, architect of the Metropolitan Life Tower and many firehouses.

The **J. Pierpont Morgan Library** (36th St. and Madison Ave., 212-685-0008) houses an extraordinary collection of sixth to sixteenth-century manuscripts, including the Book of Hours of Catherine of Cleves, the "Coptic Acts of the Apostles" (fifth-century Egyptian and considered the earliest surviving Christian miniature), the bejeweled Stavelot Triptych (supposedly part of the True Cross), and two leather boxes modestly labeled "Gutenberg Bible."

St. Malachy Chapel (239 W. 49th St., 212-489-1340) was where *Going My Way,* with Bing Crosby playing a priest, was filmed in 1944. St. Malachy's was no stranger to show business: for years it was known as the Actors' Chapel. Located near Broadway and Times Square, the chapel once held a 4:00 A.M. Mass to accommodate theater folks. The list of worshipers, besides footsore chorus girls, bartenders, and bit players, included the likes of George Cohan, Danny Thomas, and Irene Dunne. Bob Hope and Pat O'Brien served as altar boys. Douglas Fairbanks and Joan Crawford were married here. Cardinal Hayes called the church "a temple of God in the greatest playground in the world." The church was a tremendous example of the ability of Catholicism to respond to a local populace.

Built by Archbishop John Hughes, the magnificent **St. Patrick's Cathedral** (460 Madison Ave., 212-753-2261) was once dismissed as "Hughes's Folly." Critics believed it to be too distant from the city center. Well, today the heart of Manhattan surrounds the cathedral, and the splendor of the design is anything but foolish. The Gothic church was modeled after the Cathedral of Cologne. Its ornate, twin white spires rise 330 feet above the bustling city streets.

St. Patrick's Cathedral. *(David Garvey)*

The cornerstone was laid in 1858, a period when the city was predominantly Protestant. Hughes vowed to build a church "worthy of God, worthy of the Catholic religion and an honor to this great city." It was also a church worthy of Irish aspirations. The prestigious Fifth Avenue location was purposely chosen. In that era, the only reason most Irish people came to that neighborhood was as employees of the wealthy. The church was also a resounding response to the fiercely anti-Catholic "Know-Nothings" who wanted to rid the country of the "Irish menace." The impressive sanctuary made it obvious that Catholics weren't going anywhere.

The grand church is 405 feet long outside and 274 feet wide. It seats 2,200 people. Its 70 stained-glass windows were made by the finest European and U.S. artisans. The great Rose Window, 26 feet in diameter, is considered the best work of Charles Connick, an acknowledged genius in stained glass.

The St. Michael and St. Louis altar was designed by Tiffany and Company. The renowned Paolo Medici of Rome designed the St. Elizabeth altar. The Stations of the Cross won a first prize at the Chicago World's Fair in 1893. The first-rate Pièta is three times larger than Michelangelo's *Pièta* in St. Peter's in Rome. Among the multitude of statues in the church is a modern interpretation of Mother Elizabeth Seton, the first U.S.-born saint. The Memorial Rosary Confraternity of the Lady Chapel was built in 1996, one year after Pope John Paul II recited the rosary in the cathedral. More than three million people visit the cathedral each year.

Interred at the cathedral is Bishop Fulton Sheen, the father of electronic evangelists. His nationally televised weekly show, *Life Is Worth Living,* drew big ratings in the 1950s. Born in El Paso, Illinois, in 1895, Sheen turned down a full university scholarship to study for the priesthood. After being ordained, he spent a quarter century on the faculty at Catholic University, where his classes were so popular that extra chairs had to be brought in for his lectures.

He began his media career in radio in 1928; in fact, he delivered the first radio message from Radio City in New York, and he was the first to host a regular religious series on radio. In 1952 he debuted *Life Is Worth Living* on television. Since the show was aired opposite two highly rated programs by Milton Berle and Frank Sinatra, it was assumed his show would quickly die. Instead, the program drew 5.5 million households each week. Sheen received as many as 25 thousand letters a week, including correspondence from President Eisenhower. The priest donated his TV earnings to the Society for the Propagation of the Faith.

Sheen covered topics that concerned people—war, communism, love, family—in the context of God's love and wisdom. His rare gift was bringing the Word of God to people's hearts.

Also interred under the cathedral floor is Pierre Toussaint, a nineteenth-century black slave who lived in New York. He had been buried in 1853 under the bare dirt of a weathered cemetery in New York. Church authorities, convinced of his holiness, had his remains exhumed and brought to the cathedral in 1990.

Downtown

St. Andrew Church (20 Cardinal Hayes Pl., 212-962-3972) was the first parish in the city to cater to workers. In 1900 the church offered a printer's Mass at 2:30 A.M. for the night workers who worked at nearby newspapers. The church later became the first in the nation to offer a noon Mass specifically for businesspeople. The main door of the present church, built in 1939, bears the coat of arms of Pope Pius XI.

Saint Ann's Church (110 E. 12th St., 212-475-2590) was founded in 1862 when the archdiocese purchased the building, which had housed first a Baptist house of worship and then a synagogue. The French Gothic-style interior is spacious, old-fashioned, and inviting.

For years the parish was the most fashionable of the city's Catholic churches. In 1929 the **National Shrine of the Motherhood of Saint Ann** was begun at the church. Near the sanctuary is an expressive Carrara-marble statue of Saint Ann gazing down at her daughter, Mary, engrossed in a book.

Immaculate Conception Church (414 E. 14th St., 212-254-0200), built in 1894, originally served Episcopalians. The cloisterlike structure is punctuated by an elaborate tower.

St. James Church (23 E. Oliver St., 212-233-0161) was built in the 1820s to minister to the Irish in the infamous slums of the Five

Points neighborhood. The church was the birthplace of the Ancient Order of Hibernians in America, founded in 1836 to protect the Irish and their churches from anti-immigrant violence.

St. James School has a plaque on its door that honors its most famous student, Alfred E. Smith, a popular four-time Democratic governor of the state who unsuccessfully ran for president in 1928. Smith's indifference to his studies frustrated the nuns who taught him, but he lit up the stage when he performed in school dramas in the parish hall.

Next to St. James is the **Alfred Smith Boyhood Home** (25 E. Oliver St.). A plaque in the three-story brick rooming house marks the fact that Smith lived here from 1909 to 1924.

Erected in 1833, **St. Joseph Church** (Sixth Ave. and Washington Pl., 212-741-1274) is the city's oldest Catholic church. The exterior is simply designed, but the superb interior has delicate crystal chandeliers and a gilded sanctuary. The outside wall on Washington Place is made of Manhattan schist, the bedrock of Manhattan. Fr. John McCloskey, an early rector, became the first cardinal in the United States.

Maryhouse (55 E. Third St., 212-777-9617), a Catholic settlement house, was established by Dorothy Day, who cofounded the Catholic Worker movement in 1933. The legendary advocate for social justice and servant of the poor died here at age eighty-three in 1980.

As a young woman, Day rejected organized religion and had an abortion after a relationship failed. She was gradually drawn to the Catholic Church and was received into the church after a daughter was born in 1927. A freelance journalist, she founded the *Catholic Worker* newspaper in 1933 to promote Catholic social teaching and to transform society. Originally working out of her kitchen, she sold the paper for a penny, and circulation rose to 190 thousand within five years. The Catholic Worker "houses of hospitality" movement took off as well. Today, there are more than 130 in nine countries.

Day protested war, supported the civil rights movement, and

backed the United Farm Workers, and her activities lead to numerous arrests. She regularly read the Bible, corresponded with Thomas Merton, and gloried in the natural world, the beauty of God's creation. John Cardinal O'Connor of New York has backed her cause for sainthood.

Most Precious Blood Church (109 Mulberry St.) has the **National Shrine of San Gennaro** in front of it. San Gennaro was a bishop when the Emperor Diocletian declared open season on Christians in 305. Though tortured, the stalwart bishop refused to recant his faith. He was thrown into burning flames but emerged unscathed. The saint is commonly called upon to intercede in cases of fires, plagues, droughts, and other natural disasters. The parish holds a popular seven-day feast in September.

Old St. Patrick's Cathedral (268 Mulberry St., 212-226-8075) was the largest church in the city until the new St. Patrick's was completed in 1879. Consecrated in 1815, the church was badly damaged by a fire in 1866. The church was repaired but only partially restored to its original appearance. The cathedral's odd appearance is not related to the fire. The structure was only the second U.S. Gothic Revival church, and the architect, Joseph Mangin, was working with a style unfamiliar to him.

The predecessor of **Our Lady of Pompeii Church** (Bleecker and Carmine Streets, 212-989-6805) was where Saint Frances Xavier Cabrini worshiped. The gilded marble interior of the present structure, erected in 1927, is dazzling. Near the church is a square named for Fr. Antonio Demo (died 1936), who served the parish for thirty-five years.

St. Peter's Church (Barclay and Church Streets, 212-233-8355) is the oldest Catholic parish in Manhattan. During the colonial period, laws in Britain outlawing Catholicism applied to the United States. The parish was founded in 1785 after freedom of religion was established.

Elizabeth Seton was received into the Church here, and St. Peter's began the first free grade school in the city. Another notable event occurred in 1813 after Jesuit Father Kohlmann, the pastor, intervened in a dispute between a Catholic merchant named Keating and a husband and wife. Keating accused the couple of stealing. Kohlmann saw to it that Keating got his property back. The police wanted to know who had given the priest the goods, but he refused to tell them because the revelation had been made in the confessional. Kohlmann was upheld in court, and the case established the inviolability of the seal of confessional in U.S. law.

A longtime parishioner was Pierre Toussaint, a candidate for sainthood. Toussaint was born in 1766 to slaves of plantation owners in Haiti, then called Santo Domingo. At the age of twenty he was brought to New York by his owners, the Berards. The family's fortune disappeared after his master's death. Toussaint, who accumulated a decent sum of money by working as a hairdresser for the wealthy, secretly supported Madame Berard, who didn't know her wealth was gone.

Berard freed Toussaint before she died. Toussaint bought the freedom of his future wife, and he and Juliette adopted his niece when his sister died. Toussaint was indefatigable in his good works. He nursed the sick. He took in many homeless black children and taught them to play the violin. He sent money to slaves in Haiti. His reputation for charity grew, and people wrote to him for assistance. His selflessness was rooted in a deep faith. Every day for sixty-six years he attended the 6:00 A.M. Mass at St. Peter's.

The present St. Peter's Church, erected in 1836, was so extravagant and expensive that the parish accrued a debt of $135 thousand and was forced to declare bankruptcy. Archbishop Hughes then bought the property at a public auction for $46 thousand. The parish eventually paid all the claims of creditors.

Distinguished by six massive columns, the church has a granite facade, instead of the usual brownstone. A niche outside the church has a statue of Saint Peter holding the keys to the eternal kingdom.

A plaque on the rectory honors the estimable Fr. John Drumgoole, known as the "Shepherd of the Homeless Newsboys." In the 1870s he set up a shelter near Printing House Square, the newspaper district. Years earlier he had founded Mount Loretto on Staten Island, which became the largest childcare facility in the country.

The **Shrine of St. Elizabeth Seton** at the Church of Our Lady of the Rosary (7 State St., 212-269-6865) honors the woman who founded the Sisters of Charity, the first American order of nuns. Beneath the belfry of the church is a seven-foot stone statue of the first American-born saint. The church is part of a townhouse where Mother Seton and her family lived from 1801 to 1803. Built in 1793, the townhouse is the only survivor of the time when the street was an upper-crust residential district. During the Civil War the Union Army commandeered the house. After the war Charlotte Grace O'Brien, an Irish immigrant, bought the house and began the Mission of Our Lady of the Rosary, a settlement house for Irish immigrant girls.

St. Stanislaus Church (101 E. 7th St., 212-475-4576), begun in 1872, is the oldest Polish church in the archdiocese. The first Pulaski Day Parade originated from the parish. In front of the rectory is a monument to Pope John Paul II.

Upper East Side

French Canadians founded **St. Jean Baptiste Church** (1067 Lexington Ave., 212-288-5082) in 1882. The parish's first home was in a loft above a stable on East 77th Street, where the smell of horses and the rattling of harness disturbed worship so often that it came to be called the "Crib of Bethlehem."

The current church, dedicated in 1914, is a splendid classical and Renaissance-style structure. The Shrine of Saint Ann is in the crypt of the church. Babe Ruth, stricken with incurable throat cancer, once came here to pray. The church's French-style organ is one of the finest in the city.

The **Metropolitan Museum of Art** (Fifth Ave. and 82nd St., 212-879-5500) has a Raphael *Madonna,* Botticelli's *The Last Communion of St. Jerome,* and a Titian *Madonna.*

Our Lady of Perpetual Help Basilica (328 E. 62nd St., 212-832-9087), staffed by Redemptorists, is a large Gothic-style structure used for major liturgical events like the ordination or death of a bishop.

St. Stephen's of Hungary Church (414 E. 82nd St., 212-861-8500) has a carved likeness of the Magyar king atop the columns of its entrance. The interior is bathed in the soft light that radiates from the stained-glass windows behind the altar.

Upper West Side

The **American Bible Society** (1865 Broadway, 212-408-1200) contains Helen Keller's huge ten-volume Braille Bible, a replica of the Gutenberg press, and a Torah from China.

The **Church of St. Paul the Apostle** (Columbus and 60th St., 212-265-3495) is the home of the Paulist Fathers, founded in 1858 by Fr. Isaac Thomas Hecker to spread awareness of Catholicism in the mostly Protestant nations of the United States and Canada. The Gothic exterior has a remarkable bas-relief of the conversion of Saint Paul. Fifty tons of travertine are fixed against a mosaic background of Venetian glass tesserae in fifteen shades of blue.

Harlem

Our Lady of Lourdes Church (467 W. 142nd St., 212-862-4380) is a scavenger's delight. Erected in 1904, the church was built from parts of three other buildings. Its gray and white marble and bluestone facade was from the old National Academy of Design, built in 1865. The apse and part of the east wall were from St. Patrick's Cathedral when it added a chapel. The pedestals flanking the steps are from the A. T. Stewart's Department Store that stood at 34th Street and Fifth Avenue.

St. Thomas the Apostle Church (260 W. 118th St., 212-662-2693) has a wonderful arcaded porch and grand entrance stairway.

Upper Manhattan

The **Cloisters** (212-923-3700), on a wooded hilltop in Fort Tyron Park overlooking the Hudson River, resembles a medieval monastery, appropriately enough. A special branch of the Metropolitan Museum of Art, the structure houses the Met's medieval European collection. Its colonnaded walls connect authentic medieval rooms from French and Spanish monasteries. Displayed are hundreds of statues, friezes, stained-glass windows, tapestries, altar pieces, and manuscripts. The medieval devotion to God is manifest.

The **Mother Cabrini Chapel** at Cabrini High School (701 Fort Washington Ave., 212-923-3540) has mosaics around its altar that depict the selfless life of Saint Frances

Mother Cabrini Chapel.

Xavier Cabrini, America's first citizen-saint. Her remains are entombed in a crystal coffin under the altar.

Bronx

St. Anselm Church (673 Tinton Ave., 718-585-8666) is an impressive neo-Byzantine brick structure erected in 1915. The outstanding interior is a rich panorama of marble columns, mosaics, bronze lamps, and stained-glass windows over which semicircular arches sweep up to a mighty dome. Originally serving German, Italian, and Irish working-class families, the parish has ministered to African Americans and Hispanics since World War II.

Fordham University (E. Fordham Rd., 718-817-1000) opened in 1841. Its collegiate Gothic buildings serve six thousand undergraduates. The lovely campus has rolling green lawns, small gardens, and landmark buildings. The outdoor "Harvard" scenes from *Love Story* were filmed here. The university church is the architecturally distinctive Our Lady, Mediatrix of All Graces, a Gothic-revival masterpiece designed in 1845 by a teacher at the college. The stained-glass windows were a gift of King Louis Philippe (1773–1850) of France. The church's bell tower is said to have inspired Poe's poem "The Bells." The campus center is Edward's Parade, a quadrangle. Keating Hall has the look of a Gothic fortress. Rose Hill Manor House, the administration building, was once a wealthy merchant's home.

Our Lady of Mt. Carmel Church (627 E. 187th St., 718-295-3770) was begun in 1907 by an Irish priest who spoke Italian and saw the needs of new immigrants. Italians volunteered to build the church, which has many plaques honoring its donors.

Brooklyn

St. Augustine Church (Sterling Pl. and Sixth Ave., 718-783-3132) was the work of the Parfitt Brothers, designers of many churches. The exterior successfully combines a variety of materials—brownstone, brick, copper, and marble—and exuberantly mixes turrets, towers, gargoyles, and statues. The interior is no less dazzling.

The wealthy Pratt family donated the **Bishop's Residence** (378 Clinton Ave.) to the church in the early part of this century. The interior is decorated with original Tiffany glass windows. An original Murillo oil painting adorns the main stairway. The residence is the present home of Bishop Thomas Daily.

Cardinal John O'Connor once called **St. James Cathedral** (Jay and Tillary Streets, 718-852-4002) the city's "best-kept secret." Small in comparison to other cathedrals, the historic structure has a charming harmony. The parish dates from 1822. The current church, completed in 1902, incorporated some elements of the original. A plaque commemorates Pope John Paul II's brief visit here in 1979.

The adjoining cemetery has a monument to Peter Turner, one of the first great lay leaders of the city.

Fr. George Mundelein, who later became bishop of Chicago, built **Our Lady Queen of All Saints Church** (Lafayette and Vanderbilt Avenues, 718-638-7625) in 1914. Statues of two dozen saints adorn the church.

St. Stanislaus Kostka Church (607 Humboldt St., 718-388-0170), dear to Poles, has a shrine to Our Lady of Czestochowa. In 1969 Cardinal Karol Wojtyla paid a visit. Near the church between Broome and Humboldt Streets is **Pope John Paul II Square**. The parish boasts the largest Sunday Mass attendance in the diocese.

Queens

Calvary Cemetery, owned by the Archdiocese of New York, is the archdiocese's oldest and largest cemetery. The headstones date to the early nineteenth century. The cemetery scenes in *The Godfather* were shot here.

St. John's University (Grand Central and Utopia Pkwy., 718-990-6161), founded in 1870, is the second largest Catholic university in the country. The school has a proud tradition of public service; nearly a quarter of its law-school graduates are state officials. Check out Sun Yat-sen Hall, a pagoda-style structure home to the school's Department of Asian Studies.

Flushing Meadows Park was the site of the Vatican Pavilion at the World's Fair of 1964–65. Pope Paul VI visited the pavilion when he spoke to the United Nations in 1965. A commemorative prayer garden marks the site of the pavilion.

Long Island

Eastport

A hidden treasure is **Our Lady of the Island** shrine in Eastport (Eastport Manor Rd., 516-325-0661). Long Islanders usually find the underpublicized shrine by accident, though foreign pilgrims have

it on their itinerary. The main attraction is a 40-ton, 18-foot statue
of Mary holding Jesus, bolted onto a huge rock and inspired by the
Christ of the Andes statue in Rio de Janeiro. The Vigliotta family
donated most of the land and paid for the shrine's construction in
1953. Crescenzo Vigliotta was a duck farmer who had fifteen children, and one of them, Fr. Bill Vigliotta, is now in charge of the
shrine.

Western New York

Lackawanna

Our Lady of Victory Institutions (780 Ridge Rd., 716-828-
9648) grew out of the energy and piety of Fr. Nelson Baker, known
as the "padre of the poor" in the nineteenth century. A successful
feed and grain merchant in the 1840s, he had an intense religious
experience and decided to devote his life to Mary as his Victorious Lady. The poor and afflicted were his flock. He did many
good works before entering the seminary and being ordained in
1876. His children's home was nationally known. Children arrived alone from distant states, wearing tags around their necks
that read simply, "Father Baker's, Lackawanna, N.Y." Baker is a
candidate for sainthood.

Today, the complex includes a church, shrine, hospital, and
school. The elegant Italian Renaissance church was built in 1921 at
a cost of $3.5 million. The main altar has twisted columns of rare
Pyrenees red marble and an incredible 9-foot, 1,600-pound statue
of Our Lady of Victory.

Pine City

Located on a wooded hill, **Mount Saviour Monastery** (231
Monastery Rd., 607-734-1688) uses its 250 acres to raise Scottish
Blackface sheep, a hardy, rugged animal. In the 1970s the
Benedictine monks ran a dairy farm, but partly out of ecological
concerns, they switched to sheep, who survive entirely on a diet of

grass and legumes. Among the wool products for sale at the monastery are mittens.

The octagonal chapel has an altar that sits in the middle and a precious fourteenth-century statue of Our Lady, Queen of Peace.

Youngstown

Near the Canadian border is **Our Lady of Fátima Shrine** (1023 Swan Rd.). The shrine, dedicated in 1956, has a church whose dome is covered with two layers of glass and plexiglass depicting the Northern Hemisphere.

RHODE ISLAND

Tiny Rhode Island was historically important in establishing religious freedom in America. It was founded by Roger Williams, who disagreed with the harsh religious intolerance of the Puritans and was banished from them because of his views. Rhode Island was the first state to grant complete religious freedom, a principle followed by other states and later enshrined in the Constitution's Bill of Rights.

Harrisville

The **Shrine of the Little Flower** at St. Theresa's Church (7 Dion Dr., 401-568-8280) is the oldest shrine dedicated to Thérèse Martin, better known as Saint Thérèse of Lisieux, the Little Flower of Jesus. She was beatified in 1923, and the church was built just four months later. On the grounds are Stations of the Cross and Holy Stairs, made of fieldstone, limestone, and granite and patterned after those Jesus ascended during his Passion.

Newport

St. Mary Church (12 William St., 401-847-0475) is the oldest Catholic parish in the state. Designed by Patrick Keeley, the English Gothic-style church was built in the 1850s under the supervision of a member of the Army Corps of Engineers who was stationed nearby. In 1953 Sen. John F. Kennedy and Jacqueline Bouvier were married here. A frenzied crowd of three thousand people broke through the police line outside the church and nearly crushed the young bride.

Salve Regina University (100 Ochre Point Ave., 401-847-6650), run by the Mercy Sisters and located on the Cliff Walk, is one of the most beautiful college campuses in the country. Scenes from *True Lies,* starring Arnold Schwarzenegger and Jamie Lee Curtis, were filmed here.

Providence

St. Joseph Church (86 Hope St., 401-421-9137), designed by Patrick Keeley in 1853, is the oldest standing Catholic church in the state. It was founded by Irish immigrants who came here to work on the Providence and Worcester Railroad. Showman George Cohan attended the church as a boy.

The **Cathedral of Saints Peter and Paul** (30 Fenner St., 401-331-2434), built in 1889, is an impressive Gothic-revival structure with two monumental square towers. In one of the towers the first automatic Angelus clock in the United States was installed. The church has the world's largest tracker organ.

Warwick

Our Lady of Providence Center (836 Warwick Neck Ave., 401-739-6850) is the former estate of Sen. Nelson Aldrich. The movie *Meet Joe Black,* with

Our Lady of Providence Center. *(Ultima Studios)*

Anthony Hopkins and Brad Pitt, was filmed here.

Woonsocket

St. Ann Church (82 Cumberland St., 401-766-0370) is lavishly decorated with original frescoes by Giodo Nincheri, a Canadian artist. He used many parishioners' faces, though his Saint Peter bears a striking resemblance to Nincheri himself.

VERMONT

Northern Vermont
Bakersfield

In the mid nineteenth century Irish fleeing the potato famine and French Canadian Catholics escaping political unrest came to Vermont. Too poor to build new churches, they purchased homes, businesses, and schools and converted them into churches. **St. George Church** was founded in 1867 when the diocese bought South Academy, a private school built in 1840, and used it as a church. Extensive renovations in 1905 gave it a Gothic look. The parish closed in 1996; the building is owned by the Bakersfield Historical Society.

Burlington

St. Joseph Church (85 Elmwood Ave., 802-863-2388) was the first French national parish in New England. The red sandstone church was consecrated in 1901. A cock, symbolic of the denial of Peter, surmounts the cross atop the church. The symbol, rare in the United States, is common in the provinces of France, the home of the ancestors of the French-Canadians who founded the parish.

Isle La Motte

St. Anne's Shrine on Isle La Motte (off Rte. 129, 802-797-3481), a sleepy island known for its stone houses, marks the site of the region's first Mass in 1666. That year the first French settlers, including several Jesuits, came to the New World. The site includes an open-air chapel in a quiet pine grove, a marble statue of Saint Anne, and several small outdoor shrines.

Newport

A lighted figure of Mary stands between the twin granite towers of **St. Mary Church** (5 Clermont Ter., 802-334-5066). The massive stone church, built in 1904, sits atop a hill near the edge of town. The church is near Lake Memphremagog, and its dedication stone reads, "Ave Maris Stella," a nautical reference. An anchor is carved into another stone.

Stowe

Blessed Sacrament Church (on Mountain Rd., 802-253-7536) is a true gem. The little country church was built during the winter of 1949 on the property of the former Dutton Farm. "Brother" Joseph (Ira) Dutton, born in Stowe in 1843, converted to Catholicism at age forty and went to assist Father Damien at his leper colony in Molokai, where Dutton spent the last forty-five years of his life. Noted French artist André Girard told the compelling story of Dutton in a series of paintings on the exterior of Blessed Sacrament Church.

Dutton and his family moved to Janesville, Wisconsin, when he was four. He was a popular, exuberant young man. When he left town to fight in the Civil War as a Union soldier, friends gave him a valuable rubber overcoat, and the town turned out for this send-off. After the war he married an unstable woman, who ran off with another man. Dutton worked for the railroad in Memphis and became a heavy drinker. After giving up drinking, he joined the Catholic Church and committed himself to a life of penance. After two years with the Trappists in Gethsemani in Kentucky, he set sail for Molokai.

He once wrote of his new life, "I was firm in at least one resolve: to get along with everyone, to ask no special favors, not to make anyone the slightest difficulty that I could reasonably avoid and to do what I could to help my neighbor in every way." Brother Dutton took over after Father Damien died within three years of his arrival. He made sure that the leper colony had the finest possible facilities and healthcare. His fame was such that in 1908 President Theodore Roosevelt granted him a special favor. Dutton was enamored of ships, and sixteen U.S. battleships, on a trip around the world, were ordered to pass by the leper colony in battle formation. The gentle brother, who somehow never contracted leprosy, died in 1931 at age eighty-eight.

The church is full of the paintings of Girard. Most notable are the large mural of the Trinity behind the altar, the colorful ceiling, and the superb Stations of the Cross.

The **Trapp Family Lodge** (802-253-8511) is run by the youngest child of Maria von Trapp, known to Americans as Maria in the film *The Sound of Music*. The von Trapps purchased an old farmhouse in 1941 in this mountain hamlet because it reminded them of Austria. The farmhouse was the base of their worldwide musical tours. The lodge grew out of the Trapp Family Music Camp they began in 1947.

The lodge sits on 2,200 acres of meadows and woodlands. The lodge was rebuilt after a devastating fire in 1980. Maria, who died in 1987, is buried alongside her husband, Baron von Trapp, who died in 1947, in the family cemetery next to the lodge. The gift shop includes CDs by the Trapp family and a book by Maria von Trapp that tells her true story, as opposed to the Hollywood version. The film, among many historical errors, downplayed Maria's strong Catholic faith. Raised as a socialist and atheist, she was dramatically changed by a chance encounter with a Jesuit priest when she was a teenager. She left the convent only because a doctor was concerned about her health.

Southern Vermont

Stratton

The **Chapel of the Snows** (802-387-5861) on Stratton Mountain is sweetly tucked into a grove of trees. Strap on your skis and snowplow your way to God.

Weston

Weston Priory (58 Priory Hill Rd., 802-824-5409) is home of the Weston Benedictine monks, whose contemporary liturgical choral music has been popular for many years. The Benedictines display a number of Nativity scenes from around the world from September through Christmas. A Spanish scene is made from terra cotta and lacquered cloth, one from Kenya contains soapstone sheep, and another from Mexico has hand-carved wood. The gift shop contains CDs and cassettes as well as bells and sculptures. The stone chapel on the grounds is a place of prayerful solitude.

Windsor

The modern **St. Francis of Assisi Church** (30 Union St., 802-674-2157) features the *Seven Sacrament* panels, created by George Tooker, a renowned painter who lives nearby.

MID-ATLANTIC

DELAWARE

Hockessin

The first Catholic church in Delaware was a log structure built in 1772 at **Coffee Run Mission Site** (southeast of Hockessin off State 48). The structure was also used as a home by Fr. Patrick Kenny, a Dublin native who came to the area in 1804. The indefatigable Kenny attended five other missions in Delaware, Maryland, and Pennsylvania and almost single-handedly kept Catholicism alive in the region. Kenny is buried in the **Coffee Run Cemetery**. In recent times the Knights of Columbus built a tiny chapel to commemorate the first church. The site includes a wooden cross and iron bell that date from two centuries ago.

Wilmington

The **Cathedral of St. Peter** (Sixth and West Streets, 302-654-5920) began, in the words of the diocese's first bishop, as an "old and very clumsy building." It has since gradually evolved into a stately cathedral thanks to a series of additions and renovations.

The parish began around 1796. Many of its parishioners were French refugees who fled a 1795 revolt in the Dominican Republic, and early parish baptismal records are written in French. The present church was dedicated at 6:00 A.M. on September 12, 1818, by horseback-riding Father Kenny, the only priest within hundreds of miles.

46

The church was first enlarged in 1829. The bell tower and memorial stone that were installed are still here. Between 1870 and 1905 a series of improvements were made, including adding a barrel-domed roof and stained-glass windows and enlarging the sanctuary. Another major renovation occurred in 1981. What was once a 30-foot-by-40-foot tin-roofed church is now a local treasure.

Near Wilmington

Greenville

The original **St. Joseph on the Brandywine Church** (10 Old Church Rd., 302-658-7017) was built by the wealthy Du Ponts in 1841 for their Irish employees. The Du Ponts were a French immigrant family who owned local powder mills. They had a curious relationship with area Catholics. The pastor of St. Joseph once publicly tore pages dealing with Martin Luther and Sam Adams from a textbook used in the public schools because of his frustration over lack of state support for Catholic schools. A Du Pont retaliated by saying he preferred hiring Protestants rather than volatile Catholics. Yet, another Du Pont, though not Catholic, served as a trustee of the church and condemned the "Know-Nothing" movement for its stance toward "poor oppressed Irish Catholics."

DISTRICT OF COLUMBIA

Washington and Vicinity

Just west of the visitor's center at **Arlington National Cemetery** (Arlington National Bridge at Jefferson Davis Hwy., 703-692-0931) are the graves of President Kennedy and his brother Robert. JFK rests under an eternal flame near the graves of Jackie Onassis, his wife, and two of their children who died in infancy. A wall across from the plot is engraved with a quotation from his stirring inaugural address. JFK's resting place is the most visited grave site in the country. Robert's grave is marked by a simple white cross.

The largest U.S. Catholic church is the immense **Basilica of the National Shrine of the Immaculate Conception** (400 Michigan Ave., NE, 202-526-8300). Its cornerstone was laid in 1920, but owing to the Great Depression and World War II, the church was not dedicated until 1959. "America's Catholic church" was built with funds contributed by every U.S. parish.

Like the great European cathedrals, the sheer size of the church is overwhelming. The shrine's huge blue dome can be seen for miles. Inside, the vast expanse of art and chapels gives an overview of Catholicism around the world. No less than fifty-nine chapels honor Mary. The chapels explain Mary's role among various ethnic groups. On the lower level of the church is the Mary Memorial Altar, built with donations from women named Mary.

The area known as Memorial Hall contains pillars on which are inscribed the names of donors. Look carefully and you can spot Babe Ruth's name.

On the main level is an oratory donated by Irish Catholics. Decorations include a stunning Waterford crystal chandelier and a mosaic inlay made to look like illuminated manuscripts, reminiscent of the *Book of Kells.*

The **Cardinal Gibbons Statue** (16th St. and Park Rd.) pays tribute to a church leader who strove to prove that Catholics were loyal Americans second to none. Born in Baltimore of Irish immigrants, he eventually became the archbishop of Baltimore in 1877 and later the second American cardinal. Since Washington was then within his archdiocese, he became fast friends with Presidents Cleveland, Roosevelt, and Taft. Gibbons often credited the freedom in America for the success of the U.S. Catholic Church.

The **Catholic University of America** (4th St. and Michigan Ave., NE, 202-319-5000), is the national university of the Catholic Church in the United States; it is the only institution of higher education founded by the U.S. bishops. Its six thousand students enjoy a 144-acre campus, adjacent to the Basilica of the National Shrine of the Immaculate Conception. The school dates from 1887.

For those who are unable to travel to the Holy Land, the next best thing is the **Franciscan Monastery and Gardens** (1400 Quincy St., NE, 202-526-6800). The church has replicas of the Holy Sepulcher, Calvary, and grottoes of Nazareth, Bethlehem, and Gethsemane. The Altar of Calvary has a life-sized relief of Christ's crucifixion. Even more unusual is the replica of the Roman catacombs, built under the church. The poured concrete walls were airbrushed to resemble mighty stone blocks. The tour ends with the Purgatory Chapel, decorated with tile frescoes of corpses.

The monastery's gardens are a natural wonder. Strewn with roses and enclosed by cloisters, the gardens offer a retreat from the weighty political ruminations of Washingtonians.

Founded in 1789, **Georgetown University** (37th and O Streets, NW, 202-687-0100) was the nation's first Catholic college. A statue of Archbishop John Carroll, its founder, sits in front of Healy Hall. Note the stack of books under the bishop's chair. The sculptor added them later when frisky undergraduates kept putting chamber pots there.

Healy Hall, incidentally, is named after Fr. Patrick Healy, the first African American Jesuit in the United States. In 1874 he was named president of Georgetown, becoming the first African American to head a Catholic university. Healy planned and built the hall that now bears his name. The four-story structure is 312 feet long and 95 feet wide. Its spire is the highest point in the District of Columbia.

Georgetown began as a seminary with twelve students and a few professors. Today its 13 thousand students enjoy a 104-acre campus with sixty-one buildings. The school adopted its official colors of blue and gray in 1866 to symbolize the union of the North and South after the Civil War. The school mascot, the Hoya, is derived from a Greek and Latin phrase *hoya saxa,* which means, "what rocks!" That comes from a cheer that referred to the stones in the school's outer walls or perhaps from Georgetown's nineteenth-century Stonewalls baseball club.

St. Matthew's Cathedral (1725 Rhode Island Ave., 202-347-3215) should be vaguely familiar to Americans over forty. President Kennedy's funeral was held here. The church's steps were the background of the famous picture of John-John saluting his father's casket. Directly in front of the altar, on the floor, is a memorial to the slain president. It reads, "Here rested the remains of President Kennedy at the requiem mass November 25, 1963, before their removal to Arlington where they lie in expectation of a heavenly resurrection."

The parish's boundaries include the White House, and President Kennedy attended Sunday Mass here. He sat on the right side in the seventh or eighth pew from the back. On more official occasions, he sat in the "Pew of Presidents," the first row on the left side.

Considering its location in the nation's capital, the cathedral is aptly named. Matthew, a former tax collector, is the patron saint of government workers.

If a picture is worth a thousand words, the masterpieces at the **National Gallery of Art** (Sixth St. and Constitution Ave., NW, 202-

737-4215) speak volumes about faith and God. On display are Botticelli's *Adoration of the Magi,* Raphael's *Alba Madonna,* Van Eyck's *Annunciation,* and Ruben's *Daniel in the Lion's Den.* Modern art often lacks a sense of the divine; the paintings from the centuries when Christianity was unquestioned blaze with awe and wonder.

Scheduled to open in the year 2000 is the **Pope John Paul II Cultural Center**, to be located on a fourteen-acre wooded site near The Catholic University of America. The $50 million center will be part museum and part think tank. The 100 thousand-foot center will include galleries, theaters, classrooms, study areas for scholars, gift shops, and a dining area. It will serve as both a tribute to the historical ministry of Pope John Paul II and a place for scholars to apply the teachings of the Church to contemporary social problems. Adam Cardinal Maida of Detroit, whose immigrant parents were born in Poland, spearheaded the project. The center's cornerstone, a brick-shaped stone from the tomb of Saint Peter, was blessed in a ceremony at the Vatican in 1996.

Trinity College (125 Michigan Ave., NE, 202-939-5000) was one of the nation's first Catholic college for women, ushering in a wave of such institutions. It was founded in 1899 by Sr. Julia McGroarty, a native of Ireland. As superior of the Sisters of Notre Dame de Namur, she also founded fourteen convents.

The **Washington Monument** (15th St. and Constitution Ave., 202-426-6839) should interest Catholics for two reasons. Its construction history was marred by abject anti-Catholicism. And the president it memorializes was a staunch defender of religious liberty.

The monument was still under construction in 1854 when a block donated by Pope Pius IX was stolen by the anti-Catholic "Know-Nothings" of the American party. The "Know-Nothings" actually took control of the project the following year, but their mismanagement and public anger over their theft brought the work to a halt. The monument was not finished until 1884.

During Washington's presidency religious intolerance flared up. "No Popery" signs waved in New England. America was still an untried experiment, and it was uncertain if and how religious freedom should be protected. Washington, who worshiped regularly at his Episcopal church, vigorously supported the right of Americans to worship freely.

MARYLAND

Southern Maryland

Chapel Point

St. Ignatius Church (8855 Chapel Point Rd., 301-934-8245) is the oldest active Jesuit parish in the nation. A resident priest has been at this site since 1662. The current church, built in 1798, was gutted by a fire in 1866 and subsequently restored. Adjoining the church is **St. Thomas More**, a residence for priests for more than three hundred years.

Leonardtown

St. Aloysius Church (22800 Washington St., 301-475-8064) dates from 1710. Catholicism has long been predominant in St. Mary's County. In this century, too, the county has had a higher percentage of Catholics than nearly any other U.S. county.

St. Francis Xavier Church (21370 Newtowne Neck Rd., 301-475-9885), built in 1731, is the oldest Catholic church in continuous use in the thirteen original colonies. The first church on the site was erected in 1662. The cemetery established then is still in use. In 1668 the Jesuits purchased 850 acres here for 40 thousand pounds of tobacco and set up their mission headquarters for a wide region. The bell in the vestibule, dated 1691, was used until 1884.

Port Tobacco

In 1790 the **Carmelite Monastery** (5678 Mount Carmel Rd.), the first U.S. convent, was established. The family of Fr. Charles Neale, a native of Charles County, as were the nuns who began the convent, donated 860 acres to the Carmelites. Two of the original convent buildings have been restored and are open to visitors during the summer. A third building is still used as a convent.

St. Clements Island

Maryland was founded as a haven for Catholics. On March 25, 1634, the Feast of the Annunciation, English colonists landed on **St. Clement's Island**, located in the Potomac River off Colton Point. A 40-foot cross on the island marks the spot where Leonard Calvert, a member of a prominent Catholic family in England, Jesuit Fr. Andrew White, and 140 Catholic and Protestant voyagers on the *Ark* and the *Dove* landed.

White erected a large wooden cross and offered a Mass of Thanksgiving. The Protestants, the majority on the ships, held their own services. There was no friction between the two groups. Before the ships left England, the Calverts had written a set of rules for the new colony: All people would be equal before the law. All would be free to practice their faith, and there would be no state-established religion.

The Calverts cleverly named their colony Maryland. For Catholics, the name honored the Queen of Heaven. The Protestants did not protest; for them, the name was a tribute to the Queen of England. Father White established a mission in Maryland that lasted well after the American Revolution and compiled the first catechism, dictionary, and grammar in a Native American language.

The **St. Clements Island-Potomac River Museum** (Bay View Rd. in Colton's Point, 301-769-2222) has exhibits on the early history of Maryland.

St. Inigoes

St. Ignatius Church (Villa Rd. off Rte. 5, 301-863-2149 or -5400) was built in 1785 at the site of a Jesuit mission that began in 1662—the first Catholic mission in the colonies. The church was built after freedom of religion was restored in America following the revolution. Adjoining the church is one of the oldest graveyards in the country. Buried here are early Jesuit priests and Revolutionary War veterans.

St. Mary's City

St. Mary's City (on Rte. 5, 301-862-0990), the capital of Maryland from 1634 to 1695, faded from prominence and practically disappeared from the map for centuries until excavations began in the 1970s. The city, the fourth permanent settlement in British North America, is being reconstructed. The city has special significance for Catholics. It was the site of the enactment of the first laws in the New World recognizing religious tolerance. In 1649 the legislature guaranteed freedom of conscience for all Christians. (Freedom for other religions came later.) Sadly, the law was abolished the same year it was enacted when the Puritans seized control of the government and began fiercely persecuting Catholics. A *Freedom of Conscience* statue that commemorates the historic law is at the city's entrance.

Northern Maryland

Annapolis

Historic **St. Mary's Church** (109 Duke of Gloucester St., 410-263-2397) recalls both the persecution of Catholics and their determination to practice their faith. Behind the church is the thirty-five-room **Charles Carroll Mansion**. Born here in 1737, the wealthy Carroll was the only Catholic signer of the Declaration of Independence. Since Maryland Catholics could not worship in public until the Revolution (nor vote or hold public office), Carroll opened a private chapel in his home. Carroll's cousin, incidentally, was Archbishop John Carroll, the Baltimore bishop who was the nation's first prelate.

In 1821 Carroll's granddaughter oversaw the building of St. Mary's Church. The current Gothic church was built between 1858 and 1860 by Redemptorist novices, seminarians, and brothers. Saint

John Neumann, then provincial vicar for the Redemptorists, signed the deed to the property in 1852 and, as bishop of Philadelphia, attended the dedication. He blessed one of the four bells that were installed in the steeple. A stained-glass window in the back commemorates Neumann.

The remains of Saint Justin, one of the most extensive relics in the country, are buried in the church cemetery. A priest brought them to Maryland from Italy in 1873 to protect them from political turmoil. The fifteen small, brittle bones were displayed in the church until the 1960s when the church was renovated. In 1989 the remains were buried in a golden urn.

Baltimore

No other U.S. city has such a rich Catholic past. Founded here were the first seminary, the first parochial school, the first cathedral, and the first African American parish. The first priest to be ordained in America was ordained here, and the first bishop was appointed here.

The mother church of U.S. Catholicism is the **Basilica of the Assumption of the Blessed Virgin Mary** (Mulberry and Cathedral Streets, 410-727-3566). The land was formerly owned by Revolutionary War hero John Eager Howard. Dedicated in 1821, the neoclassical structure was designed by Benjamin Henry Latrobe, the architect of the U.S. Capitol. The three-domed building has a spacious interior. Built of brick and granite, it was once described by a major historian of architecture as "the most beautiful church in America."

Most of the first bishops in the United States were consecrated here, and many of the nineteenth- and twentieth-century meetings of U.S. bishops were held in the basilica. A bust of Archbishop Carroll is located in the nave, and he is buried in the church crypt. Carroll was a key figure in the Revolutionary War. He obtained the support of the French government for the American cause, later prompting George Washington to write, "Of all men whose influence was most potent in securing the success of the Revolution, Bishop Carroll of Baltimore was the man."

Baltimore was established as the first diocese in 1789, and as the first bishop, whose diocese was the entire country, Carroll led the growth of the Church in the United States. In his quarter century as a bishop, the number of U.S. Catholics quadrupled to more than 200 thousand. Under his direction the Sulpicians at St. Mary's and the Jesuits at Georgetown educated a native-born clergy. At his invitation, Augustinians, Carmelites, Dominicans, Sisters of Charity, and Visitation nuns began their work in the United States.

Carroll was a man ahead of his time. Despite attacks by bishops overseas, he advocated the use of the vernacular in the liturgy to counter distrust and prejudice against Catholics and to make the faith more accessible to worshipers. He was partly successful. The Baltimore Synod of 1791 instructed priests to read the Sunday Gospel in English.

St. Francis Xavier Church (1501 N. Caroline St., 410-727-3103) was founded in 1793 as the nation's first Catholic church for African Americans. That year five hundred Blacks arrived in Baltimore on six ships from Santo Domingo (now Haiti). Some were slaves and some were free. All were French-speaking Catholics. Sulpician Fathers, who fled the French Revolution, set up a basement chapel for the refugees at St. Mary's Seminary. The congregation received its own church in Baltimore in 1864. The parish, now run by the Josephite Fathers, moved to its current location in 1968.

Four French Sulpicians who fled the French Revolution started the first U.S. seminary, **St. Mary's Seminary** (5400 Roland Ave., 410-323-3200), in 1791. The United States then had fewer than thirty Catholic priests and fewer than fifty thousand Catholics. The persecution of the Church in France proved to be enormously beneficial for the U.S. Church. French priests and seminarians emigrated in waves, and Archbishop John Carroll put them to good use, assigning some to the sparsely populated frontier areas like Kentucky and Indiana.

Mother Seton House.

Mother Seton House (600 N. Paca St., 301-523-3443) was where the first American-born saint lived and ran a school that was the birthplace of the U.S. parochial school system.

Elizabeth Ann Seton was born in 1774 into a prosperous Anglican family with a tradition of service. Married at nineteen to William Seton, she raised five children in New York. After her husband died of tuberculosis, Seton was drawn to Catholicism. Despite strong objections from family and friends she became a Catholic in 1805. Her children were taunted, and the church she joined in New York City was nearly burned down.

By chance, she met Sulpician Fr. William Dubourg, the founder of St. Mary's Seminary, who asked her to come to Baltimore to open a school. With her three daughters she moved into the small house on Paca Street and opened the school in the fall of 1808.

Mother Seton founded the Sisters of Charity of Saint Joseph in 1809. The community closely followed the rules of the Daughters of Charity in France, with one important exception. Widows admitted to the Daughters of Charity had to entrust their children to others; Mother Seton refused to do so. She died in 1821 and was canonized in 1975.

Mother Seton House is furnished in period furniture. A stained-glass window of Mother Seton portrays her saintly demeanor.

Adjacent to Mother Seton House is the chapel from the original St. Mary's Seminary. **St. Mary's Chapel**, built in 1807, reverberates with history. Mother Seton took her vows here in 1809. The

Oblate Sisters of Providence, the first Black community of nuns, began here in 1829. The Sister Servants of the Immaculate Heart of Mary also started here.

Childs

The **"Stone Lady"** keeps an eye out for the 62 thousand vehicles per day that pass by her on busy I-95 near Childs close to the Delaware border. The 14-foot white marble statue of the Virgin Mary, hands folded in prayer, is an inspiration and landmark to travelers who zip by Childs. The Oblates of Saint Francis de Sales maintain the shrine, which is near their retreat center (410-398-3040). In front of the statue are hedges cut in the shape of a cross and the letters *V* and *J,* which stand for *"Vive Jesus,"* French for "live as Jesus lived." The statue was built in 1972 to commemorate a horrible accident that killed three people. A priest who raced from his room to assist rescuers proposed building the shrine. The money given by motorists appreciative of the shrine is used to maintain the statue and the well-kept landscaping that surrounds it.

Emmitsburg

Mother Seton School (100 Creamery Rd., 301-447-3161), founded in 1810 by Mother Seton, is the oldest parochial school in the country. Two moves away from its original building, the independent school is staffed by nuns and laity and is supported by about a dozen parishes. The school is recognized for its quality academics while remaining affordable.

The **National Shrine of St. Elizabeth Ann Seton** (333 S. Seton Ave., 301-447-6606) includes the grave site of Mother Seton, a chapel, a museum, a reproduction of a classroom from her time, and Seton House, the original home of the Sisters of Charity.

Overlooking the Mother Seton shrine is a towering, 95-foot statue of the Blessed Mother, part of the **National Shrine Grotto of Lourdes** (301-447-6122). The statue is crowned with a 25-foot gold-leafed bronze figure of Our Lady. Built in the early 1800s, the grotto was the first national Catholic shrine.

Mount St. Mary's College (301-447-6122), begun in 1808, is home to the **John Hughes Cabin**. Born in Ireland, Hughes, who later became the first archbishop of New York, built this small log structure in 1820 while taking classes at the college. He worked as a gardener to pay for his room and board. Bishop Hughes, as head of the nation's most populous diocese, urged the Irish to adopt American ways. He also vigorously defended Catholics. In 1844, a month after Catholic churches were burned in Philadelphia, anti-Irish and anti-Catholic speakers planned a rally in New York. The rally was canceled by city officials after Hughes formed groups of two thousand men to protect each church.

Frederick

Irish immigrants who labored on a nearby canal built **St. John the Evangelist Church** (116 E. 2nd St., 301-662-8288) in 1837. Fr. John McElroy, who founded Boston College, completed the building. During the Civil War the church was used to house prisoners.

Rockville

The **F. Scott Fitzgerald Burial Site** in Rockville (St. Mary's Cemetery, Veirs Mill Rd. and Rockville Pike) holds the remains of a writer whose Catholic background is often completely overlooked. It shouldn't be. True, the creator of Jay Gatsby left the church. But his artistry was divine. The archbishop of Baltimore said of him, "He was a man touched by the faith of the Catholic Church. There can be perceived in his work a Catholic consciousness of reality. He found in his faith an understanding of the human heart caught in the struggle between grace and death. His characters are involved in this great drama, seeking God and seeking love."

Warwick

One of the first Catholic churches in the colonies was **St. Francis Xavier Church** (Bohemia Church Rd. and Warwick Rd., 302-378-5800), also known as Old Bohemia Church. A Jesuit priest founded the parish in 1704, and the church building dates from 1766. The church bell is dated 1691. John Carroll, the future bishop, and his cousin Charles Carroll attended Bohemia Academy, the predecessor of Georgetown University. The church no longer has a congregation. Old Bohemia rectory is a museum with church-related artifacts.

NEW JERSEY

Northern New Jersey

Newark

The first spadeful of soil was lifted in 1898 for the **Cathedral Basilica of the Sacred Heart** (89 Ridge St., 201-484-4600). The magnificent church was not fully completed until 1954, an indication of the church's stunning artistic detail. The French Gothic-style structure is reminiscent of the cathedrals in Chartres and Rheims. The great copper spire that tops the cathedral soars 260 feet. The church covers 40,000 square feet, nearly equal to the size of Westminster Abbey in London. There are 140 stained-glass windows and three magnificent rose windows.

Some of the finest artists in the world contributed to the cathedral. Gonippo Raggi (1875–1959) of Rome, considered by some to be the foremost religious artist of his era, coordinated the design of the marble altars, woodwork, baptistry, bronze doors, and mosaics. The figure of Christ the King sits above the main entrance, and Mary Queen of Heaven is aside him. The stained-glass windows are the work of Franz Zettler, a world-renowned craftsman from Munich. The most notable is the gallery rose window titled *The Last Judgment,* a 34-foot-wide masterpiece.

The most impressive chapel is the Lady Chapel, located in the apse behind the High Altar. Zettler's stained-glass windows look over a breathtaking altar made of pure Carrara marble.

The hand-carved woodwork surrounding the sanctuary is of Appalachian oak, a wood also used for the pews. The massive narthex screen is hand-carved Indiana limestone, as is all the interior stonework.

St. John's Church (24 Mulberry St., 201-623-0822), the oldest Catholic church in the city, was built in 1826. The church had the city's first chimes, installed in 1859.

The **National Shrine of St. Gerard** at St. Lucy's Church (118 Seventh Ave., 201-482-6663) honors Saint Gerard Majella, the eighteenth-century Italian Redemptorist who is the patron saint of motherhood. His feast is celebrated with nine days of prayer, and his statue is carried through the streets for three days.

Near Newark

Elizabeth

St. Mary's Church (155 Washington Ave., 908-352-5154), besieged by rioting nativists in 1854, was saved from destruction only by the brave women of the parish who, with babies on their arms, ringed the church and dissuaded the mob.

Morristown

St. Mary's Abbey (230 Mendham Rd., 201-538-3231) has its roots in a Benedictine community established in Latrobe, Pennsylvania, in 1846. The Benedictines purchased this site from the estate of a wealthy New York banker in 1925. The modern church is a triumphant arrangement of brick, concrete, and steel. The retreat center has room for thirty-six adults.

Summit

The **Rosary Shrine, Monastery of Our Lady of the Rosary** (543 Springfield Ave., 908-273-1228) has a replica of the Shroud of Turin. The copy was made at the command of Austrian royalty in 1624. The Dominican nuns of Saint Dominic and Saint Sixtus Monastery in Rome gave the copy to the Dominicans at Our Lady of Rosary in the 1920s. The monastery's cloistered sisters have held a perpetual exposition of the Blessed Sacrament since 1926.

Washington

The **Shrine of the Immaculate Heart of Mary** (Mountain View Rd., 908-689-7330) also serves as the national headquarters of the Blue Army of Fátima. The shrine's focal point is a bronze statue of Our Lady standing on a crowned tower, 145-feet high.

Central New Jersey

Freehold

St. Rose of Lima School (51 Lincoln Pl., 908-462-2646) was where the rock star Bruce Springsteen received his education in the 1960s. Springsteen's music is steeped in Catholic sensibilities. His songs revolve around a desperate search for meaning; sin, death, redemption, and community take center stage. Sociologist Fr. Andrew Greeley calls the Boss "a major religious prophet, a Catholic

with a profoundly Catholic viewpoint." In 1997 Springsteen performed at the school in a benefit. "Get ready for a night of sin and redemption," Springsteen told the audience. "I'll take care of the sin. Father [Gerald] McCarron will handle the redemption."

Spring Lake

One would expect to find the grandeur of **St. Catharine Church** (Essex and W. Lake Avenues, 908-449-5765) in a major city. Indeed, parishioners worshiped at a modest frame structure called St. Ann's

St. Catharine Church.
(Christine Findlay Photo Graphic Arts)

in the nineteenth century. The current church was built in 1901 after wealthy entrepreneur Martin Maloney lost his beloved daughter, Catherine, from tuberculosis at the age of seventeen in 1900. Maloney had a summer residence in Spring Lake.

The Classic Revival church was modeled after the Church of Santa Maria del Popolo in Rome. The exterior features a striking classical templelike front. The 92-foot-high copper dome is topped by a gilded cross. The interior is marked by graceful marble columns and first-rate painted surfaces, many done by Gonippo Raggi. The fresco at the center of the dome shows the Pentecost, with life-size figures of the Apostles and Mary. A number of murals have Irish themes, a collaboration between Raggi and Chicago-based Celtic artist Thomas O'Shaughnessy.

Stirling

Saint Joseph's Shrine (1050 Long Hill Rd., 908-647-0208) grew out of weekend retreats for boys given in the 1920s by the Missionary Servants. The boys erected an outdoor statue of Saint Joseph and later a rustic chapel. Another chapel was built in the 1970s. There are outdoor shrines to Our Lady of Humility, Saint Anthony, Mother Cabrini, Saint Anne, the Holy Cross, Saint Martin de Porres, and Our Lady of Fátima.

Trenton

St. Mary's Cathedral (157 N. Warren St., 609-396-8447), dedicated in 1871, stands on land where much of the fighting during the Battle of Trenton of the Revolutionary War took place. A plaque at the adjoining diocesan offices recalls that the Hessian commander Colonel Rall died at his headquarters in the house that formerly stood here.

Southern New Jersey

Goshen

The early days of Catholicism in New Jersey are incorporated into **St. Elizabeth Church** (609-861-3771). The structure once was St. Elizabeth Church of Port Elizabeth, built in 1845. The church closed fifteen years later after the glass industry of Port Elizabeth failed. In 1879 the framework, altar, pews, and accessories were floated downriver on barges and then transported by horse and buggy to Goshen.

Pomona

The **Shrine of Our Lady of the Highway, Sea and Air** at Church of the Assumption (1993 White Horse Pike, 609-965-1399) is popular with motorists on the way to the seashore. The small outdoor shrine has a statue of Our Lady of the Way in a three-sided enclosure.

Salem

St. Mary (25 Oak St., 609-935-0288), dedicated in 1852, is one of the state's oldest churches. Missionary work at Salem, led by Jesuits, goes back to the 1740s.

NORTH CAROLINA

Western North Carolina

Asheville

The unusual **Basilica of St. Lawrence** (97 Haywood St., 704-252-6042) was built without beams of wood or steel. All walls, floors, ceilings, and pillars are of tile or other masonry material. The massive stone foundation and solid brick superstructure were constructed to last for generations. The Spanish Renaissance-style structure was designed in 1909 by Rafael Guastavino, who is interred in the crypt of a chapel dedicated to Our Lady.

The elliptical dome, 82 by 58 feet, is believed to be the largest unsupported dome in North America. It is built entirely of tiles.

Depicted on the main facade is Saint Lawrence, holding in one hand a palm frond and in the other a gridiron, the instrument of his torture. The brass entrance doors, installed for the eightieth anniversary of the building, were handcrafted in India.

Nearly all the windows were made in Munich. Just under the vault of the dome are ten semicircular windows that depict biblical miracles and other scenes.

Belmont

The picturesque **Belmont Abbey** (100 Belmont-Mount Holly Rd., 704-825-6675) is one of the finest examples of "American Benedictine" architecture. A chief proponent of the style was a resident monk, Dom Michael McInerney (1877–1963). He designed scores of buildings for Catholic institutions in at least thirteen states that are characterized by a restrained use of ornament and emphasize the verticality of structures. Campus buildings, especially St. Leo Hall, a 1910 creation, seem to want to take off toward heaven. The abbey's Shrine of Our Lady of Lourdes is the only pilgrimage shrine in the state. It was dedicated in 1891 after a monk was cured of typhoid fever.

Charlotte

St. Peter's Church (507 S. Tyron St., 704-372-6808) was founded in 1851 to serve the Irish laboring in nearby gold mines. The current church dates from 1878. The magnificent fresco on the front wall of the sanctuary, sure to draw admirers for years to come, was painted in 1987. The fanciful Victorian rectory, built in 1897, features a keyhole window.

Cherokee

Our Lady of Guadalupe Church (US 441, 704-488-6766) was built in 1966 on the Cherokee Reservation in the Great Smoky Mountains. The seven-sided structure symbolizes the seven-sided counsel house of the Cherokee Nation.

Central North Carolina

Fayetteville

St. Patrick Church (2840 Village Dr., 910-323-2410) was the state's first Catholic church when built in 1821. The town counted exactly twelve Catholics. The entire state had only one hundred Catholics. The first church burned within a decade; the second lasted a century. The current building, the fourth, was completed in 1963. Catholics still represent the smallest mainstream denomination in North Carolina, but today St. Patrick has forty-five hundred members, making it one of the largest in the state.

Southern North Carolina

Wilmington

The dinner conversations at the Guastavino household in 1909 must have been an architect's dream. **St. Mary's Church** (412 Ann St., 910-762-5491) was designed in 1909 by Rafael Guastavino, the namesake and son of the noted architect. The younger Rafael took a page from his father's book on architecture and gave St. Mary's a self-supporting dome, made from tiles and without steel, nails, or wood.

PENNSYLVANIA

Eastern Pennsylvania

Allentown

Saint John Neumann founded **Immaculate Conception Church** (501 Ridge Ave., 610-433-4404) in 1857. Located here, the **National Shrine Center of Our Lady of Guadalupe**, dedicated in 1974, has a reproduction of Our Lady of Guadalupe that is strikingly similar to the original in Mexico.

Conewago Township

Established in 1721, the **Basilica of the Sacred Heart of Jesus** (717-637-2721) is the oldest Jesuit chapel west of the Susquehanna. Aware that colonial law restricted Catholicism, a Jesuit priest in the 1740s who was chapel pastor took the name of Mister Manners and dressed in the drab style of the Quakers. The present chapel, a stone church in colonial style, was constructed in 1787. In the 1840s a Tyrolean artist covered the walls and ceilings with first-class frescoes.

Gettysburg

Gettysburg National Military Park (97 Taneytown Rd., 717-334-1124) has the **Father Corby Statue** (S. Hancock Ave.). Father William Corby was chaplain of the 88th New York Infantry, a Celtic unit in the Irish Brigade. Corby gave a general absolution to all his men on July 2, 1863, before they stormed into horrific battle. General absolution was customary in England for soldiers but unheard of in the United States. The statue, dedicated in 1910, shows the priest perched on a rock explaining his action to the soldiers. A replica of the statue is at Notre Dame University.

Philadelphia

The great Babe Ruth once suited up for a semiprofessional baseball team sponsored by **Ascension of Our Lord Parish** (725 E. Westmoreland St., 215-739-1670). He did so in September 1923, while the Yankees were driving for a pennant and he was fighting for a batting title. Fr. William Casey, assistant pastor, sought out Ruth for a charity game to help pay off the debt for Ascension Catholic Club, which had built a new field. Ruth, who spent much of his childhood at St. Mary's Industrial School in Baltimore, agreed to play once he learned that children would be involved.

The Yankees played the Philadelphia Athletics at 3:15 P.M. The charity game was scheduled at 6:00 P.M., since the field had no lights. That was cutting it close. Fortunately, Yankees pitcher "Sad" Sam Jones threw a no-hitter, and the Babe made it to the game on time. Ten thousand frenzied fans squeezed into the stadium, and hundreds more packed the nearby hills. Ruth did not disappoint. Playing against a team sponsored by a department store, he ripped a 600-foot shot over the fence. The umpire, however, ruled it a ground-rule double because of the short right-field fence. Ascension lost the game 2 to 1, but Ruth's box-office magic retired the club debt and gave the parish some sweet memories.

Few U.S. churches can match the historical significance of **Olde St. Augustine's Church** (Fourth and New Streets, 215-627-1838). Two Irish friars sent by the Vatican to minister to the city's growing Irish-Catholic population laid the church's cornerstone in 1796. The parish was the foundation of the Augustinians in the United States. Donors to the church included George Washington; John Barry, the father of the U.S. Navy; and Thomas Fitzsimmons, who signed the Constitution.

In the 1820s the church became the home of the "Sister Bell" of the Liberty Bell, which cracked in 1752 the first time it was rung.

The Sister Bell was an identical bell that city officials quickly ordered. The repaired Liberty Bell was placed in Independence Hall, as was the Sister Bell until the latter was moved to St. Augustine's.

St. Augustine's, the city's largest church, was a cultural center. The first Philadelphia performance of Handel's *Messiah* occurred here. Villanova College grew out of St. Augustine's Academy, a boys' school founded in 1811. The church had a library with three thousand volumes, the largest theological library in Philadelphia.

The library—and the church—went up in flames in the Nativist Riots of 1844. The Nativists, alarmed by the increasing numbers of immigrants, wanted citizenship reserved for those with twenty-five years of residency in the United States. In Philadelphia, tensions heightened over a misunderstanding. Bishop Francis Kenrick asked the city school board to let Catholic students use a Catholic version of the Bible instead of the King James version. The suspicious public accused Catholics of trying to eliminate the Bible in public schools.

Irish-Catholics and Nativists clashed twice on the street. Eleven Nativists and two Catholics died. An angry mob began burning Catholic institutions and homes. Despite the attempts of the mayor to turn back the mob, St. Augustine's was gutted. The Sister Bell was destroyed. Only the wall behind the altar remained standing. On it, in charred gilt letters, were the words "The Lord Seeth."

The friars sued the city for not providing adequate protection. The city argued that the Augustinians, as a foreign society under the jurisdiction of the pope, did not enjoy the same civil rights. The friars won and were awarded $45 thousand.

The church was rebuilt in 1847. President James Buchanan, a native of the state, made a donation. The superb ceiling frescoes, showing scenes from Saint Augustine in glory, were painted by Philip Costaggini, who painted part of the rotunda of the Capitol in Washington. Behind the altar is a painting of the Crucifixion, and above it remain the words "The Lord Seeth."

Gesu Church (18th St. and Girard Ave.) has a painting by a celebrated artist that mysteriously ended up embedded in the wall of the sanctuary. The beautiful painting *The Blessed Virgin Mary* received a gold medal at an exhibition in Warsaw in 1884. The artist was Poland's Jan Styka (1858–1925), one of the greatest painters of his time. The painting disappeared on its way to the Chicago World Exposition of 1892. It surfaced in Gesu Church in 1897. Because it was attached to the wall, Styka was forced to let it stay. He requested the inscription that is below it: "Our Lady of Poland, Pray for Us."

Erected in 1733, **Old St. Joseph's Church** (321 Willings Alley, 215-923-1733) is the oldest church in the city and, amazingly enough, for eighty years was the only Catholic church for Pennsylvania, New York, and New Jersey. St. Joseph helped establish freedom of religion in America. Its courtyard plaque reads, "When in 1733 St. Joseph Roman Catholic Church was founded and dedicated to the guardian of the Holy Family, it was the only place in the entire English-speaking world where public celebration of the holy sacrifice of the Mass was permitted by law." The church's unique status was owing to William Penn, who founded the colony of Pennsylvania in 1701 and decreed religious toleration, a freedom not granted by other colonies. Still, Catholics had to be wary. In its early decades the parish kept a low profile, and pastors went about the city in Quaker garb.

The **Blessed Margaret of Castello Shrine** at Holy Name of Jesus Church (701 E. Gaul St., 215-739-3960) is especially dear to those who suffer from physical, mental, or emotional infirmities. Margaret (1287–1320) was born dreadfully deformed. She was a dwarf, totally blind, hunchbacked and so lame she could barely walk. Her embarrassed father kept her in a small cell he built near the forest. When she was seventeen, her heartless parents abandoned her after a trip to a shrine failed to improve her condition. Margaret became a beggar, gradually drew closer to God, and became the first unmarried woman to become a Dominican Tertiary. Her own misfortune gave her empathy for others. Nearly always serene and gentle, she visited prisoners, helped the sick, and comforted the dying.

Old St. Mary's Church (252 S. Fourth St., 215-923-7930), dating from 1763, has seen many illustrious worshipers—George Washington; James Oeller, an innkeeper who popularized the word "hotel"; and John Adams. In colonial days, Catholics apparently could sing: Adams wrote to his wife, Abigail, "The music, consisting of an organ and a choir of singers, went all the afternoon except sermon time, and the assembly chanted most sweetly and exquisitely. Here is everything that can lay hold of the eye, ear and imagination, everything which can charm and bewitch the simple and ignorant. I wonder how Luther ever broke the spell."

The church cemetery was begun in 1759. Some of the family of Michael Bouvier, the great-great-grandfather of Jacqueline Kennedy, are buried here.

The **National Shrine of Saint John Neumann** at St. Peter the Apostle Church (1019 N. Fifth St., 215-627-3080) honors one of the most endearing figures in U.S. Catholicism. Born in Bohemia, John Neumann came to the United States after being ordained. A Redemptorist, Father Neumann was humble and down-to-earth. When named bishop of Philadelphia in 1852, he confided to a friend, "I'd rather die tomorrow that be consecrated a bishop."

He was a brilliant bishop. Wanting to be close to his flock, he avidly learned several languages. He spoke and heard confessions in French, German, Bohemian, Spanish, Italian, Dutch, and English. When he learned that some Irish could not confess because none of his priests knew Gaelic, he studied that language, too. An elderly Irish woman once stepped out of the confessional and proclaimed, "Ah, isn't it grand that we finally have an Irish bishop!"

Bishop Neumann assiduously championed Catholic schools. In one year enrollment in his schools jumped from 500 to 5,000. He befriended the poor, who knew he was an easy touch. The needy waited until he arrived home to ring his bell, sure they would receive that much more. No chore was too small for the bishop. He was known to clean the church in the wee hours of the morning. An archbishop once complained to Rome about his peculiar comrade: "The Bishop of Philadelphia seems a little inferior for the importance of such a distinguished city, not in learning nor in zeal nor in piety, but because of the littleness of his person and his neglect of the fashions." Indeed, the bishop owned just one habit and one pair of shoes and wore an old hat.

The bishop established eighty churches, brought seven religious orders into his diocese, and authored two popular catechisms. In 1860 Neumann died suddenly at age forty-eight after collapsing in a street. He was canonized in 1977, the first American male to be recognized so. Neumann is entombed at St. Peter in a glass coffin underneath the altar. Lights illuminate the wax facsimile molded around his skeleton.

Rosenbach Museum and Library (2010 Delancey Pl., 215-732-1600) has a marvelous double-sided altarpiece that shows the Resurrection. One side was carved during medieval times, probably in the fourteenth century, and the other, using the more naturalistic style of the Renaissance, during the sixteenth century.

Near Philadelphia

Doylestown

The **National Shrine of Our Lady of Czestochowa** (Beacon Hill and Ferry Roads, 215-345-0600) had a modern church built in 1966 to commemorate one thousand years of Christianity in Poland. President Lyndon Johnson gave the main address at the dedication before an audience of 135 thousand. The church's huge stained-glass windows are among the largest in the country. The west window shows the history of Christianity in Poland, and the east window depicts the contributions of Christians to U.S. history.

Eastern Pennsylvania

Scranton

St. Anne's Monastery National Shrine (1230 St. Ann St., 717-347-5691) grew out of the monastery, retreat house, and chapel begun by the Passionist Fathers in 1905. Hardly had the buildings been occupied when they began to tilt and crack. An old mine shaft was caving in underneath. Experts warned the priests to vacate the premises. Instead, they prayed to Saint Ann. Amazingly, a huge drift of coal broke loose and filled the shaft, halting the movement of the earth. A shrine was then built. The Lombardy Renaissance-style church was dedicated in 1929. Its rough brick and artfully smooth stone create a pleasant effect.

Conflict at **Sacred Heart of Jesus and Mary Church** in Scranton (1217 Prospect Ave., 717-343-6420) led to the formation of the Polish National Catholic Church, the first permanent schism in the United States. In 1895, 250 Polish families clashed with their pastor over finances, withdrew from the parish, and built a new church down the block they called St. Stanislaus. Fr. Francis Hodur, a popular and strong-willed assistant at Sacred Heart, agreed to be their pastor and was eventually excommunicated.

On the surface, the conflict was about church administration. The families had built Sacred Heart and wanted to retain control of the property. Clashes at other Polish American parishes in Chicago, Buffalo, and elsewhere over property rights also led to defections. Many Poles disagreed with the practice of a bishop's holding church property in his name and instead favored the trustee system of ownership in which parishioners maintained control.

But the larger underlying issue was Polish nationalism. Many Catholic Poles were set apart from the mainstream U.S. Church, partly by choice to preserve their cultural heritage and partly because they were excluded from the hierarchy, which the Irish controlled.

Probably more than any other ethnic group, Poles made a strong identification between their religion and their mother country. Like other ethnic groups, they set up national parishes in U.S. cities where they could worship in ways that reflected their homeland traditions. Their church was a piece of Poland they brought with them and would not surrender.

Another factor underlying the schism was the intense loyalty Poles demonstrated to priests. Polish priests were expected to be models of rectitude and to meticulously duplicate their beloved spiritual practices of Poles. In return, Poles gave their priests unswerving allegiance.

St. Stanislaus Cathedral (529 E. Locust St., 717-343-6017) is the mother church of the Polish National Catholic Church. At one time nearly 5 percent of U.S. Poles belonged to the PNCC, which dates from the 1890s.

Abraham Lincoln, who once unsuccessfully defended in court an Irish Catholic congregation in a dispute with their bishop over ownership of their church, is featured in a stained-glass window.

Western Pennsylvania

Bensalem

The **Blessed Katharine Drexel Shrine** at St. Elizabeth Convent (1663 Bristol Pike, 215-244-9900) contains her tomb. The foundress of the Sisters of the Blessed Sacrament was beatified in 1988.

Brownsville

Dedicated in 1845, **St. Peter Church** (304 Shaffner Ave., 412-785-7781) is the oldest continuously used church in western Pennsylvania. The sandstone church sits nobly on a hill, and its distinctive Gothic spire rises above the east bank of the Monongahela River. A first-rate stained-glass window dramatizes the first religious service in Brownsville.

Erie

Mount Saint Benedict Monastery (6101 E. Lake Rd., 814-899-0614) consists of three isolated hermitages in the woods. About 150 Benedictine sisters call the monastery home. Besides providing a peaceful place to pray, the sisters are known for their peace efforts. They work for disarmament, ecological stewardship, and social justice in solidarity with the poor and oppressed, especially women.

Footedale

The **St. Maximilian Kolbe Shrine** (412-245-7179) at St. Thomas Church resembles the prison cell in Auschwitz where the saint died after volunteering to die for another. The words "The path of freedom is marked by the cross" are above the entrance to the outdoor shrine, erected in 1982 after Kolbe was canonized.

Loretto

Prince Demetrius Gallitzin was born in 1790 at The Hague, where his father was the ambassador of the Russian government. Raised as an atheist, the prince was drawn to Catholicism through his mother, a convert. Despite threats from his family, he went to the United States and entered Saint Mary's Seminary in Baltimore. In 1795 he became the second priest to be ordained in America. He served at McGuire's Settlement, changing its name to Loretto. The **Prince Gallitzin Chapel and Home** (on Rte. 53) are kept much as they were when the "Apostle of the Alleghenies" died in 1840.

New Baltimore

St. John the Baptist Church (814-733-2210) is known as the Church on the Pennsylvania Turnpike. A pair of signs on the east- and westbound berms list Mass times. Concrete stairs lead up from the highway to the church. Erected in 1890, the church survived the building of the turnpike in the 1930s because of the savvy of the pastor. He agreed to give the state the land they needed if they created a permanent access to the church from the roadway.

Pittsburgh

The extraordinary **St. Anthony's Chapel** (1704 Harpster St., 412-231-2994) contains the skulls of martyrs Saint Stephena and Saint Macharius; the entire skeletal remains of Saint Demetrius; a piece of stone from the Holy Sepulchre, Christ's burial tomb; and more than 4,400 other religious relics. The chapel has the largest collection of relics in the world outside the Vatican.

Part of Most Holy Name of Jesus Church, the chapel is dedicated to Saint Anthony of Padua, known as "the Wonder Worker." The relics were secured by the first pastor of the parish, Fr. Suitbert Mollinger. The son of a wealthy Belgian family, the enterprising priest, concerned that the relics were being neglected, began procuring them in the 1880s on his frequent trips to Europe. The chapel was dedicated in 1892 on the Feast of Saint Anthony. That same day Mollinger suffered a stroke; he died two days later.

Nearly three thousand awestruck people visit the chapel each month. One of the most memorable pieces is a life-size Stations of the Cross, acquired in 1890, carved of wood by artists of the Royal Ecclesiastical Art Establishment in Munich.

The green-domed **Immaculate Heart of Mary Church** (3058 Brereton Ave., 412-621-5170) rises brilliantly above the neighboring asphalt-shingled dwellings. The inscriptions for the windows and Stations of the Cross for the church, founded by Poles in 1904, are in Polish. But in a nod to the universality of Catholicism, a photo of the pope is captioned in Italian: Papa Giovanni Paolo II.

Near Pittsburgh

Millvale

Explosive revolutionary paintings highlight the interior of **St. Nicholas Croatian Church** (412-821-3438). The paintings were executed from 1937 to 1941 by Maxo Vanka, a Croatian immigrant. Under the choir loft is a startling image of Mary breaking a soldier's rifle and the crucified Christ bayonetted. A set of images portray two meals: an immigrants' modest table blessed by Christ and a lavish capitalists' feast. Another painting shows Croatian mothers mourning sons killed in war and in industry.

SOUTH CAROLINA

Southeast South Carolina

Charleston

The Gothic-style **Cathedral of St. John the Baptist** (105 Queen St., 803-724-8395) was built in 1907 with Connecticut tool-chiseled brownstone. Over each entrance are unique stained-glass windows showing the papal coat of arms and the seal of the state of South Carolina. The pews are of carved Flemish oak, and the main altar is of white Vermont marble.

In the nave are 14 large two-light windows depicting the life of Christ from the Nativity to the Ascension. Above the high altar is a five-light window modeled after Leonardo da Vinci's *Last Supper.*

The parish dates from 1821. A fire in 1861 that broke out in a factory destroyed much of the city, including the church.

Established in 1789, **St. Mary of the Annunciation Church** (89 Hasell St., 803-722-7696) is the mother church of the Carolinas and Georgia. Many early members were French-speaking refugees who escaped Santo Domingo after a bloody slave rebellion in the 1790s. Tombstones in the church cemetery are written in French.

The current church dates from 1838. Union ships shelled it in 1863, causing minor damage. In 1896, when a new marble floor was put in, a shell was found buried under the sanctuary.

The magnificent main altar of the church was consecrated in 1896. At the time the entire church was handsomely frescoed. Twenty-three oil paintings by Caesare Porta of Rome surrounded the church in the balcony. The Royal Bavarian Establishment in Munich crafted the church's twenty-five stained-glass windows.

No description of Charleston and Catholicism can be complete without reference to the **Sisters of Charity of Our Lady of Mercy** (424 Ft. Johnson Rd., 803-795-2866). Bishop England founded the order in 1829 and patterned them after the Sisters of Charity in Maryland. As the bishop said of his four original nuns (as all bishops could say), "They cost me very little and do much service." The sisters operated orphanages, schools, and a hospital. The order thrived, especially for the four decades in the second half of the nineteenth century under the sterling direction of Mother Teresa Barry, still spoken of in glowing terms normally associated with the modern-day Mother Teresa.

Near Charleston

Moncks Corner

Mepkin Abbey (1098 Mepkin Abbey Rd., 803-761-8509) was founded in 1949 when publisher/philanthropist Henry Luce donated the land to the Trappist Abbey of Gethsemani. Henry and Clare Luce are buried on the grounds. The patriot Henry Laurens, who was imprisoned in the Tower of London, owned the land during the Revolutionary War. The British burned his estate; Union soldiers burned it again during the Civil War.

The abbey is the state's only contemplative monastery. Its 3,000-acre tree-lined location on the Cooper River is a favorite spot for retreats. The monks' innovative fertilizer business has received national attention. The abbey's 25 thousand-volume library attracts scholars and clergy of all faiths.

Ritter

John England, the first bishop of South Carolina, founded **St. James the Greater Church** (803-549-5230) in 1833 to serve plantation owners and their slaves. When the planters left, the parish became an anomaly, a Black Catholic parish in the heart of a rural Southern county. As the Civil War neared, the diocese somehow lost track of the little church. No priest tended to it for forty years. Incredibly, when a priest stumbled upon it in 1897, he found a thriving community led by former slaves.

Still mostly an African American parish, St. James features a massive oil painting of Peter Claver ministering to slaves. It was executed by Emmanuel Dite of France in 1894. The church's neighborhood is known as Catholic Hill.

Sullivan's Island

The first Catholic church on Sullivan's Island was the **Church of St. John the Baptist**, built in 1846. It was the only public building that survived the shelling of Fort Moultrie during the Civil War, only to be destroyed by a cyclone in 1885. **Stella Maris Church** (1204 Middle St., 803-883-3108) was constructed in 1869 partly from the loose brick of the old fort, until the federal government ordered parishioners to stop "dismantling" the old fort walls.

The church's grooved pine ceiling was designed to resemble the interior of an old slave ship. The sanctuary area, restored in the late 1970s, was done in cypress and poplar. The oak pews also date from that time. Until the fort closed in 1947, the firing of its large guns routinely broke church windows. The church's stained-glass windows were not installed until after the fort was no more.

Central South Carolina

Columbia

St. Peter Church (1529 Assembly St., 803-779-0036) was the boyhood parish of Joe Bernardin, a quiet lad of great resolve and deep faith who, of course, later became a cardinal in Chicago. Bernardin was baptized and served as an altar boy here. Pope John Paul II visited the church in 1987 during a daylong visit to the state. The present church dates from 1906; the original church was built in 1824 for immigrants who came to the area to dig the Columbia Canal.

Western South Carolina

Edgefield

An enterprising, frugal pastor built **St. Mary of the Immaculate Conception Church** (305 Buncombe St., 803-637-6248) in 1860. The priest opened a quarry for granite about four miles outside town, bought a forge, and even set up a blacksmith's shop on the construction site. He later traveled as far as Cuba and the Bahamas to solicit donations to pay off the church debt.

Greenville

The late Bob Jones was virulently anti-Catholic. He remarked when Pope John Paul II visited South Carolina that he would "as soon speak to the devil himself." But he amassed one of the finest religious art collections in the country. More than four hundred paintings are displayed in thirty rooms at the **Bob Jones University Museum and Gallery** (1700 Wade Hampton Blvd., 864-242-5100). Nearly every major artist who painted religious themes is represented.

VIRGINIA

Northern Virginia

Alexandria

Wealthy plantation owners, craftsmen, shopkeepers, and slaves founded **St. Mary's Church** (310 S. Royal St., 703-836-4100), Virginia's oldest Catholic church, in 1795. George Washington supposedly made a contribution. Slaves used the balcony.

The current church, erected in 1826, was allowed to remain open when Union troops occupied the city during the Civil War because Yankee troops prayed there. To the right of the sanctuary is a masterful Italian marble statue of the Immaculate Conception. A large marble statue of Saint Joseph stands in the rear.

Berryville

The **Abbey of Our Lady of the Holy Cross Monastery** (on Rte. 2, 540-955-1425) sits on 1,200 acres of farmland on the scenic Shenandoah River. Much of the land is leased to a cattle rancher, whose cows add to the rustic atmosphere. The abbey is known for its bread, so popular it's sold at local grocery stores. It's made from unbleached and stone-ground flour, spring water, and unsulfured molasses. The lovely prayer chapel has a choir loft, a favorite place for retreatants who desire solitude. On the monastery grounds is the Wormley Estate, a well-preserved, two-hundred-year-old stone structure.

Fairfax Station

When the cornerstone of **St. Mary of Sorrows** (5612 Ox Rd., 703-978-4141) was laid in 1858, the church's only luxury was a steeple bell, in use today, that was bought from a Baltimore firm.

Both Confederate and Union soldiers occupied the church. Jesuit Fr. Peter Kroes, a Netherlands native, stood by his parishioners and favored the Southern cause. He refused to take an oath of allegiance when Union troops occupied the city and lost his right to bless legally binding marriages, so he sent his parishioners to Washington. Fr. Joseph Bixio, his assistant, was nearly hanged as a spy. He often crossed between lines to minister to soldiers and was brought before Gen. William T. Sherman for judgment. The poised priest convinced the general his work was entirely spiritual.

The fierce Second Battle of Manassas in 1862 resulted in St. Mary's being used as a federal field hospital. Doctors used the church as an operating room. Thousands of wounded were laid on a hill and had to wait for three days until a train took them to Washington. Nursing the wounded was an idealistic young woman named Clara Barton. Her experiences during those three endless, terrible days convinced her to dedicate her life to the wounded and led to the founding of the American Red Cross.

The historic church is used mostly for weddings. A more modern St. Mary's is the main worship space.

Front Royal

The parents of a Confederate soldier who died during the war donated the money used to build **St. John the Baptist Church** (123 W. Main St., 540-635-3780). A marble tablet on the east wall reads, "Pray for the soul of John Cerrell Jenkins. Died Oct. 11, 1861. Out of whose means principally this church has been erected." The Jenkins family not only paid for the construction but donated the altar, bells, pews, vestments, and sacred vessels. At the dedication in 1884, Bishop John Keane of Richmond said, "This church was built with the money of one who gave his life for the Confederacy; its cornerstone comes from the battlefield of Manassas; its limestone framings from Fisher Hill; and its red brick was made from the soil of Front Royal, saturated with the blood of the soldiers of the Confederacy."

Middleburg

St. Stephen the Martyr Church (Rte. 748, 703-687-6433) has a plaque on a pew that marks where President Kennedy once sat.

Central Virginia

Crozet

It may seem so, but not all monasteries were founded long ago. Six sisters from Mount St. Mary's Abbey in Wrenthan, Massachusetts, began **Our Lady of Angels Monastery** (3365 Monastery Dr., 804-823-1452) in 1987. The new monastery was just the fifth house of Cistercian nuns in the country and the first in the South. The nuns lived in two log cabins until their brick structure was built in 1989. Their main source of support is the production of Gouda cheese. The contemporary chapel on the 500-acre property offers a respite from the frantic pace of modern life.

Southern Virginia

Richmond

St. Patrick Church (213 N. 25th St., 804-648-0504), built in 1866, is located in historic Church Hill. Adjacent to St. Patrick is St. John's Church, site of Patrick Henry's "give me liberty or give me death" speech.

Western Virginia

Wytheville

The original **St. Mary's Church** (370 E. Main St., 540-228-3322) dates from the 1840s. During the Civil War a skirmish flared up around the church as a priest hurried to remove the Blessed Sacrament. A seminarian accompanying the priest was shot and lost a limb, an injury that forced him to abandon his vocation. The original church was razed in 1961. Its successor, Old St. Mary's, which was dedicated in 1937, gave way to a more modern worship space in 1991.

WEST VIRGINIA

Northern West Virginia

Harper's Ferry

Situated impressively on a high point in town, **St. Peter's Church** (304-725-5558) is a solid stone church erected in 1896. Master stone-mason Edward Tearney supervised the construction. His father, John, had coordinated the building of the original church in 1833. The church survived the Civil War by flying both the Union and Confederate flags.

Martinsburg

Founded in 1825, **St. Joseph Church** (219 S. Queen St., 304-264-8947) was used as a horse stable and a prison by Union soldiers during the Civil War.

St. Mary's

The town of **St. Mary's** has a religious origin. Alexander Creel founded and named the town in 1834. He was passing by on a steamboat when he had a vision of the Virgin Mary. She pointed to the shore and said, "There you will behold the site of what will be a happy and prosperous city." He quickly bought the land but soon began doubting the wisdom of the purchase. So he sold the land and purchased property a few miles away. Fifteen years later he finally realized his original property was better situated and repurchased it. While in St. Mary's, stop and say a prayer at **St. John Church** (310 Washington St., 304-684-7669).

Wheeling

The imposing Romanesque-style **St. Joseph Cathedral** (13th and Eoff Streets, 304-233-4121) is made of Indiana limestone. The triple-arched stained-glass windows of the dome depict four archangels: Michael, Gabriel, Raphael, and Urial. The vault of the dome is frescoed with representations of nine choirs of angels. Other stained-glass windows portray the life of Christ, the four cardinal virtues, and the life of Saint Joseph.

Southern West Virginia

Boomer

St. Anthony's Shrine (Rte. 60, 304-779-2561) is dedicated to the patron saint of miners. Founded in 1928, the shrine was housed in a new, more spacious building in 1954.

SOUTHEAST

ALABAMA

Southern Alabama

Greensboro

In the heart of the Black Belt (a reference to the area's rich black soil) is the historic **Noel-Ramsey House** (Market and South Streets). French settlers Thomas and Ann Hurtel Noel built the home about 1820, and their modest dwelling place served as the initial Catholic church for local folks.

Mobile

The enormous white columns of the **Cathedral of the Immaculate Conception** (400 Government St., 334-434-1565) are a city landmark. The cornerstone was laid in 1835, and since then the church has survived an explosion during the Civil War, a fire, and an airplane disaster.

Relatively few Catholics live in the Deep South, but Catholics were actually the first settlers of Mobile. A French Catholic, John Baptiste de Bienville, came here in the name of France in 1702. The first Catholic church in what was to become Mobile was established by the Bishop of Quebec (yes, in Canada) in 1703.

The first church was no more than a wooden barn. The current cathedral was built on land that had been the burying ground for the area's first settlers. Because the diocese had little money, construction took 15 years. The Romanesque structure is 165 feet long, 102 feet wide outside, and 88 feet wide inside. The naming of the church, incidentally, came several years before the Immaculate Conception of Mary was proclaimed as a dogma of faith in 1854. The church's most notable feature is its 12 stained-glass windows, made by the Franz Mayer Company in Munich in the 1890s.

In 1865 the explosion in the harbor fourteen blocks distant from the church on Ascension Thursday blew out one side of its windows. During World War II a low-flying plane struck one of the towers. In 1954 a disastrous fire destroyed the sanctuary.

Pope John XXIII raised the cathedral to the rank of minor basilica in 1962. The designation is for churches that surpass others either in age or excellence.

Montgomery

The **St. Jude** complex (2048 W. Fairview Ave., 334-265-6791) serves the spiritual, medical, educational, and social needs of the poor. The institution was founded by Passionist Fr. Harold Purcell. St. Jude Church, built in 1938, has a 100-foot bell tower and a distinctive blue tile roof. The Ten Commandments are portrayed on the ceiling cross beams and the Creed and Sacraments on the glass windows.

Northern Alabama

Birmingham

The anti-Catholic bigotry that raged in Alabama in the earlier part of the century climaxed with the murder of Fr. James Coyle of **St. Paul's Cathedral** (2120 Third Ave. N., 205-251-1279) in 1921. He was shot in front of witnesses as he sat on his front porch; his assailant was Edwin Stephenson, a Methodist minister who was outraged that the priest had married his daughter to a Catholic. The minister, whose defense was led by future Supreme Court justice Hugo Black, was found not guilty by reason of insanity.

Cullman

The extraordinary **Ave Marie Grotto** (1600 St. Bernard Dr., 205-734-4110) consists of more than 125 small-scale reproductions of famous churches, shrines, and buildings. The miniature religious fairyland is located at St. Bernard Abbey, the state's only Benedictine abbey.

A monk, Brother Joseph Zoettl, built the amazing replicas, well-detailed but not always architecturally accurate. Born in Bavaria in 1878, he came to the abbey in 1892 and developed his hobby while taking care of the abbey's power plant. Zoettl used stones, cement, and whatever he could find to pay tribute to some of the most well-known cathedrals and monasteries. He based his representations on postcards he collected.

Amazingly, Zoettl, maimed in an accident, was a hunchback. He was still able to bend over, and his patience in constructing his art is legendary among the monks. He died in 1961 and is buried in the abbey cemetery not far from the grotto's gift shop.

Huntsville

St. Mary of the Visitation Church (222 N. Jefferson St., 205-536-6349) is an attractive building whose cornerstone was laid in 1861. A grand total of eleven families originally belonged to the parish. The church was built of native limestone laboriously hauled by mule cart and wagon from the nearby Monte Sano Mountain. The Civil War halted work on the church. Fr. Jeremiah Trecy, the founding pastor who was a native of Ireland, ministered on several battlefields and tended to the wounded of both North and South.

FLORIDA

Northern Florida

St. Augustine

One of the most memorable landmarks for U.S. Catholics is the **Cathedral of Saint Augustine** (38 Cathedral Pl., 904-824-2806). Established in 1594, it is the oldest parish in the United States. In 1565, seven hundred Spanish colonists arrived here. The colony was named St. Augustine because Florida was first sighted on St. Augustine's Day, August 28. The parish records, dating back to 1594, are the oldest written records in the country.

The church was constructed in 1797 in Spanish Mission style. Renowned New York City architect James Renwick restored the church after a fire gutted it in 1887. He added the Spanish Renaissance-style bell tower. The oil paintings representing the Stations of the Cross are copied after those in the Vatican's Pauline Chapel. Outstanding features are Spanish floor tiles, a baroque gold tabernacle from Ireland, and murals that depict the life of Saint Augustine. Beyond its individual elements, the church has the wonderful air of antiquity. Its walls seem to burst with anticipation, a portent of the glorious rise of the Church in the New World.

Near the ancient fort, Castillo de San Marcos, is the site where the first Mass in the United States was celebrated on September 8, 1565, the day the colonists came ashore. A towering 208-foot cross made of stainless steel marks the spot. The cross is beautifully lit at night. Also here is a bronze statue of Fr. Francisco Lopez de Mendoza Grajales, who said the first Mass.

Near the cathedral is **Mission Nombre de Dios** (101 San Marcos Ave., 904-824-3045), or Name of God, established in 1565. America's first Christmas was celebrated here. From the mission Jesuits and Franciscans carried the faith among the Native Americans to the north and west, often at the expense of their lives. One of the earliest martyrs was Fr. Blas Rodriguez, who was captured while saying Mass. Knowing what would happen, he pleaded to be allowed to finish. His last wish was granted, and at the end of Mass he was hacked to pieces.

Also on the grounds is the first shrine to Mary in the continental United States, **Our Lady of La Leche** (904-824-3045). The original chapel, built in 1620, was dedicated to Nuestra Senora de La Leche y Buen Parto (Our Nursing Mother of Happy Delivery). The shrine has an image of the Blessed Mother nursing the divine Child. The present chapel was constructed in 1915. A more modern structure is **Prince of Peace Church** (904-824-2806), built in 1965.

Daytona Beach

St. Paul Church (300 block of U.S. 1, near Hwy. 92, 904-252-5422) has a striking red-tile roof and dome. The two huge doors of the Spanish Renaissance church were patterned after portals of the basilica in Valencia, Spain. The church contains relics of Saint Teresa, brought from Rome, consisting of a bone, a strand of hair, and a small piece of the saint's garments.

Tallahassee

Mission San Luis de Apalachee (2020 W. Mission Rd., 850-487-3655) was the western capital of the mission system in Florida from 1656 to 1704. More than fourteen hundred Native Americans lived at the hilltop mission and nearby. Living alongside the friars and Native Americans were the Spanish governor, soldiers, and some civilians. The Spaniards burned and hastily abandoned San Luis in 1704 just two days before British troops and their Native American allies descended upon the site.

The state of Florida began reconstruction in 1983. Historic inter-preters in period costumes recreate seventeenth-century mission life.

Central Florida

Brooksville

Mass is said once a year, on All Souls' Day, at tiny **St. Stanislaus Chapel** (Centralia Rd., north of Brooksville, 352-796-2096). Pol-ish farmers built the humble church in 1931 after an earlier one burned down. The Depression brought havoc to the farmers and forced them to abandon the land and the church. Members of nearby St. Anthony Church tend to the church and the adjacent cemetery.

Orlando

It's a big, big shrine near a small, small world. **Mary, Queen of the Universe Shrine** (8300 Vineland Ave., 407-239-6600) attracts Catholics who visit Disney World and Orlando's other tourist draws. The shrine's 17 acres feature a 2,000-seat church, a Mother and Child outdoor chapel, decorative pools and fountains, and perfectly manicured gardens and grounds. The main church has an Old World cathedral design. The nave reaches up 85 feet. A mahogany arch embraces a holy water font fashioned of marble and ebony. The floor in the entrance has waves of granite splashing into the church, reflecting Florida's coastal geography. The newest addition is an art museum that displays sculptures and paintings donated to the shrine. The shine began on a Marian feast, December 8, 1983. Though one of the newest Marian sites, it draws more than 250 thousand people annually.

The shrine is an outgrowth of the "Disney church," **Holy Fam-ily Parish** in Orlando (5125 S. Apopka-Vineland Rd., 407-876-2211), which is tucked away in a hilly citrus grove area near Disney World. Vacationers by the thousands nevertheless find it each week-end. Saturday evening Mass is especially packed. The extensive stained-glass windows tell the story of Christianity from the Annunciation through the Second Vatican Council. Parish priests also say Mass at Disney hotels.

St. Petersburg

Dedicated in 1963, the **Cathedral of St. Jude the Apostle** (5801 Fifth Ave., 813-347-9702) is one of the largest and most splendid churches in the state. Seating 1,700, it was designed with a circular sanctuary 56 feet in diameter and a 12-foot nave. The sanctuary is crowned with a 62-foot-high dome, pierced with stained-glass windows that cast the Florida sunshine on the altar below. Visible for a considerable distance, the dome is covered with golden-hued aluminum and topped by a cross rising another 25 feet.

Tampa

The stately **Sacred Heart Church** (Twiggs St. and Florida Ave., 813-229-1595), built of granite and marble in 1905, features a 35-ton dome and grand columns. Above the central entrance is an inspiring marble statue of the risen Christ.

Southern Florida

Key Largo

St. Justin Martyr Church (105500 Overseas Hwy., 305-451-1316) is true to its location: its distinctive architecture evokes the colors and materials of the Keys. But don't just drive by. Inside is a beautiful fresco of the Last Supper.

Key West

James Bond fans will find **St. Mary Star of the Sea Church** (1010 Windsor Lane, 305-294-1018) vaguely familiar. Timothy Dalton and David Hedison parachuted to Hedison's wedding at the church in the opening sequence of *License to Kill*.

Miami

Miami's Cubans pray at **Ermita de La Caridad, Our Lady of Charity Shrine** (3609 S. Miami Ave.). The conical building, 90 feet high and 80 feet wide, overlooks the bay so that worshipers can face Cuba. A mural above the shrine's altar depicts Cuba's history.

North Miami

North Miami of all places is home to an eight-hundred-year-old monastery, the oldest structure of European origin in the United States, the **Cloister of the Monastery of St. Bernard de Clairvaux** (16711 W. Dixie Hwy., 305-945-1462). Purchased by newspaper titan William Randolph Hearst in 1920, the monastery was built in 1141 in Segovia, Spain, by King Alphonso VII. Hearst had the cloister's 38 thousand stones packed up and transported in 11 thousand crates. In a monumental screw-up, U.S. Customs removed the straw packing materials from each crate, because they were possibly contaminated with hoof-and-mouth disease. But the reassembly numbers were marked on the crates, not the stones. Hearst was confronted with the biggest jigsaw puzzle of all time. After an intensive effort, the stunning Romanesque-Gothic cloister and chapter house were reconstructed. Don't miss the gorgeous stone figure of Christ painstakingly sculpted by Cistercian monks long ago. Incidentally, Hearst bailed out after he learned of the unpacking fiasco. An Episcopal Church now occupies the site.

Palm Beach

Few churches in Florida are as idiosyncratically impressive as
St. Edward's (County Rd. and Sunrise Ave., 561-832-0400). Dedi-

cated in 1927, the
Spanish Renaissance
church has a monu-
mental main entrance
flanked by two towers.
The higher south tower
is domed; the north
tower has an arcade and
Spanish tile roof. The
large window over the
entrance shows Saint
Edward, sided by small-

St. Edward Church. *(James C. Hayes)*

er windows of Saint Cecilia and Saint Gregory. The three arched
doorways of the entrance facades include massive walnut doors.

On the left of the vestibule is a chapel dedicated to Saint Teresa,
and to the right is a chapel to Saint Anthony. The latter includes an
altar made from Fantastico white veined Italian marble.

President Kennedy often attended St. Edward during his winter
sojourns to Florida. A plaque marks his pew.

Western Florida

Pensacola

Historic **St. Michael Church** (19 N. Palafox St., 850-438-4985) can trace its roots back further than any other U.S. parish. A company of fifteen hundred Spaniards who landed on Santa Rosa Island in 1559 dedicated a crude chapel to Saint Michael the Archangel. Since that time, except from 1561 to 1590, St. Michael Church has been in existence. The church has changed locations five times, been under the jurisdiction of five nations, and endured numerous fires, hurricanes, and other disasters.

St. Michael's.

The current church dates from 1886. The gray stucco building has a square belfry rising majestically to a pyramidal spire. The stained-glass windows, imported from Munich at a cost of $25 thousand, today are insured for $1 million. They are considered among the most beautiful of their kind in the South. The unique bowed altar rail was preserved even amid the standard alterations to the church after Vatican II.

Sisters of Mercy have served at the parish school since 1877. In the early 1880s they temporarily left the classrooms to heroically attend to the victims of a yellow fever scourge.

GEORGIA

Northern Georgia

Atlanta

The third oldest Catholic church in Atlanta is **St. Anthony of Padua** (928 Ralph David Abernathy Blvd., 404-758-8861). Joel Chandler Harris, a popular newspaper columnist, was one of the founding parishioners in 1903. The church's wonderful stained-glass windows depict scenes from the Old and New Testament as well as the story of Saint Anthony.

The building of the **Cathedral of Christ the King** (2699 Peachtree Rd., 404-233-2145) in 1938 represented a triumph of love over hate. The mansion previously at this site served as the headquarters of the Ku Klux Klan. Constructed of limestone, the French Gothic structure was once cited by *Architectural Record* as "the most beautiful building in Atlanta."

Shrine of the Immaculate Conception. *(Derry Jacob)*

The **Shrine of the Immaculate Conception** (48 Martin Luther King Jr. Dr., 404-521-1866) was one of the few structures to survive the destructive siege of Atlanta by Maj. Gen. William Tecumseh Sherman in 1864. Fr. Thomas O'Reilly, pastor, the man who saved the church and several other important buildings, is remembered as a civic hero.

After Atlanta fell after four weeks

of shelling, O'Reilly volunteered his services at the Union field hospitals, making key contacts within the Union Army. Sherman ordered Atlantans out of their city and then proclaimed that any building with possible military use would be destroyed. O'Reilly protested. He convinced Sherman, a Catholic, that the Catholics in his army would recoil at razing churches. O'Reilly's plea saved several municipal buildings and five churches.

Immaculate Conception Church had suffered minor damage during the war, and as Atlanta furiously rebuilt after the war, church leaders deemed it best to erect a new church. The church was dedicated in 1873. O'Reilly, his health ruined during the war, had died the year before at the age of forty-one. A memorial to O'Reilly sits on the front lawn of **City Hall** (68 Mitchell St., 404-330-6394). Sherman, by the way, later visited the new church while his son was studying for the priesthood.

William Parkins, who played a significant role in rebuilding Atlanta, designed the new church, which features endearingly asymmetrical towers. The church became a shrine in 1954 after many parishioners moved to the suburbs. A fire damaged the interior in 1982, but restoration was done.

Sacred Heart of Jesus Church (353 Peachtree St., NE, 404-522-6800) is a welcome relief from the concentration of urban steel and glass that surrounds it. Ironically, a century ago the church was moved to this site because its original location had become too commercial. In 1897 the church, then a small wooden structure, stood twelve blocks west at Marietta and Alexander Streets.

W. T. Downing, one of Atlanta's most inventive architects, designed the French Romanesque-style church. Its twin red-brick spires rise 137-feet above the street. Between the two towers, a pediment contains a rose window, which has an emblem of the Sacred Heart at its center. At sunset, as rays pour through the window, the church interior glows with a pinwheel of color.

An outstanding feature of the church is its 28 stained-glass windows, made at the famous Mayer studios in Munich. Pictured are Saint Dominic, Saint Peter, Saint Monica, and other paragons of faith.

Augusta

Befitting the oldest Catholic church in Georgia, the **Church of the Most Holy Trinity** (303 Broad St., 706-722-4944) is a historical treasure trove. Catholics founded the parish when they first settled in Augusta in 1810. The original church on Telfair Street was used as a temporary hospital during the yellow-fever epidemics of 1839 and 1854; the rectory served as an orphanage for children whose parents died.

Construction of the current church began in 1857 but was not completed until 1863 because of the war. The fine marble altars, made in Baltimore, had to be smuggled through a Union blockade.

The sturdy Romanesque-style church features a tower on the left that rises three levels and a bell tower on the right with a belfry and spire. The base of the bell tower contains 180 thousand bricks. The church withstood a great earthquake in 1886 without a crack or flaw.

The church's Jardine organ, one of the few in the South, arrived in 1886. Built by George Jardine and Sons of New York, it is one of 877 organs built during the firm's 68 years of existence. It contains 1,304 pipes, making it the largest Jardine organ that still exists. The magnificent organ, the first built for a Southern church after the Civil War, was probably intended as a showpiece to stimulate sales in the South.

In the back of the church is a statue of Saint Patrick; the church was popularly known as St. Patrick Church from 1863 until 1971. That year two other parishes merged with St. Patrick, and St. Patrick's consecrated name—the Church of the Most Holy Trinity—was restored.

The church interior looks much the same as it did in 1863. The church features stuccoed brick walls and primarily a wooden floor. Three distinct arches, supported by 12 ornamental iron columns that are painted in gilt and light orange, span the ceiling. Overall, the church has a museumlike quality without any sacrifice of its reverential purpose.

Southern Georgia

Albany

St. Teresa's Church (315 Residence Ave., 912-439-2302) is a fine example of the frontier and small-town mission churches of the mid nineteenth century. Built in 1861, it is the oldest church building in Albany. When word of the Civil War came, the plasterer, a young man named Tom Churchill, laid down his trowel to fight and die for the Confederacy. The interior was not finished until after the war.

During the first half of this century, St. Teresa's was the center of the nation's largest Catholic mission area, covering 22,000 square miles in Georgia. A handful of priests lived at the rectory, journeying all through southwest Georgia, saying Mass, preaching, and teaching.

The church has an intricate tinwork ceiling. The organ dates from the church's first years and the pine pews from a 1902 restoration. The parish built a new church in 1958. The original church serves as a second church.

Savannah

The oldest Catholic parish in Georgia is the **Cathedral of St. John the Baptist** (222 E. Harris St., 912-233-4709). French colonialists erected a small frame church in the city and dedicated it to God under the patronage of Saint John the Baptist in 1799. A second church was designated as the cathedral in 1850 when the Diocese of Savannah was created. In 1898 fire destroyed a third church, built in 1873. Within two years the French Gothic church was rebuilt. Its most notable feature is its stained-glass windows, made by Austrian glassmakers.

The **Flannery O'Connor Childhood Home** (207 E. Charlton

St. on Lafayette Square, 912-233-6014) was the birthplace in 1925 of Mary Flannery O'Connor, whose Catholicism was central to her writing. The family moved in 1938. Open to the public is the parlor level, consisting of a living room, a dining room/kitchen room, and a sun room.

O'Connor, acclaimed as one of the greatest twentieth-century U.S. writers, was in her personal life unpious and quirkily funny. She was also deeply contemplative. Her novels and short stories are not, on the surface, particularly religious. But her ruminations on the mystery of life and Catholic dogma form the heart and soul of her writing.

O'Connor studied at the Writer's Workshop at the University of Iowa and lived for a time at a writer's colony. But while still in her twenties she developed lupus and thereafter suffered from declining health. She lived unobtrusively on the family farm in Andalusia near Milledgeville until she died at the age of thirty-nine.

O'Connor acknowledged that her artistic vision was inseparable from her faith. "It is popular to believe that in order to see clearly one must believe nothing," she said. "For the fiction writer to believe nothing is to see nothing. I don't write to bring anybody a message. This is not the purpose of a novelist. But the message I find in the life I see is a moral message."

She disagreed with those who claim artists must be unhampered by religious faith. "Dogma can in no way limit a limitless God. For me, dogma is only a gateway to contemplation," she said. She added that being Catholic had saved her "a couple thousand years in learning to write" because the Church taught her about the mystery of life.

Central Georgia

Milledgeville

Flannery O'Connor attended Georgia College and State University (517 W. Hancock, 912-453-5400), where she drew cartoons for the school newspaper and edited the literary magazine. The **Flannery O'Connor Memorial Room** at the college is a period room with walnut bookcases, a library table, chest, and armchair. Many of the items came from the O'Connor farm in Andalusia. The **Flannery O'Connor Collection** at the college's library displays her artwork and contains first drafts of her writings, various editions of her works, critical writings, photographs, tape recordings, films, and memorabilia.

KENTUCKY

Northern Kentucky

Bardstown

Proto-Cathedral of St. Joseph.
(Ron Briney)

Built in 1819, the **Proto-Cathedral of St. Joseph** in Bardstown (310 W. Stephen Foster Ave., 502-348-3126) is known as the "Cathedral in the Wilderness." It was the first cathedral west of the Alleghenies. The Diocese of Bardstown (now the Archdiocese of Louisville) is the oldest inland diocese in the United States, and the construction of its cathedral symbolized the great push westward of the Church.

Oddly, the French Revolution fueled the growth of the U.S. Catholic Church. Anticlerical hysteria led to an exodus of French priests to the United States. They arrived in a country with a small but rapidly growing Catholic population. In the late eighteenth century U.S. Catholics numbered only 25 thousand. Just twenty-five priests served the entire country. Bishop John Carroll of Baltimore counted the entire nation as his see. The widely scattered Catholics who lived away from the Eastern United States had to make do without a priest or saw a priest only rarely.

In 1793 Carroll ordained Stephen Theodore Badin, formerly a

seminarian in France. Badin was the first priest ordained in the United States. He was assigned to minister to Kentucky Catholics, desperate for a priest, and became known as the "Apostle to Kentucky."

Benedict Joseph Flaget, who was to become the first bishop of Kentucky, was born and educated in France, too. In 1792 he fled France for the United States, where he served in Indiana and taught at St. Mary's Seminary in Baltimore. In 1808, to his astonishment, he was appointed bishop. Exceedingly humble, he sailed back to France to beg the superior general of the Sulpicians to convince Rome they had made a mistake. Before Flaget could open his mouth, the superior general told him, "My Lord, you should have been already in your diocese. The pope has given you an express order to accept."

Flaget returned to the United States and was consecrated a bishop in Baltimore. But the U.S. Catholic Church was so poor he could not afford to travel to Kentucky. Finally, after three months, his friends raised money to send him and a group of seminarians to Bardstown in 1811.

The new bishop first built a small brick church, and, after five years of tireless fund-raising, the cornerstone of the Shrine of the West was laid. Frontiersmen constructed the church from local materials. They quarried the limestone, kilned the bricks, felled the timbers, and made the hinges, even the nails, by hand. At the consecration of the cathedral in 1819, Fr. Robert Abell, the first native Kentuckian priest, thanked "those who had enabled the bishop to erect in a country lately overshadowed by interminable forests a cathedral church that would be honorable to the Catholic faith of any people."

The exterior has four soaring Corinthian columns and a square clock tower surmounted by an octagonal bell chamber. The church's prized treasures are paintings given to Flaget by King Louis Philippe of France. The pictures were so widely known and valued that thieves stole them in 1950. The FBI later recovered them.

Covington

In 1888 a French-Canadian priest, Fr. Louis Clermont, arrived at **St. Anne's Parish** (1274 Parkway Ave., 606-261-9548) and began a novena to the church's namesake. The novena, in its 111th year, continues to this day. For nine days beginning on July 18 thousands of devotees of the saint carry her statue and lighted candles through the streets of the city. The St. Anne Shrine includes a relic said to be from a rock of Saint Anne's tomb in Jerusalem. Parishioners who toiled by lantern and moonlight after working during the day built the original church in the 1860s. The new church dates from 1932.

Built in 1901, the marvelous French-Gothic **Cathedral Basilica of the Assumption** (1140 Madison Ave., 606-431-2060) was modeled after Notre Dame in Paris. The flying buttresses, fanciful gargoyles, and waterspouts give the church a wonderful Old World charm.

The interior, modeled after St. Denis in Paris, features an inspiring arched ceiling that is pure Gothic. Most notable are the eighty-two stained-glass windows, including the largest stained-glass church window in the world. The 67-foot by 24-foot behemoth depicts the fifth-century Ecumenical Council of Ephesus, which proclaimed Mary the Mother of God. The upper tier illustrates the coronation of the Blessed Mother as Queen of Heaven and Earth.

The church also has four fine paintings by celebrated artist Frank Duveneck. The most outstanding portrays a repentant Mary Magdalene at the foot of the cross.

The Italian Renaissance-style **Mother of God Church** (W. Sixth and Montgomery Streets, 606-291-2288) has clock-bearing twin spires that jut toward heaven. German Catholics built the church in 1871. The Mayer Art Institute in Munich created the stone statues of Saints Peter and Paul and two mythological lions in front of the church. Local artist Ferdinand Muer sculpted the large crucifix behind the main altar in 1871. Parishioner Johann Schmitt, whose work is displayed at the Vatican, painted the five large murals that show the joyful mysteries of the rosary. Installed in 1876, the Koehnken and Grimm organ is a world-class example of German craftsmanship. Pope Leo XIII gave the picture of Our Lady of Perpetual Help to a parish priest during a private audience in 1882.

Near Covington

Bellevue

The town's predominant religious landmark is **Sacred Heart Church** (318 Division St., 606-261-6172). Built in 1892, the Gothic Revival-style church features a 150-foot bell tower with four clock faces. The ornate, hand-carved main altar, imported from Austria in 1924, rises to a height of 33 feet and depicts the life of Christ.

Melbourne

St. Anne's Convent (on Hwy. 8, 606-441-0679) might look familiar to fans of Tom Cruise. The convent was transformed into Wallbrooks, a facility for the developmentally disabled where Cruise's character discovers his autistic brother, played by Dustin Hoffman, in *Rain Man.*

Northern Kentucky

Louisville

The **Cathedral of the Assumption** in Louisville (443 S. Fifth St., 502-582-2971) is one of the three oldest U.S. cathedrals still in use. (The other two are in St. Louis and New Orleans.) Built in 1850, the Gothic Revival-style structure has leaded stained-glass windows and a 4,500-pound bell that an archbishop of Mexico gave to the church. The 287-foot spire holds a 24-foot cross.

In 1855 the cathedral was nearly seized by a rampaging anti-Catholic mob. Hostility toward Catholics had begun growing as thousands of German and Irish immigrants flowed into Louisville. Protestants grew alarmed when a German newspaper in town urged its readers to retain their language and customs and when a papal official toured the United States, prompting fears of a papal plot to undermine U.S. democracy. On election day, August 6, 1855, the *Louisville Journal* urged Protestants to "rally to put down an organization of Jesuit bishops, priests and other papists, who aim by secret oaths and horrid perjuries, and midnight plottings, to sap the foundation of all our political edifices—state and national." Mobs roamed the street, assaulting Irish and Germans on "Bloody Monday." Twenty-two people died.

Bishop Martin John Spalding, credited with quelling further violence, urged restraint by all sides. Catholics in Louisville rallied around the church. Mass attendance shot up. Parochial schools were "as full as an egg—thanks to Know-Nothingism," Spalding wrote.

The 400-foot steeple of **St. Martin Church** (639 S. Shelby St., 502-582-2827) has risen above the Phoenix Hill neighborhood since 1853. With its German-speaking parishioners and priests, the church was an obvious target for the anti-Catholic mobs on Bloody Monday in 1855. Rioters broke into the church, but destruction was averted when Bishop Spalding invited the mayor, a vocal anti-Catholic, to inspect the church and assure the mob there were no weapons inside.

The church was skillfully restored in 1991. As an act of repentance, the former owners of the *Courier-Journal* paid for the lighting of the steeple. The *Louisville Journal,* the forerunner of the *Courier,* ran anti-immigrant stories in the 1850s that contributed to prejudice against Catholics.

The Royal Bavarian Art Institute in Munich made the church's outstanding stained-glass windows in the 1890s. The two small chapels have stained-glass windows brought from a sixteenth-century monastery in Germany. The church has relics of Saint Magnus, a martyred centurion, and Saint Bonosa, who also died in 207. The U.S. government wanted the life-sized statues of the apostles, made of zinc, during World War I. Zinc was valuable in the defense industry, but the pastor refused the government's offer to replace the statues with marble ones. On the church grounds are images of ducks, the symbol of Saint Martin. He supposedly hid in a barn to avoid the office of bishop.

The Ursuline Sisters at **Mount Saint Joseph** (1731 Edenside Ave., 502-451-8685) have an interesting museum displaying religious articles, books, and many reproductions of famous Madonna paintings. The sisters also have utensils—one old and one new— that form hosts from white flour. The former is made of heavy cast iron and was put over an open fire, and the latter looks like an electric waffle iron.

Central Kentucky

Nerinx

In 1812 Mary Rhodes, a young woman originally from Maryland, began a crude schoolhouse for girls in an abandoned cabin in St. Charles. The cabin had a dirt floor, and charcoal was used in place of pencils. Before long other women who desired to live together as a religious community joined her. This was the genesis of the Sisters of Loretto, the first religious community of women in the United States.

A dozen years later the order moved, and the grounds of the **Loretto Motherhouse** (502-865-5811) in Nerinx include a restored cabin of Fr. Charles Nerinckx, the priest who served as their spiritual guide. The sisters numbered 130 within a decade of their founding. An admiring bishop of St. Louis said of them in 1823, "They will live by the product of their work. They themselves work in the garden, cut their own firewood, weave the cloth for their dresses, make their own shoes. Their life is very austere and very edifying."

The site today includes a retirement center, a retreat center, a library, and a wooded area with three lakes. Rhodes Hall, an art studio and gallery, is a far cry from the order's first primitive structure.

New Haven

The first and most famous Cistercian monastery in the United States is the **Abbey of Gethsemani** (on Hwy. 247, near New Haven, 502-549-3117). Its fame is largely due to the fact that Fr. Thomas Merton lived here. His spiritual autobiography, *The Seven Storey Mountain,* is one of the all-time Catholic bestsellers.

The Trappists, despite the current stature of Gethsemani, actually initially failed in their first journey into the Kentucky wilderness. A group of monks from Amsterdam made their way to Louisville in 1804. The hard journey had left them exhausted and sick with fever. The asceticism they practiced was particularly difficult in the harsh conditions of the wilderness, and after a fire they returned to France in 1813, not to come back until thirty years later.

"The great thing, and the only thing, is to adore and praise God," wrote Merton. The monks of Gethsemani, renowned for their simple lifestyle and meditative silence, are embodiments of reverence. Of course, it's not as if they deny themselves all earthly pleasures. The monastery and its grounds are aesthetically first-rate. And the abbey is famous for its cheese, bourbon-spiked fruitcake, and fudge.

Born in 1915, Merton received a first-rate education in France, England, and the United States. An agnostic, he underwent a dramatic religious experience at the age of twenty-three and three years later, in 1941, entered Gethsemani. *The Seven Storey Mountain* was published seven years later. Merton wrote extensively on contemplative life and prayer. His opposition to nuclear war, racism, and economic injustice as well as his exploration of Eastern religious traditions won him much admiration. Merton combined a thirst for God with a quest for human solidarity, making him a pivotal figure in the war-torn, spiritually alienated twentieth century. On the twenty-seventh anniversary of his entering the monastery, he was accidentally electrocuted in Thailand in 1968 while attending a religious conference. He is buried at Gethsemani.

Western Kentucky

Bowling Green

St. Joseph's Church (434 Church St., 502-842-2525) was founded in 1859 to serve Irish immigrants who came to the city to work on the railroad. The present Gothic-style edifice was built in three stages over a thirty-year period before being dedicated in 1889. The current altar was constructed from the wood of the former confessionals. The elaborate ceiling frescoes were first done by the Leber family of Louisville in 1903 and restored three times by successive generations of the family before being simplified in 1986.

MISSISSIPPI

Southern Mississippi

Bay St. Louis

St. Augustine Seminary (199 Seminary Dr., 601-467-6414), run by the Divine Word Order, was the first U.S. Catholic seminary to admit African Americans. Its alumni include six black bishops. On the grounds are a Sacred Heart Shrine and an Agony Grotto.

The **Church of Our Lady of the Gulf** (228 S. Beach Blvd., 601-467-6509) was once the largest parish in the state. The Italian Renaissance-style structure was built during 1908 to 1926. The fine stained-glass windows are from Germany.

The popular Father LeDuc, a native of France, headed the church from 1859 to 1897. During the Civil War he bravely stopped a Federal soldier from finishing off a wounded Confederate in the street. When the Yanks later threatened to burn down the town, the priest dashed into the street holding a cross. The Irish Catholic soldiers doffed their hats and extinguished their torches.

Next to the church is the outdoor **Shrine of Our Lady of the Woods**. Father LeDuc brought the statue from France in 1860.

Biloxi

The **cross and marker** on the north end of Back Bay Bridge commemorates the landing of two hundred French settlers in 1699. The Catholic contingent actually first settled in Ocean Springs and moved to Biloxi in 1719.

St. Michael's Church (177 First St., 601-435-5578) was founded in 1870 after packing plants for the fishing industry opened. The present church, erected in 1965, has a seashell roof and stained-glass windows that depict the apostles as fishermen.

The **Cathedral of the Nativity of the Blessed Virgin** (870 Howard Ave., 601-374-1717) was erected in 1902 after a fire two years earlier destroyed the entire parish complex. The parish was so poor that many schoolchildren had no shoes, and insurance from the fire netted only $580. So the pastor gamely went to Europe to raise funds. The Gothic-style church has superb German-made windows. The parish was founded in 1843.

Natchez

Holy Family Church (St. Catherine St. and Orange Ave., 601-445-5700) was the first Black Catholic church in Mississippi. It started in a small frame building on Beaumont Street in 1890 and moved to its present location four years later.

The grand **St. Mary's Church** (Union and Main Streets, 601-445-5616) is the oldest Catholic building still in use in Mississippi. The red brick Gothic Revival-style structure was completed in 1851. Prince Alex Torlonia of Rome gave the 3,000-pound bell to the church in 1849. Princess Torlonia threw her wedding ring into the molten metal as it was cast. Notable features are stained-glass windows from Germany, Italian marble altars, and excellent carved woodwork.

Jackson

The Gothic Revival-style **Saint Peter's Cathedral** (N. West and Amite Streets, 601-969-3125) was built in 1897. Founded in 1846, the parish suffered at the hands of Federal soldiers during the Civil War. A fire set at a nearby cotton warehouse also destroyed the church. Determined parishioners rented the largest hall in town, which was set afire, too. The angry pastor went to Washington after the war to file a claim for damages but was unsuccessful.

Central Mississippi

Tucker

In 1881 Bishop Janssens spent time with the Choctaws, who lived under harsh conditions after treaties with the U.S. government

deprived them of their land. The bishop sympathized with these "children of the forest." A visit to Holland answered his prayers. Dutch missionaries agreed to come

Holy Rosary Church.

to the state to minister to the Choctaw. The **Indian Mission Site at Holy Rosary Church** (Tucker Community, on Hwy. 19, six miles south of Philadelphia, 601-656-1742) began in 1883. Fr. B. J. Bekkers bought 400 acres of land for the Choctaw, built a church, and opened a school. By 1900 the church had 690 Native American members and 108 White members.

The Carmelites built the present Holy Rosary Church in 1903. In 1938 **St. Catherine Mission** was opened in Conehatta. The first Mass in the Choctaw language was celebrated in 1983 at St. Catherine.

Northern Mississippi

Columbus

The **Church of the Annunciation** (808 College St., 601-328-2927), constructed in 1863, is the oldest Catholic church in northeast Mississippi. It once served 12,000 square miles, from Corinth to Meridian. The unfinished building served as a hospital for thousands of Confederate and Union soldiers during the Civil War. A monk from St. Bernard Abbey in Alabama carved the wood altar. A 300-pound Gothic cross, made of cypress, is bolted to the pinnacle of the church facade. The parish is in the midst of a capital campaign to upgrade its facilities.

Church of the Annunciation.

Holly Springs

St. Joseph Church (College Ave., 601-252-3138), an utterly charming, bell-towered building constructed of wood in 1857, was the first Catholic church in northern Mississippi. During the Civil War, marauding Union soldiers ripped apart the pipe organ and played cards on the pulpit. St. Joseph's is known locally as the "Church of the Yellow Fever Martyrs." In 1878 the pastor and six Sisters of Charity, who ran the Catholic school, died while caring for victims of the scourge. In the 1950s the parish had separate schools for Whites and Blacks, but the schools merged in 1969. Whites, Blacks, and Hispanics all belong to the parish today. A new church was built in 1981; the original church is used as a meetinghouse.

Greenville

Built in 1908, the Gothic-style **St. Joseph Church** (412 Main St., 601-335-5251) boasts exquisite stained-glass windows by Emil Frei. The parish began in 1868 after a plantation owner donated land to the congregation.

TENNESSEE

Central Tennessee

Nashville

The stately **St. Mary's of the Seven Sorrows Church** (330 Fifth Ave. N., 615-256-1704) features a front portico supported by Ionic columns. William Strickland, who built the capitol building, designed the church in 1847. It served as the cathedral until 1914.

Western Tennessee

Memphis

The superb **Cathedral of the Immaculate Conception** (1695 Central Ave., 901-725-2700), completed in 1938, pleasantly blends stone, steel, cream-colored brick, concrete, and red tiles. Copper-covered domes cap its 112-foot twin towers. The oak pews seat 1,200.

The interior features many animal images symbolizing Christ and religious truths: a peacock (immortality—the peacock's flesh was once considered incorruptible), a stag (our Lord conquers and tramples sin—the stag is the traditional enemy of the serpent), a pelican (atonement in blood—the pelican was thought to tear its breast to feed its young), a unicorn (the Incarnation—the unicorn was said to evade all efforts at capture except by a virgin, to whom it would run), and a butterfly (eternal life after life on earth and burial—paralleling the three stages of the butterfly's life).

The colorful history of **Saint Joseph Church** (3825 Neely Rd., 901-396-9996) began when Italian-born Fr. Antonio Luiselli and twenty immigrant families founded the parish in 1878. Luiselli's wealthy family donated a marble altar, statues, and Stations of the Cross for the new church. The priest tirelessly worked among the victims of a yellow-fever epidemic. His parishioners urged him to leave the city for a while to protect himself. He "gave in" to their pleas and carried his belongings six blocks from the church before turning around.

Luiselli was the kind of priest of whom parishioners tell stories long after he is gone. He painted the potbellied stove bright red to warn children the stove was "red hot." Or so he claimed. Parishioners said the red stove was a ruse to hide the fact that the church was far too cold. Once, the story goes, ice had to be chipped away from the baptismal font before the ceremony could begin.

Luiselli died in 1901, but drama returned to the church in 1917 when a priest who did not speak Italian was appointed pastor. Angry parishioners nailed the church doors shut—the new pastor and two young altar boys were caught inside. They exited through a side window, and the bishop put the church under Interdict (a censure withdrawing sacraments and burial), perhaps the first in the United States.

Next door to St. Peter's Church is the **Magevney House** (198 Adams Ave., 901-526-4464), where the city's first Mass was celebrated in 1839, as well as the first Catholic wedding and christening. Eugene Magevney, one of the founders of St. Peter's, was an Irish immigrant who served as the city's first schoolmaster.

German immigrants who left their homeland out of fear of war and to escape conscription founded **St. Mary of the Immaculate Conception Church** (155 Market St., 901-522-9420) in 1860. The current church was built in 1864. Kate Hamilton Dawson, the daughter of Eugene Magevney, funded the peaceful Lourdes Grotto on the church's south side. A Franciscan assigned to the parish at the turn of the century crafted many of the church's wooden pieces.

The parish's Franciscans, as well as other priests in Memphis, courageously ministered to the city during its three devastating yellow-fever epidemics in the 1870s. Eight thousand died, including at least twenty priests and fifty nuns. Fr. Maternus Mallmann's letters over four days in 1878 describe the terror: "The yellow fever is causing dreadful havoc. Yesterday I prepared nine....I am not well, but I feel a supernatural strength. I do not believe that I need dread the yellow fever. My heart rejoices when I am summoned for a sick call....The fever is increasing in a horrifying manner. All are dying. Luckily the city is almost abandoned. Entire streets, entire sections are uninhabited. All are gone. I am well. I do not fear for my own person, but probably we shall escape entirely." Mallmann died less than a month later at the age of thirty-four.

Founded in 1866, **St. Patrick Church** (277 S. Fourth St., 901-527-2542) welcomed many nationally known entertainers a few decades ago due to its proximity to downtown hotels. Fred Allen, Roy Landman (a star on *Your Hit Parade*), and Lincoln Theodore Monroe Andrew Perry (known as Stepin Fetchit) worshiped here.

In the 1960s the parish served as an impromptu first-aid station for civil-rights protesters ruthlessly beaten by police. Within a few blocks of the church is the Lorraine Motel, where the Rev. Martin Luther King, Jr., was slain. In recent years, the parish has stepped up its efforts to fulfill King's dream of equality, providing affordable housing in the neighborhood and running programs for youth.

The oldest Catholic church in western Tennessee is **St. Peter's** (190 Adams Ave., 901-527-8282), dedicated in 1858. The Northern Gothic-style church was constructed around the original building, which was eventually dismantled and carried out the front doors.

GREAT LAKES

ILLINOIS

Chicago

Downtown

Chicago's beginnings were Catholic. The first known White men to come here were the indomitable explorers Louis Joliet of Quebec and Jesuit Fr. Jacques Marquette of France in 1673. The **Marquette and Joliet Monument** (on the northeast side of the Michigan Ave. Bridge) commemorates their visit. Marquette, on his second visit to what is now a jumble of skyscrapers, cars, and harried office workers, remarked in his journal, "Killed three cattle and four deer, one of which ran some distance with its heart split in two."

The model for the stunning chapel of **Archbishop Quigley Preparatory Seminary** (103 E. Chestnut St., 312-787-9343) is La Saint Chapelle in Paris, built by the extravagant Louis IX in the thirteenth century as a showcase for the Crown of Thorns. The French Gothic-style seminary was completed in 1920. Despite widespread poverty, Catholic schoolchildren donated more than $20 thousand for the chapel, some of it a penny at a time.

The chapel's magnificent stained-glass windows are referred to as the "crown jewels" of Chicago architecture. The windows are made of more than one million pieces of antique English glass. Depicted are scenes from the life of Christ, events from the Old

Testament, and various saints. The most startling window is high above the choir loft: a rose window dedicated to Mary and patterned after that of Notre Dame Cathedral in Paris. The red, violet, and gold glass shows Mary in the center surrounded by sixteen petals set with Marian symbols.

Brutally cold weather in Green Bay, Wisconsin, turned out to be Chicago's gain in the late nineteenth century. The shivering Servite Fathers, unable to adjust to the extreme temperatures, came to Chicago and founded **Assumption Church** (323 W. Illinois St., 312-644-0036). The parish was begun to serve terribly impoverished Italian immigrants, who crowded as many as a dozen families into a single-family dwelling.

The church has a distinctive pre-Vatican II look. Notable are the exquisite stained-glass windows, colorful statues, and old-time confessional, where Mother Cabrini regularly made her confession. The church is a popular choice for weddings because of its downtown location and old-fashioned ambience.

Mother Cabrini founded **Assumption School** in 1898 and unceremoniously taught religion to thousands of schoolchildren. She was relentlessly dedicated to the children, even when not feeling well. She died on December 22, one day after toiling for hours filling bags of candy for the children at Assumption School who otherwise might not have received Christmas presents. The school closed in 1945 when the area turned industrial. The former school building (319 W. Erie St.) now houses a cinema museum. The words *Assumption School* are still visible on the facade. Next to the building is the former convent where Mother Cabrini lived.

The **Cardinal's Residence** (1555 N. State Pkwy.) is a graceful mansion in the Gold Coast that has been home for Chicago prelates since 1885. Cardinal Bernardin, whose courageous bout with cancer inspired many, died in his room here in 1996, surrounded by loved ones and blessed with the peace of faith.

The residence has nineteen chimneys, a small chapel, a throne room (for papal visits), and the bishop's offices. Pope John Paul II stayed here in 1979. Another renowned overnight guest was President Franklin Roosevelt, who valued Cardinal Mundelein as his staunchest Catholic supporter.

On September 5, 1898, St. Vincent's College opened its doors with 72 students and $12 in the bank. Today, **DePaul University** (it changed its name in 1907) is the nation's largest Catholic university, with 18,500 students. DePaul has six campuses and more than 130 undergraduate and graduate degree programs.

The showcase of the downtown campus is DePaul Center (1 E. Jackson Blvd., 312-362-8000), formerly the home of Goldblatt's Department Store. DePaul purchased the shuttered building for $1 million in 1991 and spent $70 million to renovate it for classroom use and student services. The renovation helped spur the development of the South Loop neighborhood, in keeping with DePaul's tradition of civic involvement. The Chicago Music Mart, two dozen music-related retail stores, occupies the first floor.

The Lincoln Park Campus (Fullerton and Kenmore Avenues) is anchored by a quadrangle and the John T. Richardson Library, erected in 1993 as the school's first freestanding library. Outside the library is a bronze sculpture of Saint Vincent de Paul and two modern-day students. Unveiled in 1995, the Way of Wisdom symbolizes the university's commitment to "sculpt" students dedicated to the values of Saint Vincent.

Majestic **Holy Name Cathedral** (730 N. Wabash Ave., 312-787-8040) celebrated its dedication in 1875 with an exuberant procession that included 5,500 people, 18 bands, a 25-member priest choir, and a 20-piece orchestra. In 1926, during the International Eucharistic Congress, more than a million people visited the cathedral within five days to honor the Blessed Sacrament. When Pope John Paul II arrived in 1979, thousands gathered outside the church and burst into "Holy God, We Praise Thy Name." The next evening the Chicago Symphony Orchestra played for the pope in the cathedral.

A child can easily open the church's bronze doors, each weighing more than 1,200 pounds: a hidden hydraulic power source does the trick. Hanging high above the sanctuary are five red hats, or galeros, belonging to the deceased cardinals of Chicago. Pope Paul VI ostensibly ended the practice as an excess display of pride, but Chicagoans stubbornly hung beloved Cardinal Bernardin's galero after he died in 1996.

Old St. Mary's Church (21 E. Van Buren St., 312-922-3444) became the city's first Catholic church in 1833 when 128 Catholics sent a petition to their bishop in St. Louis, pleading for a pastor. The first crude structure was built near State and Lake Streets for a paltry $400. It was 36 feet long, 24 feet wide, and 12 feet high. The second church, built in 1845, served as the diocese's cathedral and bore the only cross on any city building. The cross was the first object seen by travelers approaching from the lake or prairie. The Chicago Fire destroyed the church in 1871, along with more than $1 million in diocesan property. A Protestant church was purchased as a replacement.

In 1928 plans were made to house St. Mary's in a nine-story building downtown, but the stock market crash ended that idea. In 1970 the archdiocese sold the property to Standard Oil. The parish relocated to its present downtown site, which had been a chapel of the main church. The rather ordinary building sits under the El tracks, and worshipers are periodically loudly reminded that the separation between the secular and the sacred is thin indeed.

St. Peter Church (110 W. Madison St., 312-372-5111), founded in 1846 at a nearby location, was the city's first German parish. Thirty years later Franciscans who fled Germany and Otto von Bismarck's persecution of Catholics assumed leadership of the parish. Interestingly, the old-guard German immigrants, worried about change, did not welcome the Franciscans with open arms. "If Bismarck didn't want them, neither do we" was their rallying cry. But the new pastor's first homily on the Good Samaritan helped win over the parishioners.

By the 1890s the neighborhood was so much in decline that a newspaper story on St. Peter's was titled "Midst Vice and Squalor."

Today the headline would read "Midst Wealth and Splendor." The church is located in the heart of the Loop, the city's business and financial center. The church has no parishioners and instead serves Loop workers. Four quick Masses are said near the noon hour. On Ash Wednesday, the church becomes a mob scene as thousands come for ashes.

The church's marble facade blends into the rows of office buildings, and passersby who don't look up might not even notice it's a church. The structure's sole exterior religious ornamentation is an 18-foot-tall crucifix that weighs 26 tons. The church's only window is a Gothic stained-glass window dedicated to Mary, Queen of Peace.

Five religious sisters arrived in Chicago from Ireland via Pittsburgh in 1846 and promptly opened the first Catholic school in the city. A **plaque** on the side of Willoughy Tower (8 S. Michigan Ave.) marks the spot where the Mercy Sisters began their mission of mercy to the city as they opened schools, hospitals, and orphanages in the raw frontier town.

The **Tribune Tower** (435 N. Michigan) is the headquarters of a media empire that duly reports the ups and downs of humanity, but the building itself is a testament to more eternal truths. Stones from 130 historic places are built into its outside walls on three sides. Included are pieces of Notre Dame Cathedral in Paris, Cologne Cathedral in Germany, and the Holy Door of St. Peter's in Rome. The origin of the stones is identified.

West Side

The massive **Holy Family Church** (1080 W. Roosevelt Rd., 312-738-4080), completed in 1860, was the largest church in the country for many years. The church barely missed being devoured by the Chicago Fire in 1871. The fire started nearby in the barn of Patrick and Catherine O'Leary. The founding pastor, Jesuit Fr. Arnold Damen, a popular speaker who was in Brooklyn, learned of the fire through a telegram. His church was doomed, he was told.

Damen fell to his knees in prayer and vowed that seven lights would always burn before a Shrine of Our Lady of Perpetual Help if the church were spared. Somehow the church narrowly escaped the flames, and those seven lights still burn today in the sanctuary.

A modern "miracle" spared the church in 1990 when $1 million was raised, much of it literally at the eleventh hour, to stave off the wrecking ball. The church's nave had been closed since 1984, and the Jesuits set a deadline for the community to raise money to pay for initial repairs. December 30, the day before the deadline, was, coincidentally—or providentially—the Feast of the Holy Family.

Razing the church would have been a great loss. The Victorian Gothic-style wonder is an imposing cathedrallike structure with a rib-vaulted ceiling. The stained-glass windows, the oldest in the city, date from 1860. The interior features 150 hand-carved statues and a communion rail carved from solid walnut that is a masterpiece of liturgical art. Also notable is a 6-foot, 600-pound oak statue of Saint Patrick, crafted in 1860 by Anthony Bouscher. He was a German-trained sculptor reduced to carving wooden cigar-store Indians in America before Damen discovered him and put him to work at the church. A dentist restored the statue in 1998, taking it into his suburban home for four years.

Our Lady of Sorrows Church.
(James Norris)

Our Lady of Sorrows Church (3121 W. Jackson Blvd., 773-638-5800) was the site of one of the greatest outpourings of religious devotion in the twentieth century. The Servite Fathers began a Sorrowful Mother Novena in 1937 during the Great Depression, and thousands came every Friday. One day, seventy thousand worshipers came for thirty-eight separate services at three locations inside the massive Romanesque-style church. A priest who directed the novena marveled at how "the Catholic church map of the U.S. was lit up with the sudden brilliance of a pinball machine."

The novena was the brainchild of Servite Fr. James Keane, pious, devout, and remarkably charismatic. He popularized the novena nationwide through novena clubs, a magazine, tours, lectures, radio programs, and even a movie. By the early 1940s, as World War II raged, 750 thousand people attended the novena weekly at twelve hundred churches and convents. The novena began losing steam in the mid 1950s as the Catholic Church began changing. Keane was seriously injured in a car accident in 1960, and his death in 1975 drew little attention.

The splendid interior of Our Lady of Sorrows, completed in 1902, was inspired by the work of a renowned fifteenth-century Italian architect, Donato d'Agnolo Bramante. The cavernous yet intimate church suggests God's grandeur and mercy. The barrel-vaulted ceiling, consisting of more than one thousand gold panels, rises 80 feet above the marble floor. Standing in the church can stir a mental picture of the novena's heyday. Or better yet, visit on a Friday afternoon and join in. Incredibly, eight or nine people who have attended the novena since its first day still come each week. Keane insisted the devotion would be a perpetual one, and the novenites say they will attend as long as their health permits.

The oldest church building in Chicago and one of the most beautiful is **Old St. Patrick's** (718 W. Adams St., 312-648-1021). The parish began in 1846 to relieve overcrowding at St. Mary's Church. St. Patrick's served hardscrabble Irish immigrants who escaped the potato famine in their homeland and lived in modest wooden cottages near the church.

Old St. Patrick's. *(copyright 1998 by Daniel Pesek)*

The brick-and-stone Romanesque-style structure was dedicated on Christmas in 1856. Its twin spires, unique in the city, are Romanesque and Byzantine, symbolizing West meeting East. Thomas Augustin O'Shaughnessy designed the superb stained-glass windows in 1911. The eccentric Chicago artist disdained traditional methods and instead used tiny particles of brilliantly colored glass to create translucent mosaics he aptly called "imprisoned light." The effect is spellbinding. The windows contain motifs from the *Book of Kells,* an illuminated manuscript of the Gospels created by Irish monks during the Middle Ages, and images of Saint Patrick, Saint Bridget, and other Irish saints.

The church escaped the horrific Chicago Fire of 1871 but barely survived the deterioration of the neighborhood over the years. By the early 1980s a typical Sunday Mass drew two dozen people. Fr. John Wall led a revival of the parish as the neighborhood rebounded. The parish today draws worshipers from all across the city and suburbs. One regular worshiper is Mayor Richard Daley. Each July the parish hosts the World's Largest Block Party, a title that just may be true. The success of the parties enabled the parish to complete a multimillion dollar restoration.

North Side

"Oh, wow" is a common reaction to first-time visitors to the stunning **Chapel of the Benedictine Sisters of St. Scholastica**

St. Scholastica Chapel.

Priory (7430 N. Ridge Blvd., 773-764-2413). A few years ago, it was more like "Oh, dear." The chapel's frescoes, painted in 1938, were cracked and fading. Joseph Ramirez, a local artist committed to restoring the beauty and grandeur to liturgical

art, spent nearly five years working on the frescoes after luckily finding cans of the original paint in a dark basement corner.
Ramirez also made an altar and tabernacle and designed the chapel's
chairs.

How do saints live? Quite modestly, at least according to the
room that Saint Frances Xavier Cabrini called home. Her tiny, sparse
room at **Columbus Hospital** (2520 N. Lakeview Ave., 773-388-
7338) looks as it did the day she died in 1917. The **Mother Cabrini
Shrine** displays her simple bed, the wicker chair in which she died,
and even the bloodstained gown she wore at the time of her death.
In a glass case are personal items like her religious habit and eye-
glasses. Visitors can view a videotape chronicling miracles attrib-
uted to her.

Columbus Hospital was one of sixty-seven hospitals, schools,
and orphanages founded by Mother Cabrini, America's first citizen-
saint. Her room at Columbus is smaller than most people's living
rooms, but Mother Cabrini was a true giant in U.S. Catholicism.
She lovingly cared for society's poor and outcast and founded the
Missionary Sisters of the Sacred Heart religious order. Her death,
caused by a cerebral hemorrhage, touched off widespread mourning, not unlike the grief that came with the loss of Mother Teresa.
The diminutive, frail, but tireless nun, a native of Italy, served immigrants, particularly Italians. She is the only woman honored by
having her name inscribed on the base of the Statue of Liberty.

Mother Cabrini was quiet and humble, rarely consenting to have
her photo taken. But she could be indomitable if necessary, whether
haggling with a merchant for a better price or beseeching a bishop
or benefactor to back a new project. The building of Columbus
Hospital in 1905 is a case in point. She had purchased the North
Shore Hotel to convert it into a hospital. Sensing something was
amiss, she showed up at dawn one morning and measured the property with a clothesline. Her suspicions were confirmed: the owner
had tried to cheat her by trimming the size of the lot. Later, the
contractor tried to cut corners. She promptly fired him and took

over as general contractor. She gladly hired Italian tradesmen to complete the building.

Mother Cabrini, declared a saint in 1946, is not forgotten today. More than 20 thousand people annually visit the room and adjoining chapel at Columbus Hospital. The lovely chapel is decorated with black and gold Italian marble. Dramatic stained-glass windows, frescoes, and banners depict the important events in the saint's life. The chapel has daily Mass, a weekly novena, and occasional concerts.

The magnificent **St. Mary of the Angels** (1850 N. Hermitage Ave., 773-278-2644) is a Roman Renaissance-style structure

reminiscent of St. Peter's in Rome. The eighteen-hundred-seat church, built in 1911, was popularly known as "the Polish basilica of Chicago." The church has sixty-eight stained-glass windows; it is one of only thirteen U.S.

St. Mary of the Angels. *(Don DuBroff, S.P.G.)*

churches featuring the Stations of the Cross in stained glass. The archdiocese had slated it for demolition in 1988, but parishioners mounted a furious fund-raising drive to pay for needed repairs. The church was rededicated in 1992 after repairs to the roof, dome, windows, and interior. The second phase of the restoration, scheduled to be finished in 1999, includes applying more than 100 thousand sheets of gold leaf imported from Germany.

A deadly fire roared through **Our Lady of the Angels Grade School** (3814 W. Iowa St., 773-227-8262) on December 1, 1958. Ninety-two students and three nuns were killed. Nearly one hundred others were injured, some seriously. It was the third-worst school disaster in U.S. history. On the day of the fire, sixteen-hundred students were in school. Most of them were from Italian families who came to America in the first half of the century for a better life. Frantic parents who were told of the tragedy sped first to the school, then to the hospitals, and if still unable to locate their child, to the morgue. The cause of the fire was never officially determined. The charred school building was demolished, and another was built. The tragedy led to stronger fire-code regulations. Donations poured in from across the world to help survivors, and the trust fund that was established was not depleted until the mid 1990s. In recent years survivors and family members have held days of remembrance at various locations.

The pride of Chicago Polonia is the grand **St. Stanislaus Kostka** (1351 W. Evergreen Ave., 773-278-4560), the mother church for local Poles. Finished in 1881, the church is basilica-style, with pews separated by two rows of columns. The 70-foot-high dome has a large, dramatic painting of the risen Christ, early church figures, and saints dear to Poles. The interior owes much to the 1892 Columbian Exposition, some of whose world-class artists agreed to work on the church. A German artist designed the stained-glass windows, and the chandeliers came from the Tiffany factory in New York.

In the 1890s St. Stanislaus, with more than eight thousand families, was the largest Polish parish in the world. Former notable parishioners include Sister Theresa Dudzik, foundress of the Franciscan Sisters of Chicago, and Bishop Paul Rhode of Green Bay, who became the first American bishop of Polish descent in 1908.

South Side

Nearly a quarter of the men studying for the priesthood in the United States are enrolled at **Catholic Theological Union** (5401 S. Cornell, 773-324-8000), the nation's largest graduate school of theology. CTU also trains large numbers of laity, many of whom find jobs with dioceses and at parishes and schools. A visit to the seminary offers a glimpse of future church leadership. The seminary began in 1968 when Franciscans, Passionists, and Servites closed their tranquil suburban seminaries and pooled resources to buy the old Hotel Aragon.

John Powers wrote hilariously about growing up Catholic in *The Last Catholic in America* and *Do Black Patent Leather Shoes Really Reflect Up?* He detailed the unique experience of Catholic grade schools' lessons on venial and mortal sins, Lenten loopholes, altar-boy politics, and nuns who put the fear of God in students. **St. Christiana School** (3333 W. 110th St., 773-445-2969) is where little John Powers learned his Baltimore Catechism.

Corpus Christi Church (4920 S. King Dr., 773-285-7720) was founded in 1901 to serve the "Gold Coast" Irish who built mansions along the boulevard. Author James Farrell, who explored the Irish-American experience through Studs Lonigan and other memorable working-class characters, attended the parish school. Today the parish serves African Americans.

Originally serving Whites, **St. Elizabeth Church** (50 E. 41st St., 773-268-1518) became the mother church for Black Catholics in Chicago when it merged with St. Monica Church in 1924. Fr. Augustus Tolton, the first Black priest in the United States, founded St. Monica. St. Elizabeth continues to serve Black Catholics. Located in a poor, blighted neighborhood, the church runs a number of valuable social-service programs, and its school has been a springboard to success for many.

The **Monastery of the Holy Cross** (3111 S. Aberdeen St., 773-927-7424) is an oasis of peace and prayer amid the noise and hurry of urban life. In 1991 the Benedictine monks moved into this closed parish to witness God's love in a modern, industrial setting. The monks chant the Divine Office four times daily. They sell fudge, cheese, and jellies to sustain their way of life.

Founded in 1929, the **National Shrine of St. Jude** (3200 E. 91st St., 773-768-0793) was the first shrine in the country dedicated to the saint. The shrine was the brainchild of Claretian Fr. James Tort, the pastor of Our Lady of Guadalupe Church. Many of his parishioners were laborers in the nearby steel mills who lost their jobs as the economy nose-dived. Tort had a personal devotion to Saint Jude, at that time a relatively unknown saint. He prayed to the saint for his church, under construction, to be completed, as well as for his parishioners to find comfort. During Lent in 1929 he noticed many worshipers kneeling down in prayer before a statue of Saint Jude, and he moved the image to a place of prominence above the altar. An overflow crowd attended the final night of a solemn novena that ended on the saint's feast day, October 28, the day before the stock market crashed. Word of the devotion spread quickly, and novenas attracted huge numbers throughout the Depression and World War II. The "patron saint of hopeless causes" became one of the most cherished saints in just a few years.

St. Sabina Church (1210 W. 78th Pl., 773-483-4300), a vibrant African American parish, has the largest painting of a Black Jesus in the United States. "For God So Loved the World" is part of the back wall of the sanctuary. Heading the parish is charismatic Fr. Michael Pfleger, a civic crusader who successfully protested stores that sell drug paraphernalia and the prevalence of billboards for alcohol in Black neighborhoods.

Near Chicago

Berwyn

St. Odilo Church (2244 S. East Ave., 708-484-2161) is the only U.S. parish dedicated to the souls of purgatory. Saint Odilo, born in 962 in France, was a Benedictine monk who popularized All Souls' Day. The church has a small National Shrine of the Poor Souls in Purgatory. A large stained-glass window above the choir loft depicts Saint Odilo and souls in purgatory, surrounded by four angels. The modern church was built in 1962.

Lockport

St. Dennis Church (1214 S. Hamilton, 815-838-0704), begun in 1846, was an outgrowth of the "Holy Tramps" who ministered to bedraggled Irish laborers. In 1836 construction of a 97-mile canal began to link the Illinois River and the Great Lakes. Irish immigrants did the backbreaking labor, and a cadre of priests on horseback ministered to them. Clothed in the same apparel for days, the priests carried portable altars in their saddlebags. Risking their own lives, the priests continued their ministry amid a devastating cholera epidemic in 1837.

St. Dennis's direct predecessor was a crude mission church at Haytown. The present St. Dennis, a sturdy limestone structure, dates from 1878.

Mundelein

The sprawling, secluded **St. Mary of the Lake Seminary** (847-566-6401) is the most spectacular major seminary in the country. The 1,000-acre wooded grounds include a lake, an outdoor Stations of the Cross, and a grotto. The campus's fourteen buildings are styled in classical Georgian architecture. The graceful Chapel of the Immaculate Conception was modeled after the historic First Congregational Church of Old Lyme, Connecticut.

The seminary dates from the 1920s. Cardinal Mundelein wanted to build a seminary on a scale that showed Catholics, for so long considered second-class citizens, had come of age in the United States. Protestants, who dominated the area, weren't so impressed with plans for a Catholic seminary in their midst, and the archdiocese had to fight off a lawsuit challenging St. Mary's tax-exempt status. But the neighbors soon realized that the complex was a valuable addition, and the residents of the town of Area voted to change its name to Mundelein in 1925. Real-estate developers jumped on the bandwagon, too, advertising that their plots stood near the "Athens of America."

In 1927 the seminary hosted the final day of the 28th International Eucharistic Congress, the first to be held in the United States. An estimated 718 thousand filled the seminary grounds for a Mass, the largest Catholic congregation ever assembled. The entire congress had been done on an epic scale. Catholics from around the world streamed into Chicago. The fifty-member papal group from the Vatican traveled from New York to Chicago in a special "red train," a Pullman car painted red. Thousands gathered in depots across the country to cheer it on. The choir for the congress consisted of 62 thousand schoolchildren from parish schools; half practiced at Wrigley Field and the other half at Comiskey Park. A medical team of 70 doctors and 340 nurses was on duty at the congress's gatherings. Hundreds of thousands, many forced to stand outside, attended the evening Masses at Soldier Field, where a cross at the altar rose 125 feet into the air.

The congress was a great source of pride for Catholics, an unmistakable sign that the church was robust and significant in a nation that was once overwhelmingly Protestant. The church was no longer the immigrant church of the nineteenth century, when Europe felt obliged to send its money and priests to the United States. The U.S. church was rapidly building churches, schools, and hospitals. Catholic leaders hoped the glory and pageantry of the congress would lessen anti-Catholicism. "It must be a hard bigot who has missed the poetry and the romance and the glory and the holiness of the Catholic Church during these days," wrote a priest in *America* magazine. Yet just two years later the presidential campaign of Al Smith unleashed a torrent of anti-Catholic sentiment.

Plainfield

In August of 1990 a tornado ripped through Plainfield, killing twenty-seven people from several towns. Among the dead were the principal and music teacher at St. Mary School, who were killed in the school building, and the son of the rectory housekeeper, who had driven to the parish to check on his mother. The pastor, in the garage when the tornado hit, survived with cuts on his head, even though the garage and car were destroyed. Gone, too, was much of the parish—its church, school, rectory, ministry center, and two mobile classrooms.

The parish pulled together, consoling the mourning and vowing to rebuild. The new school opened in two years, and **St. Mary Church** (129 S. Division St., 815-436-2651), a spacious, dome-shaped contemporary structure that cost $3 million, was dedicated in an emotional ceremony in August 1994, one day before the tornado's anniversary. A stained-glass window frame from the old church sits proudly in the common area.

Techny

Dedicated in 1998, the **Chapel of the Word** at the Divine Word Missionaries (1985 Waukegan Rd., 847-272-2700) is a marvelous modern expression of religious faith. Using modest materials like corrugated plastic, plywood, and pine and cherry boards, the tiny chapel seats just a dozen people. The chaotic exterior, mirroring the tensions of everyday life, gives way to an ordered and serene interior, symbolizing the peace of God.

Southern Illinois

Belleville

Our Lady of the Snows (9500 W. State Rd., 618-397-6700), located on 200 acres near the bluffs of the Mississippi River Valley, is one of the largest outdoor shrines in the country. Its most distinctive feature is a big *M*, a concrete structure that rises 50 feet above an outdoor altar. The shrine offers a multimedia presentation and special seasonal celebrations, including the Way of the Lights in the winter.

Cahokia

The **Church of the Holy Family** (120 E. First St., 618-337-4548) is the oldest church west of the Alleghenies. In 1799 Fr. Gabriel Richard built this walnut-log church, restored in 1949. A century earlier on the same site French-Canadian priests ministered to the Cahokias.

Prairie du Rocher

Dating from 1719, **St. Joseph Church** (802 Middle St., 618-284-3314) is the oldest U.S. parish dedicated to St. Joseph. The church was connected to the restored Fort Chartres, the center of the French empire in the Mississippi Valley.

Quincy

The plain stone monument, one hundred years old and weather beaten, rises from the earth at **St. Peter Catholic Cemetery**. The inscription on the stone reads, "Rev. Augustine Tolton, the first colored priest in the United States." The simple inscription hardly conveys the dramatic story and impact of Tolton.

Augustus (the name on his tombstone is wrong!) Tolton was born in 1854 in Ralls County, Missouri, the son of two Catholic slaves. Tolton and his mother, Martha Jane, escaped to the North when Augustus was seven. After being cruelly taunted at one Catholic grade school, Tolton became the only Black student at **St. Peter School** in Quincy. A statue of him stands on the school grounds (25th, 217-223-1120).

Fr. Peter McGirr, pastor of St. Peter's, preached racial tolerance from the pulpit and refused to listen to parishioners who demanded Tolton be removed from school. McGirr arranged for special tutoring for Tolton and encouraged him to pursue the priesthood. Tolton studied for the priesthood at the College of the Propaganda in Rome after no U.S. seminary would take him.

Ordained in 1886, Tolton was assigned to Quincy's St. Joseph Parish, where he headed a thriving church, attended by both Blacks and Whites. Yet the pastor of a nearby Catholic church complained to the bishop that Father Tolton was stealing his parishioners. Outside Father Tolton's presence he referred to him as the "nigger priest." The bishop sided with the White priest, and Tolton was put in charge of thirty Black Catholics who had been gathering in the basement chapel of St. Mary's Church in Chicago. Some members of the basement chapel group, overcome by joy, wept openly when Father Tolton said his first Mass there.

Tolton was successful in gaining hundreds of Black converts. Construction of a church on the city's South Side began in 1891. A local philanthropist, Anne O'Neill, donated $10 thousand for the church. Another generous donor was Katharine Drexel, foundress of the Sisters of the Blessed Sacrament in Philadelphia. Most Chicago priests also rallied to Father Tolton's side. They affectionately called him "Father Gus."

As he had in Quincy, Tolton devoted himself to the poor, visiting their rat-infested tenements nearly every day. He also crisscrossed the country as a much-sought-after speaker. He was the headliner at the first-ever Black Catholic Congress in Washington in 1889. Father Tolton, not withstanding his personal experiences, never wavered in his support of the Church. His standard message was "the Catholic Church is the church of our people." Black Catholics cherished him, and he was cheered wildly at his speaking engagements. A Black journalist of the time hailed him as "one of the most important men in America."

Father Tolton once wrote in a letter that he wished there were twenty-seven of him, so great were the demands on his time. His friends urged him to scale back his schedule, but Tolton continued to hurl himself at his duties. On a sweltering 105-degree day in July 1897, his grueling lifestyle caught up with him. Stepping away from the train station in Chicago, he collapsed and died of heat stroke. He was forty-three.

Ruma

In 1992 soldiers in Liberia savagely murdered five nuns from the Adorers of the Blood of Christ order while they were doing missionary work in the war-torn African nation. The motherhouse (2 Pioneer Lane, 618-282-3848) commemorated the tragedy with a **statue of the martyred nuns**.

INDIANA

Northern Indiana

Fort Wayne

The church in Fort Wayne owed its original vitality to Fr. Julian Benoit, born in France but a horseback-riding missionary once he came to northern Indiana in 1836. Father Benoit won the trust and respect of those to whom he ministered, including the Miamis in the Fort Wayne area. About eight hundred Native Americans who were ordered by the federal government to relocate to a reservation in Kansas refused to leave until the priest guaranteed their safety.

Father Benoit was a builder as well as a conciliator. In 1858 he designed the **Cathedral of the Immaculate Conception** (S. Calhoun and E. Jefferson Streets, 219-424-1485), where he is interred before the high altar. Outside the church on Cathedral Square is a historical marker showing the burial place of Miami Chief Jean Baptiste de Richardville.

The church's beautiful stained-glass windows, created at the Royal Art Institute in Munich in the late 1880s, show scenes from the life of Mary. Other unique features include a three-dimensional Stations of the Cross, depicting Christ carrying the cross through the ages, and a Belgian, hand-carved screen behind the main altar.

The nearby **Cathedral Museum** traces the history of the Church in northern Indiana through rare books, photographs, and other items. A small research library contains one of the largest collections of anti-Catholic books in the country. John Francis Noll, the fifth bishop of Fort Wayne, accumulated the collection.

The campus of **St. Francis College** (2701 Spring St., 219-434-3100) includes a college library housed in a magnificent mansion. The thirty-three-room structure boasts a stairway that spirals to the third floor, lavish wall hangings, hand-painted murals, and period rooms. Students who can concentrate on their homework while surrounded by such opulence belong to the head of the class.

A contemporary landmark in Fort Wayne is the **Jesuit Statue** (at the filtration plant where the St. Mary and St. Joseph rivers come together to form the Maumee River). Erected in 1976, the statue commemorates the missionary priests who explored the region in the seventeenth century.

Merrillville

The **Shrine of Our Lady of Czestochowa** is located at the Salvatorian Fathers Monastery (5755 Pennsylvania St., 219-884-0714). In the church is a large 8 foot by 12 foot painting of Our Lady of Czestochowa and an array of statues representing historical figures, including Polish saints and kings.

Munster

The **Carmelite Shrines** (1628 Ridge Rd., 219-838-7111) offer a replica of the Vatican's Private Audience Hall, twenty shrines that feature Italian sculptures, and an arboretum. Most interesting is the **Shrine to St. Maximilian Kolbe**, designed by a man who witnessed his martyrdom. Ted Wojtkowski, now living in a Chicago suburb, was imprisoned by the Nazis in Auschwitz. When a prisoner escaped, the Nazis picked out men to be executed. Father Kolbe, a charismatic Franciscan priest from Poland who ran the largest religious house in the world before being arrested, stepped forward and volunteered to take the place of one of the men doomed to die. Wojtkowski, fearing for his own life, stood two rows behind the priest. "His expression was so serene, so peaceful, not a shadow of fear," recalled Wojtkowski. "He knew what he was doing."

In 1975 Wojtkowski, president of the Polish Association of Former Political Prisoners, designed the monument. It shows Kolbe, who was intensely devoted to the Blessed Mother, pointing toward the nearby Marian Grotto. Kolbe is holding his heart, in which are ashes from Auschwitz. A plaque on the statue reads, "We lived through it to tell the truth."

South Bend

Cheer, cheer for Old **Notre Dame** in South Bend (219-631-5000). The University of Notre Dame is an emotional touchstone for many Catholics. Yet even the most ardent Domer may not know that the university's football team played a significant role in dispelling anti-Catholicism. In the 1920s, when the Ku Klux Klan was active, the Fighting Irish achieved national prominence under Knute Rockne. Catholics were stereotyped as babushka-wearing foreigners who worshiped saints, mumbled Latin, and bowed down to the pope. The football team showed Catholics as brawny, athletic young men who displayed uncommon skill and courage every Saturday. Every victory on the gridiron in the golden age of sports helped wear away the un-American image of Catholics.

Start a tour of the campus with the **Main Building,** topped by a golden dome. The structure is arguably the best-known college landmark in the world. The dome is layered in 23-carat gold leaf; the statue of Mary on top is 19 feet tall and weighs more than two tons. Completed in 1879, the building was for many years the entire university.

Next to the Main Building is the **Basilica of the Sacred Heart**. Constructed over an eighteen-year period in the 1870s and 1880s, the basilica recently received a $17 million renovation. The church serves the university community as well as functioning as a parish church for South Bend.

Grotto of Our Lady of Lourdes. *(Lucile Nichol)*

Adjacent to St. Mary's Lake is the **Grotto of Our Lady of Lourdes**, a replica of the well-known shrine in France. Father Edward Sorin, who founded Notre Dame in 1842, visited Lourdes and vowed to reproduce it on his campus. A gift from Fr. Thomas Carroll, a former student, made it possible in 1896. Boulders weighing as much as three tons were used in its construction.

Reproduced at the grotto is a letter from the humanitarian Dr. Tom Dooley, a Notre Dame grad, to Fr. Theodore Hesburgh, formerly the longtime president of the university. Six weeks before he died in 1961, Dooley wrote, "If I could go to the grotto now, then I think I could sing inside." The grotto is a popular place for students to pray before exams and for visitors to light a candle. The rosary is said daily at 6:45 P.M.

The university grew out of a mission established in 1832 by Fr. Stephen Badin. Near the lake is a sparse log cabin, a replica of his chapel. The original chapel was destroyed by a fire in 1856. The replica, built in 1906, is used for Masses and weddings. Badin is buried beneath the floor.

The **Snite Museum of Art** houses 19 thousand works of art, including nineteenth-century French oil sketches, Rembrandt etchings, and sculptures by Ivan Mestrovic. Admission is free.

Recently expanded, **Notre Dame Stadium** has been the playground of football legends since 1930. Notre Dame has won 11 national championships and produced 7 Heisman Trophy winners, more than any other university. Most modern stadiums lack soul. This stadium shakes down the thunder just sitting there on the drabbest Monday.

Dedicated in 1963, **Hesburgh Library** was once the largest college library in the world. It holds more than two million volumes and can accommodate half of the student body at any given time. On the library's south wall is a 132-foot-high mosaic of Christ surrounded by saints and scholars. Christ's upraised arms loom high over the north end of the football field, hence the name "Touchdown Jesus" for the mosaic.

To soak up the legendary atmosphere of the campus, make a final stop at nondescript **Washington Hall**, now the campus auditorium. George Gipp, who died in 1920 at the age of twenty-five and was played by Ronald Reagan in the 1940 film *Knute Rockne All American,* lived on the upper floors as a student. The ghost of the Gipper is said to wander the halls and make a ruckus after every Notre Dame victory.

Near Notre Dame is the oldest Catholic college for women in the United States, **St. Mary of the Woods University** (219-284-4000), established in 1840. Visit the **Church of the Immaculate Conception**, built in 1886. Inside is the tomb of Mother Theodore Guerin, the foundress of the college. She was beatified in 1998. The **Mother Theodore Guerin Historical Museum** is located in the motherhouse of the Sisters of Providence. On display are artifacts relating to the history of the order. Also here is a narrated exhibit of twelve scenes from the congregation's history.

Valparaiso

Seven Dolors Shrine (356 W. Seven Mile Rd., 219-759-2521), run by the Franciscans of the Most Holy Savior Custody, is situated on 160 acres. The Main Grotto has a life-sized statue of Our Lady of Sorrows with seven golden swords piercing her heart.

Central Indiana

Indianapolis

The city's oldest Catholic church and parish is **St. John the Evangelist** (121 S. Capitol Ave., 317-635-2021), founded in 1837. Diedrich Bohlen, Indianapolis' premier architect, designed the church, which was dedicated in 1871. Its architecture is pleasingly eclectic, from American Romanesque to French Gothic. For many years the church served Irish immigrants.

The church's wonderful marble altar was the result of congressional legislation. In 1880 the steamer *Scandinavia* arrived in New York from Livorno, Italy, carrying fifteen cases of marble for Bishop Francis Chatard, whose diocese was strapped for funds. A local congressman who was a Methodist minister sponsored a bill to admit the marble duty-free.

The window over the 1,400-pipe organ depicts John the Evangelist on the island of Patmos in the central panel, with musicians and musical instruments in the "petals" surrounding it. The original rose window above the organ, picturing the Baptism of Christ, was destroyed during a severe hailstorm in 1923.

Built in 1905, **Saints Peter and Paul Cathedral** (1347 N. Meridian St., 317-634-4519) is graced with classical columns out front and a coffered ceiling reminiscent of St. John Lateran in Rome. The New York architect William Whetten Renwick considered this church one of his masterpieces. The church was renovated in 1986; angry opponents claimed the church's familiar interior and artwork were being eliminated in the name of progress.

Sacred Heart of Jesus Church (1530 S. Union St., 317-638-5551) is treasured for its exquisite hand-carved wooden altars and pulpit, stained-glass windows from Munich, and Art Deco touches. The red-brick structure, built between 1883 and 1891, ministered to German immigrants.

Southern Indiana

Ferdinand

Nearly 140 Sisters of St. Benedict live at the **Immaculate Conception Monastery** (802 E. 10th St., 812-367-1411) and close to another hundred also belong to the community. Four young German-speaking sisters who came from Covington, Kentucky, to teach Ferdinand's German settlers founded the monastery in 1867.

The monastery's architectural brilliance earned it the name "Castle on the Hill." Visible for miles, the church's distinctive Romanesque-style dome majestically rises 87 feet over the town. Completed in 1924, the structure features solid oak panels, pews hand-carved in Oberammergau, Germany, stained-glass windows depicting Benedictine saints, and a heavenly host of angelic figures.

Also on the grounds are a Lourdes grotto, an outdoor Stations of the Cross, and the Rosary Steps, a walkway for recitation of the prayer. Guided tours are offered Tuesday through Sunday. The gift shop features handcrafted items from sisters and artisans in Ferdinand and Peru and Guatemala, religious articles, inspirational books, and even homemade cookies. (The sisters make sinfully rich baked goods.)

Leopold

The odd story of the **Shrine of Our Lady of Consolation** (at St. Augustine Church, off Indiana 37, 812-843-5143) dates from the Civil War. Three young soldiers from the Union Army, members of St. Augustine's, were POWs at the notorious Confederate prison in Andersonville, Georgia. They promised one another that they would build a shrine at their church if they lived. They all somehow survived, and one traveled to Belgium to examine a shrine there that he admired.

Some historians believe that the army veteran simply stole the shrine and brought it back. International tempers flared. Luckily, the Belgium king happened to be named Leopold, who was flattered that the shrine was transported to his namesake. The shrine remains in display—a statue of Mary and baby Jesus, each wearing a white gown, a blue robe, and a crown of jewels.

Madison

One of many historic buildings in Madison is the former **St. Michael Church**, maintained by a local preservationist group. Irish immigrants founded the parish in 1837. The Gothic church was completed shortly before Christmas in 1839. Its construction literally paved the way for further settlement of Indiana. It was built from stones removed from the railroad cut, which permitted the moving of passengers and cargo northward from the Ohio River.

Meinrad

The massive **St. Meinrad Benedictine Archabbey** (on State Rd. 62, just south of I-64, 812-357-6611) sits regally atop a hill. Swiss monks founded the abbey in 1854, erecting buildings that reminded them of the medieval style of monasteries from their native continent. The industrious monks themselves moved the limestone from a quarry a mile away and hand-chipped it. The result is a Europein-Indiana monastery, complete with a church where the Gregorian chant is heard and a simple but pleasing guest house for retreatants.

The abbey houses one of the largest seminaries in the country. Silence is observed at the abbey only from 9:00 P.M. through breakfast, making the abbey one of the noisier Benedictine monasteries. The grounds even include a campus bar and pizzeria.

Oldenburg

Oldenburg is called the "Village of Spires" because of its many soaring steeples, one of which belongs to the **Chapel of the Immaculate Conception** (812-934-2475.) The chapel is part of the motherhouse of the Sisters of St. Francis, an Austrian order that came to this area to teach the children of German immigrants. The cemetery is peaceful and gardenlike. Low-cut green hedges and huge shade trees guard row upon row of small white stone crosses. The convent features resplendent ceiling frescoes.

Troy

World War II prisoners of war left behind a spiritual legacy in Indiana. A grateful Herbert Jogerst, a German POW who returned to the States after the war, sculpted **Christ Over the Ohio** near Troy (above State Rd. 66) in 1957. The 18-foot statue of the Prince of Peace with arms outstretched in blessing overlooks the scenic valley of the Ohio River. Located in a summer camp for disabled children, the statue is illuminated at night.

Vincennes

Vincennes is the cradle of Indiana Catholicism; its **Basilica of St. Francis Xavier** (207 Church St., 812-882-5638) is the oldest Catholic church in Indiana. Jesuit missionaries built a 20 foot by 40 foot log church here in 1749. A replica stands next to the current church, erected in 1826.

The white-spired, red-brick church is affectionately known as the Old Cathedral. Statues of Saint Patrick, Saint Francis Xavier, and Saint Joan of Arc are located in niches above the front entrance. The first four bishops of Vincennes lie buried in its crypt. (The church is now located in the Evansville Diocese.) Bishop John Stephen Bazin's devotion to his flock led to his death in 1848. He came down with pneumonia after sitting in a damp confessional for nine hours.

Behind the cathedral is the remarkable **Brute Library**, the oldest library in the state. Bishop Simon Brute, who in 1834 became the diocese's first bishop, assembled 11 thousand rare books and manuscripts in France and brought them to America. President John Quincy Adams praised Brute as "the most learned man of his day in America." A papal bull of Pope John XXII from 1319 is the oldest manuscript. Also included are letters from Saints Isaac Jogues and Vincent de Paul, a book containing the Lord's Prayer in 250 different languages, and a certified copy of a license issued on March 6,

1833, to one Abraham Lincoln, permitting him to operate a tavern in New Salem, Illinois.

Just west of the cathedral is the Old French Cemetery and its **Monument to Fr. Jean Francois Rivet**. Rivet, who died in 1804, was a French missionary commissioned by George Washington to teach the Native Americans.

MICHIGAN

Upper Peninsula

Caspian

The **Iron County Historical Museum** (off U.S. 2 on Hwy. 424, 616-265-2617) has twenty-one reassembled buildings, including historic St. Mary's Church, moved from Gaastra.

St. Ignace

One of the U.S. church's greatest missionary priests is memorialized at the **Father Marquette National Memorial and Museum** (720 Church St., in Straits State Park, 906-643-9394) near St. Ignace. Fr. Jacques Marquette founded a mission in 1671 at St. Ignace, named after Saint Ignatius of Loyola, the founder of the Jesuits. The priest then joined Louis Joliet on an epic 3,000-mile canoe journey on the Mississippi. Father Marquette mastered several native languages and converted thousands of Native Americans while helping Joliet map the Mississippi. In 1675, while ministering to the Iroquois, the priest began a short journey to St. Ignace, but, only thirty-seven, he died somewhere along the eastern shore of Lake Michigan.

The museum includes historical exhibits and a brief film on Father Marquette. Also here is a replica of his Mississippi journal, in both French and English.

Marquette Mission Park and the **Museum of Ojibwa Culture** (500 N. State St., 906-643-9161) stands on the site where Father Marquette established his mission among Huron and Ottawas. The park has a century-old monument that marks the original burial spot of the priest. Two years after his death a group of Native Americans who had known him retrieved his remains and reburied them under the chapel he built in St. Ignace.

St. Ignatius Church (Spring and Church Streets, 906-643-7671) is known for its painting of Saint Ignatius. The Gothic red-brick church was erected in 1904.

Indian Lake

When Fr. Frederic Baraga first visited the Ojibwas in 1832, they had heard of his coming and began building a chapel of birch bark and logs. A **replica chapel**, erected in 1984, stands at Indian Lake (one mile west of M-94). Also here are a hand-carved pine statue of Baraga, a replica of an Ojibwa house, and a cemetery blessed by Baraga, where small traditional "houses" over the graves were reconstructed.

L'Anse

The **Shrine of the Snowshoe Priest** features a 60-foot-high bronze statue of Fr. Frederic Baraga, who became the diocese's first bishop. Each of the five wooden beams that undergird the structure represents a mission he founded. The gargantuan snowshoes are 26 feet long. Local Catholics still talk about how the tireless Baraga's shoes were too big to fill.

Marquette

Named after the courageous explorer, the town of Marquette was home to its own pioneer priest. Fr. Frederic Baraga, the "snowshoe priest," is buried in **St. Peter's Cathedral** (311 Baraga Ave., 906-226-6548), a twin-towered Romanesque structure. The flinty Slovenian priest (1797–1868) arrived in the area in 1831 and tirelessly canoed and snowshoed among settlements in Michigan, Wisconsin, and Minnesota. Devoting his life to the Native Americans of the Upper Great Lakes, he was also called the "apostle of the Lakelands." One of his numerous accomplishments was compiling an Ojibwa dictionary. The present church, erected in 1936 after a fire destroyed the previous building, is made of Marquette's "raindrop" sandstone.

Sault Ste. Marie

One of the oldest U.S. parishes is **St. Mary's Pro-Cathedral** in Sault Ste. Marie (320 E. Portage Ave., 906-632-3381). Fr. Jacques Marquette built the first church here in 1668. The current structure, the fifth church building, dates from 1881. A stained-glass window of the Virgin Mary was saved from the fourth church, built in 1837. Next to the church is a 210-foot concrete tower built in the 1960s. Intended to be a part of a church that was never built, it now houses a museum that includes artifacts relating to Father Baraga.

Northern Michigan

Cross Village

Tiny **Cross Village**, located on a steep bluff overlooking Lake Michigan, was named after the cross that has stood on the edge of the bluff for more than 250 years. Legend says Father Marquette planted the first cross. The present cross was erected in 1913.

In 1855 Father Weikamp established the Society of St. Francis convent on a 2,000-acre tract. The convent owned large herds, a gristmill, a sawmill, and a carpenter-blacksmith shop, producing nearly everything for the order, from the wooden shoes worn by the nuns to currant wine. The convent was abandoned in 1896, and a decade later lightning destroyed the buildings. The tomb of Weikamp is open to visitors.

Holy Cross Church (6624 N. Lakeshore, 616-526-2030), built in 1898, has an interesting wooden statue of an angel with Native American features. The statue was taken from the little log church that once was here.

Indian River

The **Cross in the Woods Shrine** (7078 Michigan Hwy. 68, 616-238-8973) features a stunning 55-foot crucifix carved from a single redwood tree. The 21-ton statue, built in 1948, is beautifully lit at night. Also here are nine miniature shrines to saints, an arresting statue of Kateri Tekakwitha, the "Lily of the Mohawks," and the world's largest doll museum.

Mio

Our Lady of the Woods Shrine (at St. Mary's Church, 100 Deyarmand, 517-826-5509) is a composite of all the major Marian

shrines in the world. The mountainous stone structure is honeycombed with grottoes and niches. Miniature shrines are dedicated to the Infant of Prague, Saint Anne de Beaupré, Our Lady of Lourdes, Our Lady of Fátima, and the Holy Family.

Our Lady of the Woods Shrine.

The first pastor, who broke ground "without a penny and two borrowed shovels," began the shrine in 1953.

Petoskey

At the bottom of Little Traverse Bay is the **Skin Diver's Shrine** (off US 131). The life-sized figure of Christ stands beneath 60 feet of water.

Posen

Posen was settled in 1870 when lumber companies lured Polish immigrants to the area. After the timber was exhausted, the Poles bought the land for $10 an acre and cleared it for farming. **St. Casimir Church** (10075 M-65 N., 517-766-2660) was the town's spiritual and social center, preserving Old World ways of worship and social relations. Up until World War I the everyday attire of women was the national costume of Poland, and for decades all but one Sunday Mass was in Polish.

Southern Michigan

Detroit

St. Albertus Church (4231 St. Aubin St.) is the mother church of Detroit Poles. The massive ornate Gothic structure, built in 1884, seems to belong in Europe among that continent's architectural jewels. The 200-foot-long and 70-foot-wide edifice seats two thousand. The domed sanctuary features a marble altar, an elaborate communion rail, and an eloquent array of angels, murals, and stained-glass windows. Altogether, there are sixty-three pieces of sculpture; the murals portray Poland's historic churches. Poles mortgaged their homes and ate skimpy meals to pay for the first wooden church on this site.

One of more than thirty churches closed in 1990 by the archdiocese, the church is maintained by the Caretakers of the St. Albertus Church Building and the Polish American Historic Site Association.

Located downtown, **St. Aloysius Church** (1234 Washington Blvd., 313-237-5810) was called "everybody's church" in the 1920s because so many worshipers were from outside the parish boundaries. Today, too, the church belongs to everybody. The parish actively serves the homeless.

The present church, erected in 1930 at a cost of $500 thousand, has bronze figures of the twelve apostles carved over the front doors. The church completely covers its 72-foot by 100-foot plot. The remarkable three-level design was necessary because of the limited land space and the need to accommodate a large congregation. The main floor is below a large balcony, which is at street level. Worshipers on each of the three separate floors can see and hear the priest.

An icon in the city, **Ste. Anne de Detroit Church** (1000 St. Anne St., 313-496-1704) dates from 1701, making it the second-oldest continuously active parish in the United States. For a century, St. Anne's was the sole church of any denomination in Detroit. The parish was founded by the hearty French explorer Antoine Cadillac, whose name today is synonymous with luxury cars, a far cry from his arduous life. An early pastor, Father de Halle, was killed by Native Americans in 1704, and the original log chapel was burned. Altogether, there were eight St. Anne churches, most of which were destroyed by fires.

Fr. Gabriel Richard, one of the most extraordinary and loved priests of his time, was pastor from 1799 until 1832. Born in France in 1767, he fled his native country during the French Revolution. Possessed of enormous energy and vision, he founded grade and high schools in Detroit and cofounded the University of Michigan. He brought the first printing press, the first piano, and the first organ to Michigan Territory. (Native Americans, fascinated by the organ, promptly stole the pipes.) In 1823 he became the first priest elected to Congress. He ministered to the sick during an attack of cholera in 1832 and succumbed to the illness. The city came to a halt during his funeral. He is buried in a chapel of the church.

The present twin-spired church was built in 1886. The neo-Gothic structure is made of red brick and white limestone. Notable are its altars of Italian marble and Mexican onyx. Once a home for pioneer families, the church today is a port of entry for Mexicans.

Peaceful **Assumption Grotto Church** (13770 Gratiot Ave., 313-

372-0762) is Michigan's oldest Marian shrine and the city's second-oldest church. "The little church in the woods," as it was first known, dates from 1832. The present church was built in 1929. A Belgium priest who had visited Lourdes and was determined to build a replica in America began the grotto in 1881. A room in the gift shop displays crutches and braces discarded by those who came here and were cured.

Blessed Sacrament Cathedral (Woodward and Belmont Avenues, 313-865-6300), built in French Gothic style, has walls partly surfaced with rock-faced limestone. The vaulted interior is made of marble and stone.

St. Bonaventure Monastery (1740 Mt. Elliott Ave., 313-579-2100) was home to Capuchin Fr. Solanus Casey, a simple, relatively uneducated but deeply empathetic priest who brought many closer to God. Casey (1870–1957), who may become the first U.S.-born male saint, was born in a log cabin in Prescott, Wisconsin. He decided to become a priest to alleviate suffering when, at age twenty-one, he came across a young woman in the street bleeding from a stabbing. After struggling with his studies, he was ordained as a simplex priest, unable to preach or hear confessions. Assigned as a doorman to a parish in New York, he soon became known as the "holy priest." His patient ear and compassionate heart led people to unburden themselves to him. After meeting with him, people reported startling medical recoveries, reconciled marriages, and inner peace. Casey served at St. Bonaventure from 1924 to 1945. The Capuchins asked him to keep track of favors received, and Father Casey filled seven notebooks by the time of his death.

You can't see it but it's there. In 1995, the ruins of a famous mission church and its equally legendary cemetery were discovered under 10 feet of water in Lake St. Clair, 2,000 feet offshore from St. Clair Shores. **St. Felicity Church**, a crude log building, has been submerged in the rain-swollen lake since 1855.

Holy Redeemer Church (1721 Junction Ave., 313-842-3450) was the backdrop for *The Rosary Murders,* a 1980 film starring

Donald Sutherland. The script was based on a novel by William Kienzle, a former Detroit priest.

Built in 1856, **St. Joseph Church** (1828 Jay St., 313-393-8212) was once was the soul of Germantown. Parishioners paid for the huge church, once the largest in the city, by pledging one year's wages. The structure has one of the few signed stained-glass windows in the country, and Charles Van Depoelle, inventor of the first streetlight for Detroit, designed its communion rail and confessional.

The impressive exterior of **Old St. Mary's Church** (646 Monroe, 313-961-8711) was built on a scale rarely seen in contemporary church architecture. Ten polished red-granite pillars intended to be part of the state capitol building in Lansing grace the basilica-style interior. Above is an inspiring circular ceiling canvas of the Immaculate Conception.

Near Detroit

Royal Oak

The controversial radio priest Fr. Charles Coughlin broadcast from a room inside the tower at the **Shrine of the Little Flower Parish** (2123 Roseland Ave., 810-541-4122). Coughlin began his Sunday afternoon programs in 1926. Coughlin once contrasted the message of Saint Thérèse (the "Little Flower") with the hatred of the Klan. Klansmen responded by burning a cross on his front lawn. An unintimidated Coughlin promised his listeners he would "raise a cross so high to the sky that neither man nor beast can burn it down." Donations poured in. By 1933, Coughlin kept his vow. Carved into the 111-foot Charity Crucifixion Tower is a 28-foot sculpture of the crucified Christ.

Coughlin, once a supporter of President Franklin Roosevelt, later personally attacked him on the air as a "liar" and "Franklin Doublecross Roosevelt." His unpriestly diatribes drew the censure of Archbishop Edward Mooney, though, strangely, Coughlin remained a hero to many.

Southern Michigan

Monroe

St. Mary of the Immaculate Conception Church (127 N. Monroe St., 734-241-1644) is the oldest Catholic church in the Lower Peninsula. The Romanesque-style structure, built in 1838, was enlarged seven years later. A $1 million restoration in 1987 included the cleaning of the church's stunning Tiffany-like ornamental windows, which were installed in 1903.

French Canadian immigrants founded the parish in 1788 as St. Antoine at the River Raisin. On the church grounds is a centennial statue of an angel recording the souls arriving in heaven. The base has a quotation from a letter of President Washington to Catholics of America.

Incidentally, Gen. George Custer grew up down the street. Custer may have died for our sins, but he wasn't Catholic. He was married in Monroe at the First Presbyterian Church.

Westphalia

A priest and five compatriots from Westphalia, Germany, explored the wilderness on foot and founded the town of Westphalia and **St. Mary's Church** (201 N. Westphalia, 517-587-4201) in 1836. The church was the state's first for German-speaking Catholics. The present church, with an attractive belfry and spire, was erected in 1869.

Western Michigan

Manistee

Guardian Angels Church (Fifth and Sycamore Streets, 616-723-2165) is a magnificent edifice built by Irish and Germans in 1889. The exterior is lit at night, highlighting its arches and corners

and creating effective shadows. Lighting artisan Peter Simon did the work. Parishioners slyly tell visitors that who better to light up a Catholic church than a man listed in the phone book as Simon Peter.

St. Mary's of Mount Carmel Shrine (260 St. Mary's Pkwy., 616-723-3345) is a French-style church constructed of thousands of pounds of rough blasted white marble. The most notable feature is a splendid 10-foot statue of Our Lady of Mount Carmel.

Guardian Angels Church. *(R. L.) (Shively)*

OHIO

Northern Ohio

Akron

St. Anthony of Padua Church (91 Mossier Ave., 330-762-7277) was built in 1940 to serve Italians. The church has five marble altars and stained-glass windows, including one honoring Mother Cabrini, who was born in Italy. The Stations of the Cross, painted in copper and placed in marble frames, were imported from Czechoslovakia.

The elegant **St. Mary Church** (750 S. Main St., 330-762-9247) is modeled after the Cathedral at Duomo Ostia in Italy, built more than fifteen hundred years ago. St. Mary's, completed in 1915, is notable for its wrought-iron lighting fixtures, gray oak pews, and gray marble baptismal font. The bell tower features small rectangular windows that increase in number and size from the lower to the upper stories.

Bellevue

Sorrowful Mother Shrine.

The **Sorrowful Mother Shrine** (4106 State Rte. 269, 419-483-3435), founded in 1850, was the first Marian shrine in the Midwest. The shrine is located on 120 acres of unspoiled woodlands. A priest who was a member of the Missionaries of the Precious Blood was attracted to the location because it reminded him of a famous Marian shrine in the Black Forest in Germany.

The chapel, built in 1914, has a barreled ceiling with fine paintings. The outdoor Pièta chapel was dedicated in 1968. Favorite spots to pray are the Way of the Cross and replicas of the Grotto of Lourdes and the Holy Sepulchre.

Canfield

Located on a well-traveled highway, **St. Anthony's Wayside Shrine** at St. Paul Monastery (Rte. 224, 330-533-5503) draws visitors from across the country. The shrine holds novenas to Saint Anthony of Padua and Mary, Queen of the Apostles.

Canton

St. John the Baptist Church (627 McKinley Ave. NW, 330-454-8044), founded in 1823, is the second-oldest parish in northeastern Ohio. Bishop Edward Fenwick said the first Mass in the area in 1817 under an oak tree at the home of John and Catherine Shorb. A chair in the church is made from that oak tree; the Shorbs are buried under a simple tombstone in the old cemetery adjoining the church. The present church, erected in 1871, is a fine example of high Victorian style. The Brooklyn architects also designed St. Patrick's Cathedral in New York. The parish school opened in 1876; its present structure was built in 1898. Sweeping lawns surround the parish complex.

Carey

The **Basilica and National Shrine of Our Lady of Consolation** (315 W. Clay St., 419-396-7107) dates from 1875. The Romanesque-style church, dedicated in 1925, has a soaring bell tower, a huge rose window, and generous triple-arched doors. The centerpiece of the shrine is a statue of Our Lady of Consolation, secured from the mother shrine in Luxembourg. The Virgin carries the scepter in her right hand and with her left hand holds the Child, who, with the orb cradled in his left hand, raises his right hand in a blessing.

Carthagena

The **St. Charles Motherhouse** (419-925-4516) is at the center of a remarkable region known as the "Land of the Cross-Tipped Churches." Devout German-Catholic farmers settled in the region in the 1840s and built dozens of distinctive Gothic and Romanesque churches. Most have square towers, eight-sided, peaked belfries, and domes topped with gold crosses. The steeples often rise more than 100 feet. The churches contain gilded altars, frescoed walls, painted ceilings, and stunning stained-glass windows. The villages are named after Saint Henry, Saint Rose, Saint Joseph, and Saint Peter.

The St. Charles motherhouse once was a seminary for the Society of the Precious Blood, whose priests served in some of the area parishes. The impressive Gothic Revival-style structure has a five-story octagonal dome topped with a gold ball and cross. Today the building serves as a retirement home for Precious Blood and diocesan priests. The more than 250 tombstones in the adjoining cemetery, reserved for members of the Precious Blood, testify to the vibrancy of the Church in the area for more than 150 years.

Cleveland

St. Andrew Abbey (10510 Buckeye Rd., 216-721-5300) contains a fine modern chapel. The soaring, sky-lit structure combines the concepts of Vatican II with respect for the architectural designs of the past.

The **Cleveland Museum of Art** (11150 East Blvd., 216-421-7340) contains priceless religious works. The medieval collection includes wood and stone religious sculptures, altarpieces, and crosses. The single most illustrious item is the Guelph Treasure, nine sacred objects dating from the early eleventh century from the Cathedral of St. Blasius in Brunswick, Germany. The collection of fourteenth- and fifteenth-century European paintings include *The Holy Family with the Infant St. John* and *St. Margaret* by Filippino Lippi and two panel paintings of Saint Anthony Abbot and Saint Michael also by Lippi. Renaissance highlights include Titian's *Adoration of the Magi* and Tintoretto's *Baptism of Christ.* Also here are El Greco's *Christ on the Cross with Landscape* and *Holy Family.*

Founded in 1892, **St. Elizabeth Church** (9016 Buckeye Rd., 216-231-0325) is the oldest Hungarian parish in the United States. Fr. Charles Boehm, the first pastor, arrived directly from Hungary. He edited a Magyar prayer book and founded an influential newspaper in that language. The 1,344-seat church, erected in 1918, is 200 feet by 65 feet.

The solid-looking **Holy Rosary Church** (12021 Mayfield Rd., 216-421-2995) has served Italians since it was built in 1905. The main altar has a bas-relief of the Last Supper, and the baptismal font shows the baptism of Jesus.

The 232-foot-high main bell tower of **St. Michael Church** (3114 Scranton Rd., 216-861-6297) is a neighborhood landmark. Built in 1889, the stone Gothic-style church was for many years the largest in the city. The pointed bell towers and turrets give the church panache. Two large archangels crown the central portal. Inside are fifty polychrome statues. The altar is modeled after the Church of St. Francis in Borgo, Italy.

St. Paul Shrine (4120 Euclid Ave., 216-431-8854) began as St. Paul Episcopal Church in 1875. The Episcopalians knew a thing or two about church construction. The structure has a 120-foot tower with highly exaggerated turrets and pinnacles. Decorative supporting wood trusses also add a Victorian Gothic flair. The Cleveland Diocese bought the building in 1931 when the congregation moved. The Monastery of the Poor Clares of Perpetual Adoration is attached to the shrine.

One of the largest Gothic-style churches in the country is **St. Stanislaus** (Forman Ave. and E. 65th St., 216-341-9091). The brick church has served Poles since 1886. The pastor who built it was removed because the cost was considered too extravagant. His loss was Cleveland's gain.

St. Stanislaus's was the city's first national Polish parish. National parishes were established in the second half of the nineteenth century in the United States to help immigrants retain their faith while adapting to a new country. Immigrants felt out of place at English-speaking parishes, wanting to celebrate their own festivals, exalt familiar patron saints, and join the same sodalities they belonged to in Europe.

The immigrant groups, claiming a forced Americanization was diluting their faith, sometimes clashed with the Irish-dominated hierarchy. Bishops, in turn, were impatient with the immigrants. A bishop from Cleveland once warned of the danger of "the Church in the Mississippi Valley bound hand and foot to the wheel of Germanism." But over time acculturation occurred and hostilities lessened.

Extraordinary churches commonly stand in bustling urban centers. Not so with **St. Stephen Church** (1910 W. 54th St., 216-631-5633), located in a quiet residential neighborhood. The massive Gothic church was built entirely of stone in 1873. The structure is 165 feet long and 74 feet wide. The height from floor to ceiling is 75 feet. Six great treelike pillars on either side of the main aisle branch out into numerous columns. The oak pulpit was displayed at the World's Colombian Exposition in Chicago in 1893. The altars and statuary, carved from oak, were imported from Munich. The hand-carved wood statuary have Germanic facial features. The Virgin Mary has blonde hair, instead of the traditional dark color. The Bavarian Institute of Art created the stained-glass windows.

Near Cleveland

Highland Heights

Saint Paschal Baylon Church (5384 Wilson Mills Rd., 216-442-3410) has won awards for architectural excellence. The church has copies of Rodin's work; Rodin was an unsuccessful aspirant in the Blessed Sacrament community, which administers the parish. The **St. Anne Shrine** is located here.

Lorain

Built in 1907, **St. Ladislaus Church** (1412 E. 29th St., 216-277-8187) is believed to be the first U.S. church made of reinforced concrete. The church is the home of a Hungarian museum.

University Heights

The **John Carroll University Library** (20700 N. Park Blvd., 216-397-1886) has more than one thousand items relating to G. K. Chesterton. Robert Jordan Bayer, a newsman and traffic expert who had amassed the material in his Chicago-area home, donated the initial collection.

Northern Ohio

Mansfield

Life-sized Old and New Testament figures speak with wisdom and reverence at the **Living Bible Museum** (500 Tingley, 800-222-0139). A favorite of visitors is an ancient man with a Bible in his lap who reads aloud Psalm 23 in a slow, moving manner. The non-denominational museum has twenty-six exhibits altogether.

Maria Stein

Fr. J. M. Gartner visited Rome in 1872 when anarchy reigned in Italy. Churches and convents were being looted, and sacred objects were being sold in pawnshops. Appalled, Gartner gathered what precious objects he could. They eventually were donated to the Sisters of the Precious Blood, who enshrined them in the **Chapel of Relics** in Maria Stein (2291 St. John Rd., 419-925-4532). The present chapel was built in 1892. Hundreds of relics are displayed at the high altar.

Massillon

The **National Shrine of St. Dymphna** (3000 S. Erie St.) honors
the patron saint of those who suffer from mental and nervous disor-
ders. The shrine, dedicated in 1939, is on the grounds of Massillon
State Hospital.

Southern Ohio

Cincinnati

Immaculata Church on Mount Adams (30 Guido St., 513-721-
6544) was built in 1861 as a permanent memorial to the dogma of
the Immaculate Conception. **Holy Cross Church** was constructed
in 1895. A 100-year tradition, on Good Friday pilgrims climb the
180 steps to the top of Mount Adams, saying a Hail Mary on each
step and an Our Father on each of the five landings. At the top is the
Shrine of the Cross.

Old St. Mary's Church (123 E. 13th St., 513-721-2988), dedicated in 1842, is the oldest church in Cincinnati. It was established
by German immigrants led by Fr. John Martin Henni, who later
founded both the diocese of Milwaukee and Marquette University.
Cash-poor parishioners did most of the construction themselves.
The women baked the bricks in their own ovens, and the men felled
and hewed whole trees that formed the beams that still span the
church above the plaster ceiling. The church, 142 feet long and 66
feet wide, was once the largest in the Ohio Valley. The dedication
ceremonies, which included the first Catholic procession in the city,
lasted eleven hours.

The church is eclectic in style—Greek Revival, Baroque, and Romanesque. The clock in the steeple, installed in 1842, is one of the
oldest clock towers in the country. Resident Levi Coffin, a key figure
in the Underground Railroad who personally helped more than three
thousand slaves escape to Canada, cast the bell in the tower. Installed
in 1843, the bell served for decades as the fire alarm for the north-

eastern part of the city. The three large oil paintings of Mary over the altar, rotated regularly, are hoisted into place by pulleys.

St. Paul Church (Spring and E. 12th Streets, 513-543-0488) dates from 1850. The brick Classical Revival-style edifice features Doric pilasters, round-arched windows, and a steeple topped with a clock tower. The church was rebuilt in 1900 after a fire but closed in 1974 after membership dwindled. In 1981 the Verdin Company, a longtime manufacturer of bells and clockworks, purchased the church. Today, the restored building houses the Verdin headquarters and a bell and clock museum.

Cathedral of St. Peter in Chains.
(Halden Tompkins)

The glory of Greek architecture shines at **St. Peter in Chains Cathedral** (Eighth and Plum Streets, 513-421-5354). Built in 1845, the church was inspired by several classical Greek buildings, including the Tower of the Winds in Athens. The exterior has a Corinthian colonnade, and huge Greek columns dominate the interior.

A mosaic of Christ, one of the largest in the country, adorns the sanctuary. With his hands raised in blessing, Christ gives the keys of authority to Peter. To the left, Peter is shown imprisoned in chains in Jerusalem. To the right, he is imprisoned in Rome with Paul. In the center is a quotation from the Acts of the Apostles: "Peter was being kept in prison...bound with chains."

A figure of Saint John Neumann, who coconsecrated the cathedral, hangs in the baptistry. Two other historical figures met in the church in September 1976, when Archbishop Joseph Bernardin welcomed Cardinal Karol Wojtyla to the cathedral.

At one time the church was the largest, most costly church west of the Alleghenies. But as early as 1910 the neighborhood around the church had deteriorated, and in 1938 it was abandoned as a cathedral. By 1950 it was slated for demolition. Archbishop Karl Alter wisely decided to renovate the structure.

Dayton

The **University of Dayton** (300 College Ave., 937-229-1000) is one of the nation's ten largest Catholic universities, enrolling about ten thousand students. Its **Marian Library**, located on the seventh floor of Roesch Library, holds the world's largest collection of printed material on Mary. Also here are multicultural statues and replicas of Mary, paintings, stamps, postcards, Christmas cards, and medals.

Somerset

Ten families founded the red-brick **St. Joseph Church** (5757 Rte. 383, 614-743-1317), the oldest parish in Ohio, in 1818. The church dates from 1840. An unusual statue in the sanctuary shows Mary, the baby Jesus, and Saint Dominic with a dog at the Madonna's feet. Dominic's mother once had a vision in which she saw the dog. Two cemeteries with old gravestones flank the church.

WISCONSIN

Northern Wisconsin

Green Bay

Heritage Hill State Park (2640 S. Webster Ave., 920-448-5150) recreates life as it was in the state. The "living museum" includes a nifty replica of a bark chapel used by early Jesuit missionaries.

St. John the Evangelist Church (114 St. John St.), begun in 1832, is the oldest continuous parish in the state. Fr. Samuel Mazzuchelli, an extraordinarily productive missionary in Wisconsin and Iowa, established the parish. The Romanesque-style church has beautiful white marble throughout the interior.

Jesuit Fr. Claude Allouez, who landed on the western shore of Green Bay, celebrated the first Mass in the region on December 3, 1669. Allouez began a mission that flourished for twenty years. A **statue** on the lawn of the Brown County Courthouse (Walnut and Jefferson) portrays the priest, an early fur trader, and a Native American.

Near Green Bay

Robinsonville

The **Chapel of Our Lady of Good Hope** (4047 Chapel Dr., 414-866-2571) was founded in 1859 after the Blessed Mother appeared to Adele Brice, a young Belgian girl. "I am the Queen of heaven, who prays for the conversion of sinners," she told Brice. "Gather the children and teach them the catechism that they may know and love my son." Brice's father built a little log shrine, replaced two years later by a frame chapel. Brice and others later opened a school to teach religion.

Though Brice never became a vowed religious, she did wear a habit, and people called her "Sister Adele" and greatly admired her. When fires engulfed the area in 1871, terrified farmers fled to the chapel. Sister Adele exhorted them to carry the statue of Mary around the grounds and to pray the rosary. A sudden downpour saved their farms.

The chapel was rebuilt in 1942. Today, it is on the grounds of a Carmelite monastery.

De Pere

The **National Shrine of St. Joseph** at St. Norbert Abbey (1016 N. Broadway, 414-337-4300) honors the mission begun in the area by Fr. Claude Allouez in 1669. It was from here that Marquette and Joliet began their expedition.

Northern Wisconsin

Algoma

An early pastor, Fr. Adalbert Cipin, carved the exquisite altar at **St. Mary's Church** (118 Church St., 920-487-5001). He served at most of the area's Bohemian parishes, including five at one time. Cipin, a gifted musician, began a St. Cecilia Society at his parishes. Besides his altars, he left a legacy of parishes where music at liturgies remains superior.

Hurley

St. Mary of the Seven Dolors Church (404 Iron St., 715-561-2606) has a statue of Our Lady whose heart is pierced with seven swords of sorrow. The image reflects the area's terrible mining accidents and fires.

Stangelville

Czech immigrants founded **St. Lawrence Church** (414-388-3471) on a site they believed was touched by God. In the 1860s a group of settlers saw a large tree unearthed by a road construction crew accidentally fall into a crowd. A man lost his cap but not his head. The Czechs quickly built a rough log church on the spot. The present church, erected in 1892, has a wonderfully ornate altar.

Central Wisconsin

Rudolph

Fr. Philip Wagner, who was healed at Lourdes, created the heartfelt **Grotto Shrine** (6975 Grotto Ave., 715-435-3120) in 1928. The 4-acre shrine includes statues of Mary and Saint Bernadette and the handmade Wonder Cave, whose Path of Faith highlights the commandments, the sacraments, prayers, virtues, and good works.

Southern Wisconsin

Benton

Dominican Fr. Samuel Mazzuchelli contributed mightily to the growth of the Catholic Church in Wisconsin from 1835 to 1864. The native of Italy evangelized among the Native Americans, founded parishes and schools, brought the first teaching nuns to the state, and in 1847 helped found the state's first religious order of women, the Sinsinawa Dominican Sisters. The priest was an accomplished amateur architect who designed and built close to twenty churches and secular buildings in the Midwest. He built **St. Patrick's Church** and rectory (608-759-2131) in 1864. He is buried in the church graveyard.

Dickeyville

The fantastically elaborate **Dickeyville Grotto** (305 W. Main St., 608-568-3119) was the product of one priest's ample love of God and country. Fr. Matheus Wernerus, pastor of Holy Ghost Parish, built the shrines on the parish grounds. A native of Germany, Father Wernerus began working on the sixteen grottoes in 1918, the year World War I ended, and finished thirteen years later.

Dickeyville Grotto.

The main grotto consists of thousands of colored stones, molten glass, and precious gems embedded in cement. Father Wernerus was not picky when it came to materials. He used antique heirlooms of pottery and porcelain, stalagmites and stalactites, seashells, petrified sea urchins, corals, quartz, iron, lead, onyx, amethyst, and coal. The items are woven in intricate patterns. An American and a Vatican flag, made of glass set in concrete, flank the grotto.

The Patriotism Shrine has ornate images of Christopher Columbus, Abraham Lincoln, and George Washington. The Shrine of the Sacred Heart is a replica of an altar used at the Eucharistic Congress in Chicago in 1926. A curved walkway has niches with statues of the Apostles.

Eagle

Old World Wisconsin (S103 W37890 Hwy. 67, 414-594-6300) is a recreation of a nineteenth-century farmstead and village. Included is **St. Peter's Church**, built in 1839 to serve German immigrants in Milwaukee. The church, part Greek Revival and part

Gothic, has been restored to its 1889 splendor. Note the peculiar recessed aisle, intended to keep the frigid Wisconsin winter air from creating a draft.

La Crosse

They don't make them like they used to? The impressive **Cathedral of St. Joseph the Workman** (Fifth and Main Streets, 608-782-0322) was dedicated in 1962 but inspired by churches from long ago. The contemporary church has a Gothic soul. The twenty-two interior Gothic arches are made of Bedford Stone. The steeple, topped by a 17-foot aluminum cross, soars to 216 feet. The Celtic ceiling designs, taken from the Book of Kells, consist of various crosses done in gold leaf. Above the high altar is a bronze canopy created by Carl Wyland, a internationally known German craftsman. Our Lady's Chapel, 42 feet by 48 feet, has three first-rate stained-glass windows that depict Marian apparitions.

The Franciscan Sisters of Perpetual Adoration built the lovely **Maria Angelorum Chapel** at St. Rose Convent (912 Market St., 608-782-6301) in 1906. A series of paintings shows scenes from the history of the three orders founded by Saint Francis.

Madison

The oldest Catholic church in Madison is stately **St. Raphael's Cathedral** (222 W. Main St.). Its cornerstone was laid in 1854 after the pastor toured the state for donations, collecting $1,200 and 20,000 feet of lumber. The Romanesque Revival-style edifice has a lofty 235-foot-high steeple.

Milwaukee

The burial site and a statue of Fr. Stephen Eckert, O.F.M. Cap., a major force in the African American community, are at **St. Benedict the Moor Church** (10th and State Streets, 414-271-0135). Saint Benedict was the city's first Catholic church for African Americans.

Calvary Cemetery (5503 W. Bluemound Rd., 414-258-0058)

contains the graves of a number of pioneering Catholics, including Fr. Giles Taraszewicz, pastor of St. Casimir Parish and a larger-than-life figure in the Polish community. His funeral procession was the largest in the city's history.

St. Francis de Sales Seminary (3257 S. Lake Dr., 414-747-6400) is the oldest seminary building still in use in the United States. Archbishop John Martin Henni founded the seminary in 1856. Henni Hall, completed that year, contains Christ the King Chapel, class-rooms, student rooms, and more.

A little bit of France is found in the heart of Milwaukee at the **St. Joan of Arc Chapel** at Marquette University (14th St. and Wisconsin Ave., 414-288-6873). Dating from the fifteenth century, the chapel originally stood in France's Rhône River Valley. In the 1920s it was transported to a Long Island, New York, estate, where it was rebuilt. In 1965 it was again laboriously reconstructed at Marquette. Incorporated in the chapel is the invaluable Joan of Arc Stone, before which the fiery saint prayed. The building also contains historic and religious items from as far back as the eleventh century.

Also on the Marquette campus is the splendid **Gesu Church** (1145 W. Wisconsin Ave., 414-288-7101), a diocesan parish run by the Jesuits. Dedicated in 1894, the Gothic-style church was patterned after the Cathedral of Chartres in France. Illuminated at night, the church is one of the city's most visible treasures. The excellent pipe organ was brought from the Studebaker Theater in Chicago.

The Marquette **library** (1415 W. Wisconsin Ave., 414-288-7256) has an extensive special collection relating to the Catholic Worker Movement and cofounders Dorothy Day and Peter Maurin. The materials comprise more than 150 cubic feet, including the personal papers of Day and Maurin, records of Catholic Worker communities, photographs, audio and videotapes of interviews, talks, television programs, and peace demonstrations, and a wide variety of publications. Day (1897–1980) was a radical journalist who converted to Catholicism, and Maurin was an itinerant French worker/

scholar with a vision of the world "where it is easier to be good." Founded in New York in 1933, the Catholic Worker Movement is a faith-based, grassroots group that works for peace and social justice through nonviolence.

Cathedral of St. John the Evangelist. *(A. Fazio)*

The magnificent **St. John's Cathedral** (802 N. Jackson St., 414-276-9814), erected in 1847, was the first church in Wisconsin built specifically as a Catholic cathedral. Its stunning Baroque-style tower, added on in 1893, is one of the most photographed towers in the Midwest. The original clock tower, torn down because it was deemed unsafe, was designated the city's official timepiece in 1858. A devastating fire in 1935 gutted the church's interior. Restoration was finally completed on September 16, 1942, when the clock in the tower, stopped at 2:45 A.M by the fire, was set in motion again. Another disaster in parish history was the sinking of the *Lady Elgin* steamship in Lake Michigan in 1860 as it was returning to Milwaukee from Chicago. Three hundred parishioners perished.

Resourceful working-class Poles built **St. Josaphat's Basilica** (2333 S. Sixth St., 414-645-5623) out of materials salvaged from the demolished Chicago post office and custom house. Parishioners purchased five hundred railway flatcars of marble, limestone, granite columns, and finished metal and woodwork. It took a full month to ship the 200 thousand tons of building material. Legendary pastor Father Grutza greeted the shipment dressed in the blacksmith outfit that he wore before he was ordained. He then drove the first team that dumped the initial load. Like the anonymous builders of the medieval cathedrals, parishioners excavated the church site with pick and shovel. Dedicated in 1901, the grand Neo-Renaissance-style structure was the first Polish basilica in North America. Its enormous copper-clad dome, larger than the Taj Mahal, was once the fifth largest in the country. World-renowned Gonippo Raggi did the lavish interior.

Old St. Mary's Church.

The mother church of Milwaukee's substantial German-speaking population is **Old St. Mary's Church** (836 N. Broadway, 414-271-6180). St. Mary's, the oldest Catholic church still in use in Milwaukee, was built in 1846 and then enlarged in 1871. Key to the founding of the parish was the St. Anna Frauenverein (St. Anne's Women Society), whose members were attending St. Peter's but wanted a parish for Germans. The society remains active today.

Above the altar is *The Annunciation,* a painting donated in 1848 by King Ludwig I of Bavaria. The three bronze church bells, named Mary, Mary Ann, and Mary Magdalen, were cast in Munich and purchased in 1868. The wood-carved main altar dates from 1848. The Franz Meyer Glassworks in Munich executed the *Madonna of Milwaukee* mosaic on an exterior wall, dedicated in 1982.

Father Marquette statue at Pere Marquette Park.

The School Sisters of Notre Dame, who came from Bavaria accompanied by Fr. John Neumann, opened **Old St. Mary School** in 1851.

The intrepid explorer-priest Fr. Jacques Marquette hauled his canoe up the riverbank in 1674 in what became downtown Milwaukee. The place is now called **Pere Marquette Park**, appropriately located behind the Milwaukee County Historical Society (910 N. Old World Third St.).

The growing number of Poles in Milwaukee in the mid 1800s were forced to worship at German or Czech parishes, where the language and customs were foreign to them. Finally, in 1866, a group of Poles purchased a Lutheran church. One of them raffled off his gold watch, raising $250 for the new parish. **St. Stanislaus Church** (524 W. Mitchell St., 414-645-8170) was the third Polish parish founded in the United States. A Warsaw architect designed the present church in 1872.

Near Milwaukee

Elm Grove

Notre Dame Convent (13105 Watertown Plank Rd., 414-782-1450), housing the order's provincial offices, is modeled after a Bavarian castle. The American founder of the School Sisters of Notre Dame, Mother Caroline Friess, is buried along with two thousand other sisters in the 89-acre cemetery. The precocious Friess arrived in the United States in 1847 as a twenty-six-year-old and was put in charge of the order's North American mission.

Hubertus

A huge wooden cross stood atop a hill in the rolling Kettle Moraine countryside in southeastern Wisconsin in the 1850s, and a recluse who worshiped at the cross experienced a miraculous cure. That was the genesis of **Holy Hill, the National Shrine of Mary, Help of Christians** (1525 Carmel Rd., 414-628-1838). Discalced Carmelite Friars run the shrine, highlighted by a double-spired, neo-Romanesque-style church. One hundred seventy-eight winding stairs lead to the top of an observation tower in one of the spires. The grounds include an outdoor Stations of the Cross, a Lourdes Grotto, and a wall covered with crutches and walkers, left by pilgrims who no longer needed them.

Kenosha

St. Mary Church (75th St. and 39th Ave., 414-694-6018) is designed in Georgian Colonial style, an unusual design for a Catholic church. The present church was built in 1953 from brick, Indiana limestone, and reinforced concrete. The stainless-steel cross atop the steeple tower rises 125 feet above the ground.

St. Mary Church.

Waukesha

* The **Schoenstatt International Center** (W 284 N. 746 Cherry Lane, 414-548-9061) is the site of a German-based Marian movement. The chapel is a reproduction of a twelfth-century chapel in Germany.

Southern Wisconsin

St. Nazianz

The **Tomb of Father Ambrose Ochwald** recalls one of the most quixotic figures in U.S. Catholic history. Ochwald led a group of Bavarian Catholics to this small village to establish a Catholic utopian community in the 1850s. The commune flourished under Ochwald's leadership but collapsed after he died. The Salvatorian Fathers took over the buildings (206 Church, 414-773-2794). The commune's original stone church is still in use.

NORTHWEST AND GREAT PLAINS

IDAHO

Southern Idaho

Boise

In the early 1880s two priests ministered to the entire Idaho territory and its fifteen hundred Catholics. In 1884 Fr. Alphonse Glorieux, the president of St. Michael's College in Portland, was appointed bishop of the Idaho area, and within a decade the Catholic population had grown to seven thousand, led by ten priests. Bishop Glorieux set about replacing the simple frame cathedral in Boise. The result is the impressive **Cathedral of St. John the Evangelist** (804 N. Ninth St., 208-342-3511). The Romanesque Revival-style structure, begun in 1906, was modeled after the German cathedral in Mainz. The bishop refused to allow the parish to go into debt, so the cathedral was built in stages. It was completed in 1921, four years after Glorieux died.

The church is 170 feet long and 95 feet wide. The exterior walls are Boise sandstone, mined in a local quarry. The spectacular stained-glass windows depict the life of Christ and a multitude of saints.

Boise's first Catholic Mass was celebrated at **O'Farrell's Cabin** (Fourth and Fort Streets) in 1863. John O'Farrell built this structure for his seventeen-year-old bride. He apparently was a talented builder: his cabin also housed the area's first school.

Oreana

Oreana boasts a population of eight, so it's not a surprise that **Our Lady Queen of Heaven Church** (two miles south of Hwy. 78 at the base of the Owyhee Mountains, 208-467-6798) holds only an occasional service. Stop by the Trading Post for the key. The walls are paneled in apa-tone wood from Japan. Like the exterior, the floors are made of native stone. The crucifix behind the altar hangs on a sandblasted juniper tree.

The church was originally a store built by a rancher in the late 1800s. The empty building was given to the diocese in 1961.

On the Owyhee Mountains is **Our Lady of Tears Church**, part of the abandoned mining town Silver City (off Idaho Rte. 45). Mass is held once a year at the church, built by Episcopalians in 1898.

Northern Idaho

Coeur d'Alene

The Coeur d'Alenes welcomed the Jesuit missionaries to Idaho in the mid nineteenth century. They believed the "Big Prayer" of the priests would help them triumph over their enemies. The priests, of course, were more interested in victories over sin. Fr. Pierre DeSmet, in a quick first visit, taught them the Ten Commandments by having ten of them stand in a circle and each memorize one commandment. Accustomed to communal activities, they flawlessly learned the commandments.

In 1850 the Jesuits established the **Cataldo Mission** (Old Mission State Park, off Rte. 90, near Coeur d'Alene, 208-682-3814), also called Sacred Heart Mission. The remarkable Fr. Anthony Ravalli designed the splendid church. A native of Italy, Ravalli had a charismatic personality and was a gifted physician, scientist, mechanic, and artist and a master of improvisation. The church's European-style chandeliers were fashioned from tin cans; wooden ceiling panels were stained blue with huckleberry juice; wallpaper was made from East Coast newspapers. The pine altars were painted to look like marble.

The exterior is even more impressive, even though Ravalli and his crew of Native Americans used only simple tools like augers, axes, pulleys, penknives, and a few ropes. The church was built of huge logs latticed with saplings, woven with grass, and held with wooden pegs, not nails. Six pillars stand triumphantly in front. The facade has a sunburst design just below the soaring cross.

The mission had no pews: The Coeur d'Alene preferred to sit on the floor, and they called the structure the "House of the Great Spirit." They had never seen anything remotely like it, and it filled them with awe, as it does modern visitors.

Cottonwood

The 97-foot twin towers of the **Priory of St. Gertrude** (208-962-3224) rise proudly over the Camas Prairie. The Benedictine sisters painstakingly built the picturesque chapel in 1920, carefully chiseling each piece of the blue porphyry stone and placing them together by hand. The German altar was also a product of patient craftsmanship. No nails were used; each part was mortised and glued.

St. Gertrude's Museum offers a surprising bounty of fine art, like Ming ceramics, a Czechoslovakian chandelier with 160 crystals, and a French cabinet that appeared in the 1892 World's Fair in Chicago.

Lewiston

St. Joseph's Mission (part of Nez Perce Historical Park, off Rte. 95, near Lewiston, 208-756-2432), built in 1874 for the Nez Perces, is a white-frame structure with a gleaming cross over the bell tower. The Nez Perce come here on the last Sunday of May for a memorial Mass.

Priest Lake

The Jesuit priests who came to the Northern Idaho wilderness in the nineteenth century put their stamp on the land and water. **Priest Lake** is part of God's country. The 7,000-foot peaks of the Selkirk Mountain Range rise proudly over the clear lake waters, which themselves rest 2,400-feet above sea level. The town of **Priest River** and the river itself are located southwest of Sandpoint. Like a perfectly constructed cathedral, the remote, ruggedly handsome wilderness shouts to the heavens the glory of God.

IOWA

Eastern Iowa

Davenport

St. Anthony's Church (Fourth and Main Streets, 319-322-3303), built in 1853 and later expanded, is a city landmark. The solid design of the rough-cut stone building reflects the sturdiness of the pioneers who built it. The church's original bell is housed below the copper sculpture on the church's front lawn. The sculpture depicts, among others, a Sister of Charity of the Blessed Virgin Mary (the order began teaching at the parish school in 1844) and Fr. Samuel Mazzuchelli, the indefatigable Italian Dominican missionary who founded the parish.

Near Davenport

Eldridge

Nestled in the cornfields is the cloistered **Carmelite Monastery** (17937 250th St., 319-285-8387), where about a dozen women live. The community moved to the area from Baltimore in 1911. The grounds include a garden, a fruit grove, and a tiny bird sanctuary. The nuns earn income by selling altar bread to local churches.

Eastern Iowa

Dubuque

A Catholic undoubtedly held the first Christian service in Iowa. Fr. Jacques Marquette celebrated Mass when he made his trip down the Mississippi with explorer Louis Joliet in 1673. But it took 160 years before Irish Catholic settlers, who came to Dubuque to work the mines, raised funds for a church. St. Raphael Church was built in 1835 under the supervision of a legendary Italian priest, Dominican Fr. Samuel Mazzuchelli.

Dedicated in 1861, the current **Cathedral of St. Raphael** (231 Bluff St., 319-582-7646) has ornate, steeply pitched vaulting. The Stations of the Cross are from Munich, and the stained-glass windows are from London. An Italian artist painted the exceptional frescoes on the back of the sanctuary wall and the figures of the saints in the nave. Also noteworthy are relics of early saints displayed in the Corridor of the Saints.

Cathedral of St. Raphael.

St. Raphael's Cemetery, directly behind the church, was the first Catholic burial ground in Iowa. Some of the tombstones date from 1839. Near the cemetery is the foundation of a seminary building never completed.

The **Church of the Nativity** (1225 Alta Vista St., 319-582-1839) features a polished limestone floor and a brick wall depicting nine angels. An artist in Chartres, France, created its forty-two stained-glass windows.

Near Dubuque

Dyersville

The **Basilica of St. Francis** (104 Third St., 319-875-7325) is the only minor basilica in a rural U.S. community. This twin-spired church with sixty-four stained-glass windows is one of the finest examples of Gothic architecture in the Midwest. The main altar is made of Italian marble and Mexican onyx.

New Vienna

The majestic 200-foot steeple of **St. Boniface Church** (7401 Columbus St., 319-921-2465) towers over the town. The steeple has four clocks and four bells, valuable timepieces for New Vienna when the church was built in 1884. In far earlier times, steeple height expressed a "finger-pointing-to-God" message. Parishioners built the church, hauling white amnesia limestone by horse and wagon from a quarry and patiently laying it stone by stone.

Peosta

New Melleray Abbey (6500 Melleray Circle, 319-588-2319) is situated in rolling farmland. Its three dozen Cistercian (Trappist) monks rise at 3:15 A.M. to pray and carry on in similar fashion most of the day. Its "parent" abbey is Mount Melleray Abbey in Cappoquin, County Waterford, Ireland.

Petersburg

The three lofty spires of **Sts. Peter and Paul Church** (1625 300th Ave., 319-875-7992) tower over the town and surrounding farm fields. Built in 1906, the Gothic church was among the first to be consecrated in Iowa.

St. Donatus

The oldest Way of the Cross in the nation consists of fourteen brick alcoves situated along a winding path behind **St. Donatus Church** (97 E. First St., 319-583-0092). Each alcove contains an original lithograph showing Christ's journey on Good Friday. Immigrants from Luxembourg settled the town, bringing their architectural traditions. The church, nestled against a wooded hillside, has an Old World charm. The chapel behind the church is a replica of Chapel du Blichen in Luxembourg.

Eastern Iowa

Festina

Built in 1885, **St. Anthony of Padua Chapel** (on a country road east of Fort Atkinson) is one of the world's smallest churches. The stone structure is 14 by 20 feet and holds four tiny pews that seat two people each. The church was built because Johann Gaertner's mom promised God she would build a chapel if he survived Napoleon's Russian campaign, and he did. Under old cedar trees in the back is Gaertner's grave.

Harper

A concrete Jesus sculpture hanging on a metal cross in the cemetery of **Sts. Peter and Paul Church** (seven miles southeast of Harper, 515-636-3883) had withstood the elements just fine since 1911 until a bolt of lightning shattered the concrete in 1993. A local artist created a life-size bronze statue in 1997 that is expected to last one thousand years. The church was built in 1898; the parish dates from 1857.

Ottumwa

The stately **St. Mary of the Visitation Church** (N. Court and Fourth St., 515-682-4559) was built in 1930. The Gothic Revival-style structure, constructed of Bedford limestone, stands on a site where Native Americans once cultivated maize.

Spillville

Czech immigrants built **St. Wenceslaus Church** (1224 Fifth St., 319-562-3637), a reproduction of a cathedral in Kuttenberg, Czech Republic, in 1904.

Central Iowa

Des Moines

McGinnis and Walsh of Boston, the same architects responsible for the National Shrine in Washington, designed the Romanesque-style **Basilica of St. John** (1915 University Ave., 515-244-3101). Dedicated in 1927, the church resembles the Basilica of St. Paul Outside the Walls in Rome.

Most diocesan central offices are not worth a visit, but the **Catholic Pastoral Center** (601 Grand Ave., 515-243-7653) is the rare exception. Designed by Ludwig Mies van der Rohe in 1962, the building served as a bank until the diocese took ownership in 1993.

Western Iowa

West Bend

The largest grotto in the world is the incredible **Grotto of the Redemption** in West Bend (First Ave. W., 515-887-2371). The

grotto, which covers a city block, contains the world's largest collection of minerals, gems, fossils, and shells. The value of the material is more than $2.5 million.

The grotto was the lifetime work of Fr. Paul Dobberstein. As a seminarian he fell gravely ill with pneumonia, and he promised to build a magnificent shrine to the Blessed Mother if she interceded

Grotto of the Redemption.

for him. He began his work in 1912 and doggedly continued until his death in 1954. Fr. Louis Greving began assisting on the grotto in 1946 and kept working himself for fifty years. More than 100 thousand visitors see the grotto annually.

Because there are few rocks in the area, Father Dobberstein had to travel to other states in search of materials. Eventually, he constructed the grotto with stones from every state and from all over the world. There is alexandrite from the emerald mines of the Takowaya River in Russia, green jade from China, lapis lazuli from the Near East, and even a specimen from Admiral Byrd's expedition to the South Pole.

Nine separate grottoes decorate the grounds; each portrays a scene from the life of Christ. Not to be missed is a replica of Michelangelo's *Pièta.* Adjacent to the grotto is Sts. Peter and Paul's Church. Inside is a wondrous Christmas Chapel made by Father Dobberstein. It contains a Brazilian amethyst that weighs more than 300 pounds. The church's main altar, hand-carved from bird's-eye maple, won first place at the Chicago World's Fair in 1893.

MINNESOTA

Southern Minnesota

Minneapolis

The angelic **Basilica of Saint Mary** (88 N. 17th St., 612-333-1381), built in 1914, was the first U.S. church to be designated a basilica. (Basilicas are so designated because of their special religious or historical significance. The United States has thirty-four.)

The basilica's interior has 675 angels. Glass, marble, steel, bronze, plaster, and wood angels burst into view from all points and angles. The exterior is almost as long as a football field. A statue of Franciscan Fr. Louis Hennepin stands in front of the basilica. Hennepin, a Belgian missionary who arrived in the area in 1680, was probably the first European to view the Mississippi River's Falls of St. Anthony, now in the heart of the city.

Today, the basilica ministers to 3,400 households, one of the nation's largest downtown congregations. Even more interesting, well more than half of the members are young adults, a testament to the church's ability to adapt itself to current needs.

Bitterly cold Minnesota weather is no excuse not to attend Mass at **St. Olaf Church** (215 Eighth St., 612-332-7471). The building is linked to the Skyway, the city's above-street enclosed walkway. Built in 1955 from Mankato limestone, the church has a modern Vatican II look that was ahead of its time.

Our Lady of Lourdes Church (1 Lourdes Pl., SE, 612-379-2259), the oldest continuously used church in the city, was built in 1854 as a Universalist Church. In 1877 French Canadian Catholics who came to town to mill logs and grain purchased it. It was the

first U.S. church named for Our Lady of Lourdes. In the late 1960s
French-Canadians rallied to the aid of the church when it was scheduled to be torn down. They raised funds by selling *tourtieres* (meat
pies). The subsequent renovation included the installation of the
rose window that depicts Father Hennepin as he first viewed the
area on July 4, 1680. The church still makes and sells *tourtieres,*
and French Christmas carols are sung at Christmas.

St. Paul

The architect to the King of Bavaria, Joseph Reidl, designed **Assumption Church** (51 W. Seventh St., 612-224-7536). Reidl modeled the limestone church, built for German immigrants in 1873,
after the historic Ludwigskirche in Munich. The German Romanesque Revival-style structure is the oldest Catholic church in
St. Paul. Its twin towers are a city landmark, and its richly adorned
sanctuary is a marvel. The parish, founded in 1854, was the first
German-Catholic parish in Minnesota.

Emmanuel Masqueray, who also drew up the plans for the city's
celebrated cathedral, designed **St. Louis Church** (506 Cedar, 612-
224-3379), built in 1909. St. Louis Church is a masterpiece on a
smaller scale. The main feature of the limestone and brick edifice is
a pair of graceful towers.

One of the true architectural marvels of the U.S. Catholic Church
is the splendid **Cathedral of St. Paul** (Summit and Selby Avenues,
612-228-1766). Built in 1915, the Renaissance-style structure was
modeled after St. Peter's Basilica in Rome. The designer was
Emmanuel Masqueray, the French architect who won renown for
his work on the 1904 World's Fair in St. Louis. The cathedral's 96-
foot-wide green dome rises 306 feet. Seating 3,000, the church is
307 feet long and 216 feet wide. The exterior walls are made of
Rockville granite from St. Cloud. The writer F. Scott Fitzgerald,
who saw the church before its white bricks were faced with stone,
humorously described it as a "plump white bulldog on its haunches."

The ornate Neo-Baroque interior is a swirl of marble carvings, stained-glass, and paintings. Six chapels are dedicated to the patron saints of the state's pioneering ethnic groups: Saint Anthony for the Italians, Saint John the Baptist for the French Canadians, Saint Patrick for the Irish, Saint Boniface for the Germans, Saints Cyril and Methodius for the Slavs, and Saint Thérèse of Lisieux for the French. Large statues of the four evangelists occupy the niches of the church's four main piers.

Outside, at one of the entrances, is a 60-foot-wide carved-granite relief of Christ and the apostles. Twelve-foot-high figures of Peter and Paul flank Christ.

Near Minneapolis/St. Paul

Hopkins

Not all superb churches are old. The **Church of St. John the Evangelist** (6 Interlochen Rd., 612-935-5536), completed in 1969, likely will be much admired in 2069 and beyond. The church has high-paneled ceilings, curving brick walls, and oak furnishings. Its harmonious interplay of space and light is an exemplary reflection of post-Vatican II sensibilities.

Central Minnesota

Cold Spring

Built in 1951, **Assumption Chapel** in Cold Spring (Rte. 23) has a plaque showing the Blessed Mother ascending into heaven while grasshoppers below bend their knees in homage. The original chapel, destroyed in a tornado, was built after grasshoppers ravaged the area for two summers in the 1870s and farmers prayers' to Mary for relief were answered.

St. Cloud

Benedictine monks who came to the area in 1856 to minister to German immigrants began **Saint John's University** near St. Cloud

(320-363-2011). Most of the campus buildings, dating from 1866 to 1920, possess a typical collegiate charm. The more contemporary structures, designed by Bauhaus architect Marcel Breuer, are appealing, too. St. John's Abbey Church has a 112-foot-high bell tower whose style is reminiscent of the early Spanish missions. The original monastery bell hangs in the belfry.

The Romanesque-style **St. Mary's Cathedral** (25 Eighth Ave. S., 320-251-1840) has a fine statue of the diocese's patron. The church was constructed in 1931.

Western Minnesota

St. Joseph

Bucolic **Mount Saint Benedict Monastery** in St. Joseph (104 Chapel Ln., 320-363-7100) sits on a hill overlooking the Red Lake River. The sisters first arrived in St. Cloud in 1857 from Germany via Pennsylvania and came to this site in 1863.

Today, nearly two hundred sisters live in the monastery, built in 1924. They serve as healthcare providers, artists, musicians, spiritual directors, counselors, and writers. Some teach at the adjacent College of St. Benedict, opened in 1913.

The **Monastic Heritage Museum** has a spinning wheel made in Germany in 1875, historic vestments, breviaries, chalices, and a number of other artifacts.

Northern Minnesota

Warroad

St. Mary Church (218-386-1178) is the nation's largest log church, built in 1954 with donations from all across the country. It was constructed near the site where Jesuit Fr. Jean Aulneau and his companions were massacred in 1735.

MONTANA

Western Montana

Butte

A helicopter put the 90-foot **Our Lady of the Rockies** in place. The 51-ton Marian statue atop Saddle Rock, 8,500 feet above sea level, is beautifully lit at night. Bob O'Bill conceived the statue, dedicated in 1985, after his wife recovered from serious surgery.

Flathead Indian Reservation

Located in gorgeous Mission Valley, **Saint Ignatius Mission** (east of Rte. 93, 406-745-2768) has as a backdrop the spectacular Mission Mountains. Built in 1891, the church still ministers to the Flatheads.

Father DeSmet founded the mission in 1844 in Cusick, Washington, and moved it in 1854 to its current site at the request of the Flatheads. The mission was immediately successful. On Easter in 1855 more than one thousand Flatheads, Pend d'Oreille, and Kootenai arrived for Mass, and a sea of wigwams took root. The mission grew rapidly. It became the site of the first Jesuit theologate and industrial art school in the Northwest, the first Catholic school in Montana, the first home for a women's religious community (the Sisters of Providence) in the state, and the first hospital, sawmill, flour mill, printing press, carpenter shop, and blacksmith shop in the region. By the 1890s the mission's school for boys enrolled 320.

Only a few buildings remain today. The church, with its 100-foot-high belfry and stunning murals inside, retains its original splendor. The murals, a catechism in paint, tell the entire biblical history of humanity. The gifted painter was Brother Joseph Carignano, the mission cook.

Helena

The **Cathedral of St. Helena** (530 N. Ewing St., 406-442-5825) is one of the most immense and most beautiful buildings in the state. Built in 1908, the Gothic structure was modeled after the famous Votive Church of Vienna. Its two 218-foot-high towers are roofed with red tiles.

Six popular saints guard the front doors. Fifty-six stained-glass windows dominate the interior. The most exquisite is the rose window located high in the front of the building. Depicted are the ten musician angels of Fra Angelica.

The wealthy owner of a gold mine in Marysville paid for nearly a third of the church's $600 thousand construction tab. The architect, a resident of Washington, D.C., who was unfamiliar with Montana winters, failed to provide an adequate heating system, and wintertime Masses were held in the basement until 1941. Also part of the cathedral lore was the foolhardy pilot, trying to win a bet, who steered his plane in between the twin spires. He made it, but only by inches.

Madison County

The sturdy, attractive **St. Mary of the Assumption Church** (406-842-5588) was built of locally quarried stone. The small-town church is a fine example of how first-class architecture is found not just in large cities.

Missoula

The inviting interior of **St. Francis Xavier Church** (420 W. Pine St., 406-542-0321) provided early pioneers in the Rocky Mountain West a welcome relief from their harsh existence. The warm colors are a respite from the often overcast valley, and the ornate gilt scrollwork on walls and capitals reflects any ray of light admitted to the brick church.

The interior's artist was Jesuit Br. Joseph Carignano, a native of Turin, Italy. Working for the church as a cook and an artist in the Pacific Northwest, he left generations of worshipers at many churches a sense of the divine and a comprehensive catechetical understanding.

At St. Francis's, Carignano was able to implement an old Italian ideal called *un bel composto*—presenting the totality of the Church's teaching through artistic means like painting and sculpture in a beautiful whole. The church walls are emblazoned with a pictorial study of scripture stories, a depiction of all the symbols of the liturgy, and an inspirational portrayal of the lives of the saints. Amazingly, as church records of grocery deliveries show, Brother Carignano used egg tempera as his medium on the plastered walls.

Stevensville

St. Mary's Mission (west end of Fourth St., 406-777-5734) was the first mission in the Northwest. Jesuit Fr. Pierre DeSmet built a modest log church in 1841 with the help of the Flatheads. St. Mary's was the first step in conversion among a number of tribes, including the Cheyenne, Crow, and Sioux. The mission represents not only the introduction of Christianity to the western frontier but White settlement, which followed shortly after the arrival of the priests.

Ironically, though the coming of the pioneers eventually proved to be disastrous for Native Americans, the Jesuits came after repeated pleas by the Flatheads to come west. Having heard about the "black robes," their name for the Jesuits, they believed the priests carried special powers that could help them. Years before the Lewis and Clark expedition passed through Montana in 1816, medicine men supposedly had visions of the coming of the "black robes."

In 1831 four braves traveled to St. Louis in an unsuccessful attempt to persuade priests to travel back to their lands. Two more trips were also fruitless. There simply were no missionaries to spare. Finally, in 1839, another Flathead delegation met with Father DeSmet in Council Bluffs, Iowa, and he received permission to evangelize in Montana. On his journey west, a special guard of ten braves met Father DeSmet and escorted him to the main village. He received a rousing reception. Old men wept, young men danced and shouted, and children rushed to greet him.

The first site of the mission was along the Bitterroot River, near the spot where a dying Flathead child had a vision of a "house of prayer." The mission prospered. The industrious Father DeSmet traveled 300 miles to the state of Washington to get seeds for wheat, potatoes, and oats, and the Flatheads learned to farm. A mission band was started and included accordions, a clarinet, and a bass drum. In 1845 Jesuit Fr. Anthony Ravalli, brilliantly talented as a physician, architect, woodworker, and horticulturist, arrived to help the mission.

The golden era was over by 1850. The Flatheads became hostile to the priests who indicated good intentions toward the Blackfoot, their enemy. White trappers who sold whiskey to Native Americans made the situation worse. The priests were forced to move the mission in 1866 to its present location in Stevensville. Old St. Mary's Chapel (still standing) was built that year using logs from the original church.

The mission complex also includes the home of Fr. Ravalli, an Italian who arrived at St. Mary's in 1845. Ravalli was the state's first doctor, surgeon, and pharmacist. His house served as the pharmacy. He dispensed medicine through an opening in the west wall, making his home the state's first drive-up business.

On the grounds, too, is the home of Chief Victor of the Flatheads, who died in 1870. The simple structure houses a Native American museum.

The new St. Mary's Church, dedicated in 1954, has stained-glass windows that present the history of the mission. Windows tell of two appearances by the Virgin Mary and one by Saint Francis Xavier.

Eastern Montana

Ashland

St. Labre Indian School (Mission Rd., 406-784-2746), run by the omnipresent Jesuits, is located on the Northern Cheyenne Indian Reservation. The school is partly staffed by Jesuit lay volunteers.

Crow Indian Reservation

A tent, which the Jesuits used for celebrating Mass, cooking meals, and sleeping when they arrived in 1887, preceded **Saint Xavier Mission Chapel** (23 miles south of Hardin, 406-638-2641). The wooden chapel is not far from where Custer and his troops fell in a hail of arrows in 1876.

Wibaux

St. Peter's Church (406-365-4569), dedicated in 1885, was later enlarged using native lava rock. The castlelike house of God appears to be able to withstand anything thrown at it by Mother Nature.

NEBRASKA

Eastern Nebraska

Aurora

The **Plainsman Museum** (210 16th St., 402-694-6531) has exhibits on the area's history, including a replica of a prairie chapel.

Omaha

The impressive **St. Cecilia Cathedral** (701 N. 40th St., 402-551-2313) is one of the ten largest cathedrals in the nation. The massive structure, 255 feet long and 158 feet wide, was built in 1907 with three million bricks and one hundred tons of steel. Noted architect Thomas Kimball chose a Spanish Renaissance design to recall the Spanish explorers who journeyed through the region in search of the mythical kingdom of Quivera. The cathedral's twin towers rise 222 feet; the building seems to reach toward the sky, especially as seen from directly in front—an effect deliberately created by Kimball.

Our Lady of Nebraska Chapel north of the nave has a statue of Mary holding a stalk of corn. The chapel's north wall has three sixteenth-century stained-glass windows from the Cathedral of Pampeluna in Spain. They show Saint Christopher, Saint Mary Magdalene, and Saint Barbara carrying a three-tiered castle symbolizing the Trinity.

Albin Polasek, who also designed the 7-foot marble crucifix above the main altar, created the circular bronze medallions for the Stations of the Cross located on the pillars of the nave. Instead of the more typical expression of suffering, Christ is shown looking toward heaven in merciful prayer, "Father, forgive them...." Tradition has it that Polasek was stumped as to how to carve the face of Christ when a stranger wandered in asking for work as a carpenter. As they talked, Polasek became fascinated with the man's features and knew how he wanted to proceed. The carpenter was to return the next day but was never seen again.

Sacred Heart Church (2218 Binney St., 402-451-5755), built in 1902, is a Gothic Revival-style structure.

The newest church in Omaha evokes the classic churches of Europe rather than the typically short and squat churches of today. The French Gothic-style **St. Vincent de Paul Church** (14330 Eagle Run Dr., 402-496-7988) was dedicated in 1998. The style was chosen to link worshipers with the seventeenth-century French cleric. The church has an 88-foot bell tower, cloistered walks, and a Children's Courtyard.

Near Omaha

Bellevue

St. Columbans Mission (north end of Calhoun St., 402-291-1920) is the national headquarters for the Society of St. Columbans. Nearby is Our Lady of Lourdes Grotto. Antique oriental art is displayed in the administration building, and the chapel has brilliant stained-glass windows.

Boys Town

Boys Town (off W. Dodge Rd. exit from I-680 on 137th St., 800-625-1400) remains a wonderful home for needy youth and is also a great place to visit. Its Hall of History tells the story of Fr. Edward Flanagan, the young Irish priest who started the home in 1917. On display is the horse-drawn circus wagon that Father Flanagan's Juvenile Entertainers used to tour the Midwest in the 1920s. The troupe was a positive activity for the boys and was invaluable in publicizing the financially strapped home. Also here is the Oscar won by Spencer Tracy for his portrayal of Father Flanagan in the 1938 film *Boys Town.*

The clicking of cameras is a constant at the famous **Two Brothers Statue** on the campus. The statue shows one boy carrying a smaller one on his back. The inscription is "He ain't heavy, Father, he's m' brother." Father Flanagan selected the image because a disabled boy named Howard Loomis often relied on other boys for a lift.

The **Father Flanagan House**, built in 1927, contains personal memorabilia. The boys hoped for a chance at kitchen duty when Father Flanagan entertained movie stars, pro athletes, and politicians.

The **Garden of the Bible** is lined with markers containing quotations from the Old and New Testaments. The campus also has two Gothic chapels, where Protestant and Catholic services are offered. "Every boy must learn to pray. How he prays is up to him," Father Flanagan said.

Father Flanagan, a first-class scholar educated in Rome and Innsbruck, came by his life's work almost by accident. He ran a shelter in Omaha for homeless and jobless men when he realized most of them had come from broken homes. He went to juvenile court, and soon five boys were entrusted to him. He opened a home and with the help of a hardworking secretary began a shrewd publicity campaign in the Midwest. Father Flanagan and the boys' band hurried to the train station and met every celebrity that passed through town, be it Jack Dempsey, Babe Ruth, or Tom Mix.

In 1921, needing more space, he bought Overlook Farm on the rolling prairies west of Omaha. For years the home struggled to make ends meet. The bishop once threatened to close the home, and a despairing Father Flanagan became ill and was hospitalized several times. But by the mid 1920s Boys Town was on firm footing, and Father Flanagan's motto that "there is no such thing as a bad boy" was a nationally honored piece of wisdom. The priest changed the way America thought of troubled children. He pioneered alternative education and vocational training instead of prison.

Girls were admitted into Boys Town in 1979, and today 850 youths live on campus, which has 76 family homes, 2 schools, fire and police departments, and even its own U.S. Post Office.

Eastern Nebraska

Schuyler

Set amid gently rolling hills in rural Nebraska, **St. Benedict Center** (off Hwy. 15, 402-352-2177) is a modern ecumenical retreat/conference center run by the Benedictines of Christ the King Priory. The center offers heartfelt Benedictine hospitality. The gift shop includes items from around the world.

Western Nebraska

Keystone

Keystone Church (off US 30) was the sole church in America in the first part of the century that served both Catholics and Protestants. The frame church had reversible pews: the Catholic altar was on one end, the Protestant on the other. No longer in use, the building is open on Sundays during the summer.

NORTH DAKOTA

Eastern North Dakota

Jamestown

The **Basilica of St. James** (622 First Ave. S., 701-252-0119) is the only basilica in the state and just one of thirty-four in the country. Its structural splendor is especially noticeable in the windswept plains of North Dakota.

Wahpeton

Mary's appeal cuts across all lines. The **Shrine of Our Lady of the Prairies** at the Carmelite nuns' monastery (17765 78th St., SE, 701-642-2360) has an outdoor statue of Mary walking barefoot through a wheat field and holding a sheaf of wheat. An annual pilgrimage is held in August on the Sunday closest to the Feast of the Assumption.

Western North Dakota

Medora

Marquis de Mores, a wealthy Frenchman who established the town he named for his wife, built **St. Mary Church** in 1884 because he wanted her to have a church, too.

Richardton

Rising above the treetops of Richardton are the majestic twin steeples of the red-brick church of **Assumption Abbey** (701-974-3315), a large complex of buildings constructed by the Benedictine monks between 1899 and 1909. Kathleen Norris wrote about the abbey in her popular books *Dakota: A Spiritual Geography* and *The Cloister Walk.*

The monks' days are set aside for work, prayer, and reading. They tend to several hundred cattle, run a print shop, and craft pottery. In Benedict's era during the sixth century, work was for slaves. Benedict, however, excused no one from work, and labor was elevated to a holy endeavor. Even the garden tools are treated as if they were sacred because the monks believe that everything is connected and linked to the Divine.

The quiet and simplicity of the abbey not only gave Norris food for thought but also slaked her spiritual thirst. Many visitors commonly report such experiences.

Near Richardton

"They come and find, the tired travelers, green herbs and ample bread, quiet and brother's love and humbleness, Christ's peace on every head." That is an ancient description of the Benedictine monastery at Monte Cassino, and the sentiment holds true at the **Sacred Heart Monastery** (701-974-2121), just west of Richardton. Two dozen or so Benedictine women live at the monastery, set amid rolling prairie hills and endless sky.

A few years back friends donated two llamas to the monastery, and the sisters now tend more than a dozen. They sell them to sheep farmers, zoos, or pet lovers.

OREGON

Northwest Oregon

Portland

The **Cathedral of the Immaculate Conception** (18th and Couch, 503-228-4397) is the fourth edifice to serve as the cathedral. A fifth site was considered in the suburbs. Instead, the cathedral, erected in 1926, underwent an extensive restoration in 1996. The stained-glass windows in the transept, depicting the four evangelists, Saint Patrick, Saint Dominic, and others, date from an earlier cathedral built in 1885. A new stained-glass window in the nave shows Saint John Neumann. The first Mass at the initial site, located at Third and Stark Streets, was celebrated at midnight, Christmas Eve, 1851.

The unique **National Sanctuary of the Sorrowful Mother** (85th and N.E. Sandy Blvd., 503-254-7371) has two levels, one at the street, the other atop a 150-foot cliff. A ten-story elevator connects the two. On the lower level is a natural amphitheater facing the cliff and containing a marble replica of the *Pièta*. Also below is a Chapel of Mary, Our Mother with a 110-foot bell tower. The upper level includes the Sorrowful Mother Grove and St. Anne's Chapel, whose walls are lined with Marian paintings.

Near Portland

Oregon City

A vibrant mural on the side of **St. John the Apostle School** (516 Fifth St., 503-656-5123) tells of the growth of the church in the state. The school was previously called the McLoughlin Institute in honor of the man called the Father of Oregon. Dr. John McLoughlin came to Oregon City in 1846 to live peacefully on his land claim but instead helped develop the area and the Church.

Tualatin

The low-slung **Church of the Resurrection** (21060 S.W. Stafford Rd., 503-638-1579) was formerly an equestrian center. The church

no longer looks like a stable, but during the Easter season a horse trough is displayed, to remind parishioners both of the church's roots and Jesus' humble birth. The church offers a great view of the Tualatin River Valley.

Church of the Resurrection.

Northwest Oregon

Rockaway Beach

The charming **St. Mary's by the Sea Church** (275 S. Pacific St., 503-355-2661) faces the ocean. The church is said to be closer to the sea than any other church in the continental United States. St. Mary's was built in 1927 with a nautical motif. The walls and ceilings are paneled like a ship's cabin, using knot-free cedar boards. The lighting fixtures are replicas of anchors. A stained-glass window behind the altar depicts a lighthouse beacon shining on an anchor. The sanctuary area is reminiscent of a captain's quarters, with corbels supporting the walls. The holy water fonts represent two Spanish galleons. Next to the church, watchfully facing the water, is a simple statue of Mary.

Salem

St. Joseph Church. *(Tom Bockelman)*

St. Joseph Church (721 Chemeketa St. NE, 503-581-1623) has been at this site since 1864. The present church, dedicated in 1952, is majestically modern. A Sunday Mass is said in Vietnamese.

Near Salem

Albany

The old **St. Mary's Church** (503-926-1449) has more than one hundred stained-glass windows. Above the main doors are illuminated statues. The Gothic Revival-style structure dates from 1898. The new St. Mary's Church, dedicated in 1992, is an attractive modern version of the first church. The two share a white wood exterior, a tall steeple, and abundant use of wood and stained glass inside.

Gervais

While they awaited a more permanent residence, the first home for the Benedictine Sisters of **Queen of the Angels Monastery** (840 S. Main St., 503-845-6141) was an abandoned saloon in Gervais. Their monastery in Mt. Angel, built in 1887 on a 30-acre site, used stones from a nearby quarry and bricks made from clay dug on the grounds. The tireless sisters built and ran several parish schools and a college. Their buildings at the monastery were damaged in the 1993 earthquake.

Mt. Angel

St. Mary Church (575 E. College St., 503-845-2296) is fondly known as "the jewel of the Willamette Valley." The gorgeous church, dedicated in 1912, was designed in the neo-Gothic style. The majestic spire soars 200 feet. The renowned Emil Frei Glass Works in St. Louis made sixteen of its twenty-two stained-glass windows. The most photographed is the Choir of the Angels, four windows in the loft. The elaborate main altar, Baroque in style, is made of wood but painted to look like marble. At Christmas several pews are removed to accommodate a Nativity set, purchased by schoolchildren in 1912, and on Good Friday the tomb with Christ's body is displayed.

St. Benedict

Mount Angel Abbey (503-845-3030) sits on a hill the Native Americans called Tapalamaho, meaning "a place for communion with the Great Spirit." Swiss Benedictines renamed the hill Mt. Angel when they began their monastery in 1883. The complex includes a seminary, fine library, and museum. Each evening the entire community recites the Litany of Saint Joseph. The lower church has an unusual baked clay statue of Saint Joseph.

St. Paul

French Canadian trappers settled in 1830 in the Willamette Valley near the present town of St. Paul. They and the Iroquois immigrants dutifully built a church and then drew up a petition asking the bishop for a priest. They were told that no priests were available. Carry on "the best way you can," the bishop wrote. Finally, after more appeals, Fr. Francis Blanchet, the future archbishop of Oregon City, arrived on January 6, 1839, and promptly celebrated the first Mass. Blanchet and Fr. Modeste Demers had come to a small community eager for God. They held a three-week mission in the crude church, baptizing dozens of mixed-blood children and their Native American mothers, marrying their parents, and establishing a cemetery.

In 1846 Demers blessed the cornerstone of **St. Paul Church** (20217 Christie St. NE, 503-633-4611), the first brick church in Oregon. More than 60 thousand bricks were used for its construction. It measured 100 feet by 40 feet with a belfry that soared to 84 feet. The bell, cast in Belgium and shipped around the Horn, has the inscription "God, thus your praise go to the end of the earth."

St. Paul Church has been enlarged and beautified over the years, and in 1993 the "spring-break quake" severely damaged it. The church was rebuilt; its bricks were washed and used once more. Today, the colorful red-brick church sits majestically surrounded by a spacious lawn. Near the church is a replica of the original log chapel.

Sublimity

Massgoers at **St. Boniface Church** (375 E. Church St., 503-769-5664) pass through an archway of greenery that leads to the main doors. The cross atop the steeple of the church, erected in 1889, is the highest human-made point in the region.

Southwest Oregon

Medford

Sacred Heart Church (449 S. Irving St., 541-779-4661), a robust, bilingual parish, began as a small offshoot of what is now its own mission. St. Joseph's in Jacksonville, one of the state's oldest churches, was founded in 1858. Sacred Heart was established in 1890 and by 1910 became the main parish after Jacksonville's mining industry failed. The present church, dedicated in 1929, has a stunning interior.

Myrtle Point

Sts. Ann and Michael Church has an interior fashioned largely from myrtle wood. The walls, ceiling beams, and pews share the same distinctive hue.

SOUTH DAKOTA

Eastern South Dakota

Alexandria

St. Mary of Mercy Church (240 Fifth St., 605-239-4532) is notable for its **Fátima Family Shrine**. The other outdoor granite sanctuaries depict Saint Joseph with the Child Jesus, the Sacred Heart, and an Angel Adoring the Eucharist. Also here is a marble statue of the Angel of the Family and of Youth.

Marvin

Blue Cloud Abbey (605-432-5528) was named for a well-known Christian Sioux. Built in 1967 of sandstone, the Benedictine abbey has a granite mural of the Virgin on its exterior. A provocative abstract mural in the visitors' lounge portrays the coming of Benedictines as missionaries among the Native Americans a century ago. Also check out the Military Miniatures Gallery, whose exhibits were created by Fr. Matthew Kowalski, a resident.

Sioux Falls

Augustana College (2001 S. Summit Ave., 605-336-0770) has an impressive **Statue of Moses**, the only casting made from Michelangelo's original.

The largest church in South Dakota is the formidable **St. Joseph Cathedral** (N. Duluth Ave. and Fifth St., 605-336-7390). Emmanuel Masqueray, who designed the cathedral in St. Paul, designed the French- and Romanesque-style structure in 1916. The church's two tall towers offer a fine view of the city.

The city's **Statue of David** in Fawick Park (11th St. and Second Ave.) is a full-scale bronze casting of Michelangelo's famous creation.

Western South Dakota

Bethlehem

In a cave in the Black Hills is a replica of Jesus' birthplace. Ten thousand people annually visit the **Shrine of the Nativity** (605-787-4606), run by the Benedictine Fathers.

Howes

Native Americans nurtured a deep spirituality long before Europeans set foot in the New World. One of the roles of the **Sioux Spiritual Center** (605-985-5906), run by the Jesuits, is developing Catholicism within the rich Lakota culture. A task force discusses using Lakota culture in the liturgy and the relationship between Catholic theology and Lakota beliefs. The center also offers weekend retreats and Canku Wakan, a four-day retreat developed by the Lakotas and modeled after the Cursillo.

Pine Ridge Reservation

The Pine Ridge Indian Reservation includes the **Red Cloud Indian School** (605-867-5491), built by Jesuits in 1888. The Jesuits and Franciscan sisters have run the school since then. The school was named after the great Oglala chief who invited the Black Robes to begin a school. The interior of nearby **Holy Rosary Mission Church** features a multitude of traditional designs by gifted Sioux artist Felix Walking.

Rosebud Reservation

The Native Americans were sent to reservations in the 1880s after the U.S. Army had quelled any resistance. The government assigned Episcopalians to minister to the Sioux at Rosebud. But the great chief Spotted Tail asked President Grant to send the "black robes." So in 1885 Jesuits and Franciscans from Germany began **St. Francis Mission and School** on the Rosebud Reservation (605-747-2361), which still serves the Sioux today.

The success of the mission was largely due to Jesuit Fr. Eugene Buechel, an indefatigable priest who traveled by horse and wagon to Native American camps. Father Buechel, known as Black Eagle to the Native Americans, recognized the workings of the Spirit in Native American traditions. Decades ahead of his time, he ministered within the cultural traditions of the Sioux. The priest intensely studied the Lakota language, a Sioux dialect, and wrote religious books in that language.

The photographs and artifacts of Sioux life collected by the priest are housed in the **Buechel Memorial Lakota Museum** (605-747-2745). On display are ghost shirts worn in ceremonial dances and a rattle with the inscription "The devil is my enemy but I trust in Jesus." Also here are copies of Buechel's books—a Lakota Bible history, a prayer book and hymnal, a Lakota grammar book, and a Lakota dictionary.

The mission is not far from a marker noting the site of the notorious Wounded Knee Massacre in 1890, in which the U.S. Seventh Cavalry killed 250 Sioux men, women, and children, most of them unarmed.

Spearfish

Josef Meier, whose German ancestors have participated in the biblical drama for generations, produces **Great Hills Passion Play** (US 14), performed with Lookout Mountain as a backdrop. The production has a cast of 250, not counting camels, sheep, donkeys, and doves.

WASHINGTON

Eastern Washington

Colville Indian Reservation

The rescue of a Native American child led to the success of **St. Mary's Mission** (4 miles east of Omak off Hwy. 155, 509-826-6401). In 1896 Fr. Stephen DeRouge was met with hostility from the Okanogan and Chelan tribes until he saved a child who had fallen into the fast waters of Omak Creek. Chief Smitkin even provided land to build the mission. A new church was constructed in 1915. Its side altars were shipped from France around the Horn. Behind the graveyard is an old cemetery with rough wooden crosses.

Kettle Falls

The Jesuits built **St. Paul's Mission** (US 395, 509-738-2356) near Kettle Falls in 1847 to serve the Native Americans who fished for salmon in the Columbia River. The priests had to close the chapel

from 1858 to 1862 because a gold rush brought White settlers, often disruptive due to alcohol. It reopened but fell into disrepair in the 1870s. It was reconstructed in 1939 using hand-hewn logs.

Republic

Like a castle in a fairy tale, **Immaculate Conception Church** (756 S. Portland, 509-775-3935)

Immaculate Conception Church.
(Tom's Photos)

211

rises from nowhere on a heavily forested hillside. European cathedrals inspired the miners who built the church in 1913. Wooden pillars cut from the surrounding wilderness support the high-dome ceiling. The soaring steeple was repaired in 1950 after a lightning bolt zinged it.

Spokane

Bing Crosby grew up in Spokane and attended **Gonzaga University** (509-328-4220) as a pre-law student. The **Crosby Student Center** on campus houses a collection of Crosby gold records, awards, memorabilia, and a replica of the Oscar he won for his clerical performance in *Going My Way,* a Catholic film if there ever was one. The building, originally the Crosby Library, was his gift to the university. Crosby souvenirs are sold in the student center. A bronze statue of der Bingle stands outside the center, and his boyhood home now houses the Gonzaga Alumni Association (E. 508 Sharp). Crosby's generosity to Gonzaga is all the more remarkable considering officials kicked him out for throwing a piano through a fourth-floor window. That just goes to show he could carry a piano as well as a tune.

The **Immaculate Heart Retreat House** (S. 6910 Ben Burr Rd., 509-448-1224) has a large bell tower that cleverly symbolizes "to Jesus through Mary." The tower was designed as a stylized lily. The spire forms an *M,* representing Mary, and the stamens of the lily form a cross. The spacious grounds have hosted tens of thousands of retreatants since the place opened in 1959.

The **Redemptorist Palisades Retreat** (4700 SW Dash Point Rd., 206-927-9621) sits 100 feet above Puget Sound and its maritime traffic of container ships, pleasure craft, and Coast Guard vessels. The grounds include 700 feet of tidal beach, accessible by a steep stairway. Along the shore is an old wooden barge beached long ago. The forty-eight private rooms are named after spiritual leaders like Gandhi, Thomas Merton, Martin Luther King, Jr., and Moses.

Western Washington

Seattle

Architectural brilliance surrounds the students at the **Holy Name Academy** (728 21st Ave. E., 206-323-4272). The domed building, designed by the talented C. Alfred Breitung, is a fine example of Beaux Arts style.

Immaculate Conception Church (820 18th Ave., 206-322-5970), founded in 1891 by the Jesuits, was moved three years later to what is now called the Garrand Building on the campus of **Seattle University**. Seattle College grew out of the parish school. In 1933 the institution became the first coeducational college in the Northwest. The name changed to Seattle University in 1948 when an influx of World War II veterans caused enrollment to jump to nearly three thousand. The Lemieux Library contains a vivid mural by local artist Val Laigo. At the center of the campus quadrangle is Centennial Fountain.

St. James Cathedral (804 Ninth Ave., 206-622-3559) is notable for what is missing. Its magnificent dome collapsed after a snowstorm in 1916, just seven years after the church was built. The Italian Renaissance-style structure has twin towers. Installed in 1994 in the south tower is an original bell from Our Lady of Good Help, the first Catholic church in the city. The pioneer church's 1870 statue of Our Lady of Seattle is in the cathedral's Marian shrine.

The tall, tapering belfry of **St. Joseph Church** (732 18th Ave. E., 206-324-2522) is reminiscent of Seattle Tower downtown, both designed by Joseph Wilson. But the church was done inexpensively in cast concrete; the Great Depression forced Wilson to scale down his plans. There is nothing scaled down about the excellent stained-glass window in front.

St. Mary Church (611 20th Ave. S., 206-324-7100) is an eclectic-style red-brick structure built in 1910. The inner-city, bilingual parish prides itself on its strong commitment to social justice.

Prefontaine Fountain (Third Ave. between Yesler and Jefferson) is the legacy of Msgr. Francis X. Prefontaine, who founded the city's first Catholic church. He left $5,000 to the city to erect the fountain near the site of the small chapel where Mass was said until Our Lady of Good Help was built. The fountain was finally built in 1926, two decades after plans were begun.

Near Seattle

Bainbridge Island

St. Cecilia Church (1310 Madison Ave. N., 206-842-3594) dates from 1843. The parish has a long history of serving Filipinos, who came to the island around 1880 to escape armed conflict in their homeland and found work at the Port Blakely Mill Company. During World War II, nearly three hundred Japanese Americans who lived on the island were ordered into detention camps, and the Filipinos managed their farms and saved their crops.

Edmonds

Rosary Heights (23120 Woodway Park Rd., 206-542-7511) is the home of the Dominican Sisters, including Sr. Mary Jean Dorcy. In the 1940s and 1950s she wrote best-selling books for both children and adults. *The Shepherd's Tartan* and *Spring Comes to the Hill Country* were two of the most popular.

Suquamish

St. Peter Mission (360-779-4291) is the burial site of Chief Sealth, a convert to Catholicism, for whom Seattle is named. A pair of long canoes mounted atop poles marks the chief's tomb.

Western Washington

Toledo

A replica of the ingenious "Catholic ladder" is displayed outside **St. Francis Church** (139 Spencer Rd., 360-864-4126). Fr. Francis Blanchet, who came here in 1838 and later became Oregon's first archbishop, carved symbols of the Church on a four-sided piece of wood. The "ladder" gave the Native Americans a quick summary of the faith. He eventually substituted paper for the wood. Catholic ladders became popular among missionaries of the West and were eventually printed in French, Spanish, Russian, and other languages. The red-brick church at the mission dates from 1932; fire destroyed the previous three.

Vancouver

Vancouver's Gothic jewel is **St. James Church** (218 W. 12th St., 360-693-3052), formerly a cathedral before the diocesan see moved to Seattle. The church is home to the state's oldest Catholic congregation. Frs. Francis Blanchet and Modeste Demers, the first two priests to come to the Pacific Northwest, arrived in 1838. The first church, dedicated in 1846, was built close to the

St. James Church. *(Justin Studio)*

walls of Fort Vancouver. A few years later Father Blanchet filed a 640-acre land claim, which led to a long dispute between the Church and U.S. Army that was not resolved until an act of Congress in 1905.

The present church was dedicated in 1885. Bishop Blanchet suggested the design of the church based on his trip to Belgium, where he witnessed a church being built. The interior's generosity of space, accentuated by rows of dazzling stained-glass windows, gives the church a sense of majesty. The main altar is an artistic triumph of hand-carved oak, built by Belgium artisans and shipped around the Horn.

WYOMING

Eastern Wyoming

Cheyenne

The Gothic Revival-style **St. Mary's Cathedral** (2107 Capital Ave., 307-635-9261), erected in 1909, was built with gray sandstone.

Western Wyoming

Daniel

Fr. Pierre DeSmet celebrated Wyoming's first Mass on July 5, 1840, at a quiet spot on a rise above the Green River. He constructed a makeshift altar from boughs and decorated it with flowers and even bows and arrows. A **small chapel** (one mile east of Daniel at US 87 and US 89) of wood and rock commemorates the site. The Knights of Columbus erected the simple monument.

Moose

The **Chapel of the Transfiguration** (307-733-2603), erected in 1925, is a simple one-room log structure. The window behind the altar offers a stunning view of the Tetons.

Wind River Reservation

Saint Stephen's Mission (3 miles south of Riverton off Rte. 789, 307-856-5937) is located on the state's only Native American reservation. Fr. John Jutz began the mission in 1884 when he erected a tent and an altar to say Mass for Arapaho chief Black Coal and his family. The interior and exterior church, built in 1887, are decorated with bright Arapaho geometric designs.

SOUTHWEST AND SOUTH CENTRAL

ARKANSAS

Central Arkansas

Little Rock

The pride of Catholics in Little Rock is the **Cathedral of St. Andrew** (617 Louisiana St., 501-374-2794), where history and beauty surround the worshipers. Built in 1878, the English Gothic church has a steeple that soars to 220 feet. An impressive replica of Michelangelo's *Pièta* stands in the vestibule. The exterior is granite, quarried from nearby Fourche (Granite) Mountain. The statue of Saint Andrew on the front lawn was dedicated in 1982.

On the carpet just inside the church is the shield of the Diocese of Little Rock. The inverted crosses on the shield represent the crucifixion of Saint Peter, and the *X* cross symbolizes the crucifixion of Saint Andrew, brother of Saint Peter. The two did not feel worthy to be crucified as Christ was and had their crosses altered at the time of their deaths.

In the choir loft is a huge pipe organ with 3,775 pipes, one of the finest in the state. The rose window is dedicated to Saint Cecilia, the patron saint of music.

The church's stained-glass windows depict popular saints. All are original except two that had to be replaced after a devastating tornado in the 1950s. The strong winds also blew away the cross on the steeple. Church leaders replaced it with a lighter cross made of bronze.

Northwestern Arkansas

Eureka Springs

The hilly, sprawling Victorian village in the Ozark Mountains is the state's premier tourist town. **St. Elizabeth Church** (30 Crescent Dr., 501-253-9853) was listed in Ripley's "Believe It or Not." The street is so pitched that the entrance to the church is through the bell tower.

The main draw in Eureka Springs is the **Great Passion Play** (Hwy. 62 E., 800-882-PLAY), which bills itself as America's foremost outdoor drama. More than five million people have watched the story of the life, death, resurrection, and ascension of Christ. The show features live animals, colorful costuming, and multilevel staging.

A 10-foot by 10-foot section of the **Berlin Wall** is on the grounds of the Great Passion Play. An East Berliner had painted on it the words from the 23rd Psalm in German: "Though I walk through the dark valley, I will not fear." In an officially atheistic nation, the unknown Christian made a bold demonstration of faith.

The **Bible Museum** is also on the grounds of the Passion Play. Located in the lower level of Smith Memorial Chapel, the museum contains more than 6,000 Bibles in 625 languages and dialects. The impressive collection includes an actual Gutenberg Bible Leaf and an original 1611 King James "He" Bible. A videotape presents the history of the Bible.

The **Sacred Arts Center** (501-253-2525) is located next to the entrance of the Passion Play amphitheater. The center houses more than one thousand works of Christian art from all over the world.

The art mediums include French enamel, inlaid marquetry, sculptured marble, ivory, wood carvings, porcelains, and icons.

Overlooking Eureka Springs is the **Christ of the Ozarks Statue**, the second largest statue of Christ in the world. The seven-story statue stands 67-feet high and weighs more than one million pounds. Emmit Sullivan, one of the creators of Mount Rushmore, sculpted the statue, dedicated in 1966.

Subiaco

Rising dramatically from acres of lush farmland is the handsome **Subiaco Abbey** (Hwy. 22, 501-934-4295). The sole monastery in Arkansas, the abbey has a red-tile roof and was built from locally quarried limestone.

Monks from the Archabbey of St. Meinrad in Indiana founded the Benedictine monastery in 1878. Facilities include a retreat house, a chapel, a library of spiritual books and tapes, and a coffee bar. The spacious grounds include a Lourdes Grotto and an outdoor Way of the Cross. The athletically inclined can use the outdoor pool, tennis courts, and basketball court.

Before his death in 547, Saint Benedict had a vision that the way of life he founded would endure all over the world. The existence of the Subiaco Abbey in the remote foothills of the Ouachita Mountains gives credence to his vision.

Winslow

Our Lady of the Ozarks Shrine (22741 N. Hwy. 71, 501-634-2181) is a stone structure built in 1941. Inside the church is a statue of the Blessed Virgin holding a rosary, and outdoors a statue stands on a pedestal facing the highway.

COLORADO

Northern Colorado

Allenspark

The **Chapel on the Rock** is a large stone structure with Mount Meeker as a backdrop. It was built in 1935 on an immense rock formation near where a priest saw a meteor drop from the sky. Pope John Paul II visited the adjoining **St. Malo Retreat Center** (10758 Hwy. 7, 970-586-6061) in 1993 during the World Youth Congress.

Aspen

St. Mary Church (104 S. Galena St., 970-925-7339) is a solid, two-story brick church set on a stone foundation. Dedicated in 1892, the church was originally needed to serve newcomers who swarmed to the silver mines. Church leaders can recount the legend of the aspen tree, on which Christ was supposedly crucified. The tree was henceforth banned from the Holy Land to frigid, mountainous regions, and thereafter its trunk and branches could never grow straight enough to shape a cross.

Beckenridge

Homilists at **St. Mary Church** (105 S. French St., 970-668-3141) know their sermons must be riveting: outside the stained-glass window behind the altar are snow-covered peaks, luxurious ski resorts, and trendy shopping areas. Completed in 1985, the church has a graceful high cathedral ceiling. The parish began in 1880 in a small frame building whose shell was constructed in a dozen days. A subsequent pastor blasted the crude structure as "a disgrace to the name of St. Mary." At least the church survived. A rowdy pioneer town in 1891, Beckenridge saw its Methodist church blown to pieces after the minister crusaded against alcohol abuse.

Denver

A priest who fled religious oppression in Germany founded **St. Elizabeth Church** (1060 11th St.), the city's second Catholic community, in 1878 for his compatriots. The German Gothic-style edifice, built of lava stone, has a spire standing 162 feet. In 1908 an anarchist shot the beloved pastor dead while he was saying Mass. In that same era the Franciscans at St. Elizabeth's rode the rails on one-month stints to small, priestless towns in Colorado. Today the church is the campus chapel for 30 thousand students from three colleges that share a downtown site.

One of the most memorable figures in Colorado Catholicism made the **Cathedral of the Immaculate Conception** in Denver (1530 Logan St., 303-831-7010) possible. Fr. Hugh McMenamin, first as an associate pastor and then rector, coordinated fund-raising for the church beginning in 1905. Father Mac, a small man with flowing white hair, became famous for his pornography raids, riveting sermons, denunciations of the Ku Klux Klan, and ability to raise funds. He held a grand "carnival of nations" that raised thousands for the cathedral and then squeezed the arms of some of Denver's leading citizens. The debt for the church was retired in 1921 when millionaire miller John Mullen wrote a check for $110 thousand, covering his donation by raising the price of his flour a penny a pound, of course. His granddaughter, concerned about preserving the church's appearance, unsuccessfully sued the church in 1974 when it was modernized.

The impressive French Gothic cathedral borrowed its design from some of Europe's great churches. Its two slender bell spires soar 210 feet. Marble from Carrara, Italy, was used for the altars, pedestals, statues, pulpit, and communion rail. The vaulted ceiling rises 68 feet over the nave. The church's seventy-five stained-glass windows are from F. X. Zetter's Royal Bavarian Art Institute in Munich. The likes of these windows will never be seen again. The firm and its artistic secrets were destroyed during World War II.

The cathedral was long a showcase for high society. In the 1940s ushers wearing pinstriped trousers and white gloves led prominent citizens to their reserved pews, guarded by purple velvet drapes.

Near Denver

Arvada

Established in 1920, the **Shrine of St. Anne** (7555 Grant Pl., 303-420-1280) is the only shrine/parish in the Archdiocese of Denver. The shrine contains the nations' largest relic (a wrist bone) of Saint Anne, the mother of Mary. The cozy church, decked in red brick and white terra cotta trim, features rosy, translucent Romanesque windows.

The Ku Klux Klan targeted the shrine in the 1920s. Klansmen burned crosses in front of it and harassed Fr. Walter Grace. The Klan even succeeded in having Grace imprisoned for two years on false charges. During Prohibition, he was charged with forging an altar wine permit and serving wine socially. The Knights of Columbus and Holy Name Society responded to Klan rallies by holding their own march from Regis College to the shrine for an outdoor Mass.

Boulder

As played by Sidney Poitier, Homer Smith in *Lilies of the Field* was an upright Black man who built a chapel for struggling German nuns and taught them to sing rousing choruses of "Amen." The story was fictional, but novelist William Barrett based his book on the **Convent of St. Walburga** (6717 S. Boulder Rd., 303-494-5733), which was near his home in Denver.

The convent's first three nuns fled Nazi oppression and came to Boulder in 1935 from Bavaria. They eventually sent for more of their sick and half-starved Benedictine sisters. The nuns tirelessly converted a treeless prairie into a pleasant home. They planted hundreds of tiny shade trees and fashioned a chapel from a run-down barn.

The twenty or so contemplative nuns raise beef cattle, sheep, and llamas. They also tend a garden, embroider vestments, and bake bread. A variety of retreat programs are offered. The simple but satisfying moments enjoyed here leave many visitors in a mood to sing out, "Amen."

Golden

"I can do all things in Him who strengthens me," said Mother Cabrini. The first U.S. citizen-saint did a lot, founding sixty-seven hospitals, orphanages, and schools, including a home for orphans near Denver. Located on land purchased by the saint, the **Mother Cabrini Shrine** (20189 Cabrini Blvd., 303-526-0758) features a recreation of her room, including artifacts like her cane. Also here is an inspiring 22-foot-high Christ statue that looks out toward the mountains. In front of the statue is an image of the Sacred Heart, fashioned from local white rocks by Mother Cabrini herself.

Grant

The **Christ of the Rockies** (off US 285) is a stunning 52-foot-high, 26-ton statue that is brilliantly illuminated at night.

Northern Colorado

Leadville

St. Joseph Church (Second and Maple Streets, 719-486-1591) was founded in 1878 as a civilizing influence when Leadville was a mining boomtown overrun with saloons, beer halls, and gambling houses. The church burned down in March 1923, but was rebuilt so quickly that for the first Mass on Christmas Eve the bell, not yet installed, was struck with hammers. The remarkable Fr. George

Trunck painted the religious murals inside from 1924 to 1946. He was an artist, writer, and diplomat, having served as part of the peace delegation that wrote the Treaty of Versailles finalizing World War I.

Longmont

Ecumenism is alive and well at **Spirit of Peace Parish** (1500 Hover Rd., 303-772-6322). The parish has shared its worship space with Westview Presbyterian Church since 1982. Small Christian communities form the backbone of the parish, which uses most of its funds to serve the community. The parish is a sterling example of the Church's diversity and commitment to social justice.

Snowmass

Rugged wilderness encroaches upon the well-known **St. Benedict's Monastery** (1012 Monastery Rd., 970-927-3311), nestled in the Rocky Mountains in a valley 7,800 feet above sea level. Owls and coyotes can be heard nightly. The Trappist monks pray a good part of the day and find time to ranch as well as bake the enticing Snowmass Monastery Cookies. The monastery's 4,000 acres offer hiking and cross-country skiing.

Fr. Thomas Keating, popular author and advocate of centering prayer, lives here. So, too, does Father Theophane, who wrote *Tales of a Magic Monastery*. The isolation and serenity of the monastery makes it easy to see how centering prayer became a fixture here.

Vail

Skiers fill the pews of the **Vail Interfaith Chapel** (19 Vail Rd., 970-476-3347), a mission of St. Patrick's in Minturn. Prayers at the ski Masses are said to Saint Bernard, the patron saint of Alpinists. Celebrities like Gregory Peck and Jimmy Connors have been spotted here in ski attire. The packed Midnight Mass on Christmas Eve is sometimes said at the Vail skating rink or a ski lodge.

Central Colorado
Manitou Springs

The dollhouselike **Our Lady of Perpetual Help Church** (218 Ruxton Ave., 719-685-9388) was built in 1903. The former rectory is an actual castle, built by an eccentric French priest in the 1890s. The Manitou Springs Historical Society owns the castle, modeled after European sites and called Miramont.

Southern Colorado
Conejos

Founded in 1850, **Our Lady of Guadalupe Church** (US 285, 719-376-5985) was the state's first Catholic church. Its priests traveled to twenty-six small towns, saying Mass in homes. The current church, built in 1857, has a Lourdes grotto in the churchyard.

Lake City

Saint Rose of Lima Church, a striking building on an elevated site in a mountainous region, was built in 1877 for Italian miners.

Pueblo

French and Spanish explorers arrived in Pueblo in the sixteenth century but left no trace of their Catholicism. Jesuits established the first Catholic church, St. Ignatius, in 1872. The church was rebuilt in 1912 after it burned down and was later renamed **Sacred Heart Cathedral** (11th St. and Grand Ave., 719-544-5175). The extraordinary stained-glass windows, crafted by Emil Frei of St. Louis, include depictions of Jesus giving the keys of the Kingdom to Peter, the Sermon on the Mount, and the Good Shepherd. The rose window shows Saint Cecilia, patroness of music.

Silverton

There's gold in them prayers! Or at least uranium. In the 1950s lead mines in southwestern Colorado closed, leaving families in dire straits. Led by their pastor, parishioners of **St. Patrick's Church** (1005 Reese, 970-325-4373) erected a shrine on the slope of Mount Anvil. A 16-foot statue of the Sacred Heart of Jesus became known as the **Christ of the Miners** (off Hwy. 110). Shortly after the shrine was dedicated, uranium was discovered and the local economy rebounded.

KANSAS

Eastern Kansas

Atchison

Rooms with a view are available at **St. Benedict's Abbey** (913-367-5341). The abbey overlooks the Missouri River. Built of limestone quarried locally in 1929, the structure has loping corridors that stretch for more than 300 feet.

St. Benedict Church (Second and Division Streets, 913-367-0671), reminiscent of churches in western Germany, has two towers flanking its main door and a tall arched nave separated from the side aisles by a row of arches.

The **Benedictine Sisters of Mount St. Scholastica** (801 S. Eighth St., 913-367-6110) dates from 1863 when seven Benedictine sisters from Eichstatt, Germany, arrived and opened St. Scholastica Academy. They've been praying, working, and serving the area ever since. The chapel has an impressive interior with a grandly scaled nave.

Baldwin City

The **Baker University Library** (8th St., 913-594-6451) has a rare collection of Bibles, including two first editions of the King James version and notable American Bibles. Also here are clay cuneiform tablets from the time of Abraham and a medieval synagogue scroll.

Bazaar

Bazaar, population one hundred, was the nearest town to the plane crash that killed **Knute Rockne** on March 3, 1931. The forty-three-year-old legendary Notre Dame football coach perished with seven other passengers while headed to California to visit motion-picture studios. A memorial marks the crash site.

Council Grove

The Sante Fe Trail was a pioneer version of an interstate highway. Begun in 1821, the 780-mile trail ran from Independence, Missouri, to Sante Fe, New Mexico. The town of Council Grove was an important stopping point. The **Madonna of the Trail Monument** (Main and Union Streets) commemorates the pioneer mothers who braved the journey. The statue shows a woman holding a musket in one arm and a baby in the other, as a small boy clings to her skirt. Dedicated in 1928, the name of the statue honors the Virgin Protector.

Hermit's Cave (two blocks north of Main St. on Belfrey St.) was the home of Mottea Boccalini, a quirky but devout Franciscan friar who trekked from one Native American tribe to another, preaching the Gospel and administering last rites to settlers on the Sante Fe Trail. On the walls of the cave Boccalini carved his name, a cross, and the words *Jesu, Maria,* and *Capri* (his hometown in Italy). The friar was found dead in another cave in New Mexico with a dagger in his heart.

Leavenworth

St. Mary College (4100 S. 4th St., 913-682-5151) occupies a 240-acre campus. Worth a look are St. Mary Hall, built in 1870, and Annunciation Chapel, dedicated in 1914.

St. Mary's

Jesuits founded **St. Mary's Mission** (208 W. Bertrand) for the Potawatomies in 1848. The town of St. Mary's grew around the mission. A historical marker (on US 24 on the east side of town) honors the work of the Jesuits. The mission operated a manual labor school, which developed into St. Mary's College in 1869. In

1931 the college became a Jesuit seminary. Today, the Society of St. Pius X, a group of disenchanted Catholics, runs a school here.

At the entrance to the campus is a memorial arch dedicated to Lt. William Fitzsimmons, an alumnus who was one of the first three U.S. soldiers killed in World War I. A boulder on the campus marks the site of the first cathedral between the Missouri River and the Rocky Mountains. Built of logs in 1849, it became the church of Bishop Miege, known as the "Bishop of the Indians."

Just west of the former St. Mary's College is the **Church of the Immaculate Conception** (913-437-2408). Inside is a valuable painting, the *Immaculate Conception,* executed by Benito, an Italian court painter of the early sixteenth century. Pope Pius IX gave the painting to the Potawatomi in 1854.

Central Kansas

Lyons

Fr. Juan de Padilla, a native of Spain, was one of four Franciscans who accompanied Coronado in the mid 1500s on his futile search for cities of gold in the New World. Padilla had no interest in gold; souls were his target. He left Coronado's party and walked back to Kansas with four companions to evangelize among the Native Americans. Hostile Native Americans killed him, making him one of the first Christian martyrs in the United States. Padilla urged his companions to flee when they came under attack. They watched as he fell to his knees and crossed himself before a storm of arrows struck him. The **Padilla Cross** (on US 56 four miles west of Lyons) honors him near his place of death. Erected in 1950, the large stone cross "denotes the four corners of the world brought to Christian unity" when Padilla carried the cross into the New World.

Western Kansas

Catherine

Nearly a dozen Catholic churches built by German-Russian immigrants grace the small towns off I-70 between Russell and Hays. Most are built of post rock, the region's unique stone with brown streaks. All the churches feature stained-glass windows and a tower with a cross on top. Their ornate altars are hand-carved. **St. Catherine Church** (913-625-7536), by far the largest structure around, dominates the tiny town of Catherine.

Fort Dodge

Fr. Juan de Padilla of Spain celebrated the first Mass held west of the Mississippi on June 29, 1541. Erected in 1975, the **Coronado Cross** (a mile and a half east of Fort Dodge) marks the historic spot.

Victoria

The fiery orator William Jennings Bryan appropriately dubbed **St. Fidelis Church** (601 10th St., 913-735-2777), once the largest church west of the Mississippi, as the "Cathedral of the Plains." The twin towers of the beautiful Romanesque Revival-style structure rise majestically above the flat land. Germans from the Volga region of Russia who fled oppression built the church of native limestone in 1911. Each family was assessed $45 and six loads of stone.

LOUISIANA

Northern Louisiana

Carmel

Tiny **Rock Chapel** is located one-half mile into the woods as a refuge for meditation and prayer. Carmelite monks built it in 1891, but it became lost in the wilderness after 1910. Local Catholics rediscovered and restored it in 1961. Overlooking Bayou Loop, the chapel has colorful murals and frescoes.

Central Louisiana

Alexandria

Located in the heart of the city's historic district, **St. Francis Xavier Cathedral** (626 Fourth St., 318-445-1451) has a long and rich history. The first church was built in 1817. For several years Catholics were the only denomination in the city with a church, yet they had no resident priest. The second structure, erected in 1834, survived the torching of most of the city in 1864 by Union troops when the pastor boldly defied the soldiers at the front steps of the church. The current edifice, the first bricked church in the city, was dedicated in 1899. The mortar for the church was dug from a sand bar in the middle of the Red River.

St. Francis Xavier Cathedral.

The floors are made from native pine. The rose windows, the largest in the state, compare favorably to those in European cathedrals.

Southern Louisiana

Baton Rouge

St. Joseph's Cathedral (Main and Fourth Streets, 504-387-5928), restored three times since 1853, appealingly blends old and new. Worth noting are the fine stained-glass windows, the Stations of the Cross in mosaics, and a mahogany crucifix by sculptor Ivan Mestrovic. The church was once seized and sold for a debt because of a squabble by lay members.

Lafayette

Vermilionville (1600 Surrey St., 800-99BAYOU) is a recreation of Cajun and Creole culture in a southern Louisiana bayou village from 1765 to 1890. Among the many replica buildings is La Chapelle des Attakapas, based on eighteenth-century churches at Pointe Coupee and St. Martinville. The simple church has a white wooden altar and black, wrought-iron chandeliers. The priest's house, called Le Presbytere, has a bed, a kneeler for praying, religious pictures, a desk, and a small fireplace.

Near Lafayette

Grand Coteau

The **Academy of the Sacred Heart** (318-662-5275) was the site of a miracle that led to the canonization of Saint John Berchmans. This shrine is the only one in the United States situated on the exact spot where a miracle occurred.

The miracle occurred in 1866 for Mary Wilson, a critically ill member of the order. The nuns prayed to Blessed John Berchmans for his intercession. Mary later recounted how she saw a figure at her bedside. "Are you Blessed John Berchmans?" she asked. "Yes,

I come by the order of God," he replied. "Your sufferings are over. Fear not!" Mary's doctor's sworn statement read: "Not being able to discover any marks of convalescence, but an immediate return to health from a severe and painful illness, I am unable to explain the transition by any ordinary natural laws."

Begun in 1821, the academy is the world's oldest Society of Sacred Heart School. During the Civil War, 20 thousand Union troops under Gen. Nathaniel Banks were quartered in Grand Coteau. Fortunately for the school, Banks's daughter was attending a Sacred Heart school in New York, and urged by his wife, he placed the school under his protection.

The academy, located on 250 acres, continues today as a boarding and day school for women. The formal gardens, laid out in 1831, were patterned after the gardens of a French bishop. The rows of pine and moss-hung oaks that shadow the paths of the academy were planted about 1850 to provide shade to the priests as they walked to the school's chapel to say Mass.

Southern Louisiana

New Orleans

Built in 1855, **St. Alphonsus Church** (2030 Constance St., 504-522-6748) closed more than fifteen years ago but was considered too precious a landmark to raze. The Friends of St. Alphonsus, who rent the building from the archdiocese, give tours and hold cultural events here. The Redemptorists built the church in 1858 to serve Irish peasants who came to New Orleans to escape the potato famine.

Italian Francesco de Rohden, who painted the frescoes at St. Alphonsus in Rome, did the altar painting of Saint Alphonsus. The Royal Bavarian Institute in Munich designed the exquisite stained-glass windows. But the most striking feature of the church is the wondrous main altar, hand carved by the Munich craftsmen.

There is virtue as well as vice in the French Quarter. The triple-steepled **St. Louis Cathedral** (615 Pere Antoine Alley, 504-525-9585), named for the French king who led two crusades, is the oldest active cathedral in the country. The current structure dates from 1794, though it was remodeled and enlarged in 1851. The stained-glass windows in front of the church were gifts from the Spanish government. The huge mural over the altar shows Saint Louis announcing the seventh crusade.

The previous church was one of more than 850 buildings that went up in flames during the Good Friday Fire of 1788. A Spaniard who made his fortune in real estate, Don Andre Almonester y Roxas, offered to bankroll a new church—with the condition that the congregation pray for him after his death. Roxas is buried beneath the marble floor.

Pope John Paul II held a prayer service here in 1986. To honor the occasion, a pedestrian mall in front of the cathedral was renamed Place Jean-Paul Deux.

Like most other buildings in the French Quarter, the cathedral has its own ghost story. A priest from centuries ago who enjoyed earthly pleasures is said to dance through the aisles, singing hymns and chanting.

Behind the church is the **Cathedral Garden**, between Pirate Alley and Pere Antoine Alley. A statue of the Sacred Heart of Jesus stands at the center of the garden.

Built by the Irish in 1871, **St. John the Baptist Church** (1139 Dryades St., 504-525-1726), has an eye-pleasing brick exterior and eye-popping stained-glass windows, imported from Munich.

The German-Baroque **St. Mary's Assumption Church** (2030 Constance St., 504-522-6748) has a 142-foot tower that changes from a square to an octagonal shape at the roof level. The red-brick church, built in 1860, contains beautiful frescoes and stained-glass windows. The wedding in *The Witching Hour,* based on an Anne Rice book, was filmed here. The church houses the **Father Seelos Center**. The German-born priest, a candidate for sainthood, served in Pittsburgh with Saint John Neumann and died in New Orleans in

1867 after contracting yellow fever. Seelos, who is buried in the church, was known for his ability to bring peace to confessors.

The **National Shrine of St. Ann** (2101 Ursulines Ave., 504-822-8112) has an unusual Lourdes-type grotto in which Our Lady looks down from her niche in the rock, as Bernadette saw her. But Mary's eyes are bent toward the chapel of her mother, Saint Ann, whose altar and statue shine out from the cave below. The shrine began in 1902 on the 50th anniversary of the parish.

Built in 1826, **Our Lady of Guadalupe Chapel** (411 N. Rampart St., 504-525-1551) was originally called the Chapel of the Dead. It was constructed near the city cemeteries as a burying chapel for victims of a yellow-fever epidemic. Note the statue of "St. Expedite" to the right of the entrance. Legend has it that a crate arrived marked "expedite," and the statue inside was erected as such.

Irish immigrants founded **St. Patrick Church** (724 Camp St., 504-525-4413) in the 1830s after they discovered God spoke only French to French Quarter Creoles at St. Louis Cathedral. An Irish architect, who was inspired by England's York Minister, designed the Gothic Revival-style church.

Saint Roch Chapel (1725 St. Roch Ave., 504-596-3050) was built in 1875 out of gratitude after parishioners at the Church of the Holy Trinity were spared from a devastating yellow-fever epidemic. "Turn to Saint Roch. He will protect you," Fr. Peter Thevis told his flock. Young women pray here and invoke the saint's intercession, for he is supposedly skilled at finding them a good husband.

The **Ursuline Convent** (1100 Chartres St., 504-529-3040) is the oldest nunnery in the state and the old-

Old Ursuline Convent.

est building in the Mississippi River Valley. The Ursulines arrived from France in 1727, and their huge convent, sprawling more than half a city block, was dedicated in 1745. The nuns brought a civilizing influence to New Orleans, considered not much better than Sodom and Gomorrah in those days. They also proved invaluable in caring for the sick of the city's cholera and fever outbreaks.

But the Ursulines hold a special place in the city's history for another reason. In 1815 British forces threatened to take the city in the famed Battle of New Orleans. Matched against the sixty ships and fifteen thousand troops of the British was a ragtag U.S. force of five thousand men led by Gen. Andrew Jackson. While the British cannon began pounding the city, a crowd that spilled out into the streets gathered to pray in front of the nuns' statue of Our Lady of Prompt Succor, brought from France by one of the nuns. The superior of the order vowed to have a Mass of thanksgiving celebrated every year if the Americans were victorious.

As luck—or providence—would have it, a fog that hid the British forces lifted at an inopportune time for the British, exposing their positions. And the regiment leading the attack forgot the scaling ladders needed to jump a rampart. The fighting lasted less than half an hour, and the Americans suffered only six fatalities. Jackson himself regarded the triumph as sent by heaven. For years afterward the nuns received baskets of fruit and meat from Southerners on the anniversary of the battle.

The nuns sold the convent in 1824. Today, the restored building holds the archives of the New Orleans Archdiocese. Open for visits are the formal gardens, the first floor of the convent, and the chapel, known as Our Lady of Victory Church or St. Mary Italian Church. The herb garden inspired one of the nuns to become the first pharmacist in the United States.

The celebrated statue is now part of the **National Shrine of Our Lady of Prompt Succor** (2635 State St., 504-866-1472) at the new Ursuline Convent, a striking Gothic building. A Mass of thanksgiving is still said every year on January 8. Also at this location is

Ursuline Academy, founded in 1727, making it the oldest girls' school in the country.

Xavier University (Palmetto and Pine Streets, 504-486-7411) is the only traditionally Black Catholic university in the Western Hemisphere. Mother Mary Katharine Drexel, a Philadelphia heiress who devoted her life and fortune to Blacks and Native Americans, founded the university in 1915. Whites had driven Southern University, the state college for Blacks, out of the city. The archbishop of New Orleans invited Drexel to open a school in the city. She had to back away from several sites because of resistance from Whites.

Pope John Paul II visited the school in 1987. The university is known for producing many doctors and teachers.

Near New Orleans

Covington

Novelist Walker Percy (1916–1990) is buried in the small cemetery at **St. Joseph Abbey**. The cemetery is for the Benedictine monks and members of the confraternity, laypeople closely involved with the monastery. A deeply Catholic writer, Percy is best-known for his first novel, *The Moviegoer,* which examines a young man's troubled quest for meaning in life. Percy was cynical and fatalistic until he converted to Catholicism at the age of thirty-one. A resident of Covington, Percy dedicated himself to achieving racial justice and subtly proclaiming the Gospel through art. He was the only American on the Pontifical Council for Culture.

Violet

Our Lady of Lourdes Church (6305 E. St. Bernard Hwy., 504-682-3046), a picturesque white clapboard building, faces the Mississippi River. A hurricane in 1915 blew down the first church. Amazingly, all the church's statues of saints were left standing.

Southern Louisiana

Convent

Silence is golden at **Manresa Retreat House** (Hwy. 44, 504-562-3596), run by the Jesuits. Retreatants who arrive on Thursday bask in the quiet until Sunday afternoon. A retreatant once called the place "the house of silence and the sacred God, where nobody speaks to anybody and everybody speaks to God." The buildings, with their noble proportions and dazzling whiteness, were built in the spirit of Greek Revival. The main three-story plastered-brick structure has twenty-two massive Doric columns. The buildings originally belonged to Jefferson College, which opened in 1831.

Plaquemine

Madonna Chapel.
(Pam Blanchard)

Measuring 6 feet by 8 feet, the **Madonna Chapel** near Plaquemine (on Hwy. 405 in Bayou Goula at Point Pleasant, 504-545-3635) is one of the nation's smallest churches. Since 1904, Mass has been said once a year, on August 15, the Feast of the Assumption. An Italian immigrant, Anthony Gullo, built the chapel after his gravely ill child survived. The key to the chapel is sometimes found in a wooden box mounted on the wall near the door or on top of the door frame.

St. Francisville

Our Lady of Mount Carmel Church (504-635-3630), completed in 1893, was built from plans drafted in 1871 by P. G. T. Beauregard, a leading Confederate general.

St. Martinville

Residents of St. Martinville, founded by Acadian families in 1765, have long cherished their Catholic faith. On Sundays Mass is traditionally announced an hour ahead of time by the ringing of a light bell. Thirty minutes later a heavier one warns residents again, and just before Mass the largest bell and the two smaller ones call people to worship.

St. Martin de Tours Church in St. Martinville (133 S. Main St., 318-394-6021) is the mother church of the Acadians. The building contains some furnishings from the original structure of 1765, including original box pews, altar, and a marble baptismal font that is believed to be a gift from Louis XVI. Many of the parishioners in the eighteenth century were royalists who fled the French Revolution. Slaves built the current church, a simple structure of cement-covered brick, in 1832.

At the rear of the church is a statue of Evangeline, an Acadian who was the subject of a Longfellow poem. The actress Dolores del Rio posed for the statue when she portrayed the heroine in an early movie filmed here. Cast members later presented the bronze monument to the town.

Western Louisiana

Natchitoches

Immaculate Conception Church (Second and Church Streets, 318-352-3422), built in 1857, is domed and spired. The interior is lit by French crystal chandeliers, and its wooden spiral staircase also came from France.

MISSOURI

Southeast Missouri

Cape Girardeau

One of the most unique churches in Missouri is **Old St. Vincent's Church** (741 Forest, 573-335-7667). Erected in 1853, the church was designed in an English Perpendicular Gothic Revival style. A tornado leveled the first church on the site, constructed in 1838, in 1850.

Kelso

St. Augustine Church (201 S. Messmer, 573-264-4724), built in 1889, was superbly restored in 1979. The beautifully grained walnut altars and Stations of the Cross, made in Germany, were gilded with gold.

New Hamburg

German immigrants escaping religious persecution founded **St. Lawrence Church** (1017 State Hwy. A, 573-545-3317) in 1847.

St. Lawrence Church.

America proved to be more of the same. The church they built near Benton was burned. They completed another wooden church in 1848. It now stands near the present church, erected in 1859. Each family was required to deliver eight wagons of stone, donate $5, or take every tenth day off to quarry, haul, and lay stone or cut wood at the sawmill. The church's pillars were made of trees that were covered with boards. During the Civil War, a Confederate guerrilla force burned the church, which was then rebuilt. The church was last renovated in 1994.

Perryville

St. Mary's of the Barrens Seminary (1811 W. St. Joseph St., 673-547-8344) played a key role in the westward spreading of the Catholic faith. Begun in 1818, the seminary was the first institution of higher learning west of the Mississippi. Its graduates became pioneer missionaries and bishops. The seminary closed in 1986.

The first **Church of St. Mary's of the Barrens** was a small log cabin built by Vincentian Fr. Joseph Rosati in 1818. The simple church has been restored.

The present St. Mary's, built in 1837, was a parish church until 1965. The Venerable Felix de Andreis, the first superior of the Vincentians in the New World, is buried beneath the church floor.

Near Andreis's tomb is the **Shrine of Our Lady of the Miraculous Medal**. The devotion stems from the appearances of Mary in 1830 in Paris to Saint Catherine Labouré, a novice of the Daughters of Charity of St. Vincent de Paul. Once Mary appeared standing on a globe with dazzling rays of light shining from her hands. An oval frame appeared around Mary and bore these words, "O Mary, conceived without sin, pray for us who have recourse to thee." The vision turned around and a letter *M* surmounted by a cross and twelve stars appeared. Our Lady asked that a medal be fashioned similar to the apparition and promised blessings to all who wore it. Devotion to the medal spread rapidly after the first one was struck in 1832.

A museum is also on the grounds. A rare-books collection includes a priceless portion of the Gospel of St. John from the Gutenberg Bible.

St. Louis

Built in 1866, **St. Alphonsus "Rock" Church** (1118 N. Grand Blvd., 314-533-0304) got its name from the large amount of stone used in its construction. The church has a 237-foot steeple, a mammoth bell that weighs five tons, and an impressive main altar. Here, too, is the **Shrine to Our Lady of Perpetual Help**, blessed in 1922.

Built in 1903 "On the Hill," **St. Ambrose Church** (5130 Wilson Ave., 314-771-1228) serves a famous Italian neighborhood that has produced a legion of baseball stars, as well as a disproportionate number of men in arms during World War II. A statue of Milanese immigrants graces the church front.

A large crowd of people, some in tears, gathered outside **St. Anthony of Padua Church** (3140 Meramec St., 314-353-7470) in April 1994, as flames roared through the city landmark. The church was so treasured that a St. Louis newspaper later selected the fire as the top story of the year. But the devastating fire somehow left intact the walls, stained-glass windows, altar, and much of the interior, and within twenty months the grand church was restored to its former glory. The Franciscan Friars who built the church in 1908 borrowed its German Romanesque-style from the German Rhineland. The church is 226 feet long, and its two towers rise 175 feet into the air. Stained-glass window master Emil Frei created the exquisite windows.

Calvary Cemetery (5239 W. Florissant, 314-381-1313) contains the graves of Archbishops Kain and Peter Richard Kenrick, humanitarian Tom Dooley, Union General Tecumseh Sherman, author Kate Chopin, and ex-slave Dred Scott.

The **St. Francis Xavier (College) Church** (3628 Lindell Blvd., 314-977-7300) has excellent stained-glass windows done by Emil Frei, Jr.

St. John Apostle and Evangelist Church (15 Plaza Square, 314-421-3467) is the only church whose windows contain the stars and stripes and stars and bars. The pastor who built the church in 1858 became the chaplain of the First Missouri Confederate Infantry Brigade.

St. Joseph Shrine (1220 N. 11th St., 314-231-9407), built by German immigrants in the 1840s, was once the largest parish in the city. The church was the site of an authenticated miracle. In 1864 gravely ill Ignatius Strecker, whose wife heard a powerful sermon on then-Blessed Pater Claver, was cured after being blessed with a relic of Claver. One of Strecker's descendants, a namesake, became archbishop of Kansas City.

The Church of Hagia Sophia in Istanbul was the inspiration for the magnificent **St. Louis Basilica** (4401 Lindell Blvd., 314-533-2824). Built between 1907 and 1914, the Byzantine-Romanesque structure features a huge green dome, flanked by twin towers and two half-domes. Mosaics cover the church's domes, arches, ceilings, and walls. The spectacular art is considered the world's greatest collection of mosaics.

The first Mass in St. Louis was said in 1764 at the site of the **Old Cathedral** (209 Walnut St., 314-231-3250), also called the Basilica of St. Louis, located adjacent to Gateway Arch Park. Two log churches and a brick cathedral preceded the current structure, a Federal-style church built in 1834. The church is the only property of early St. Louis still used for its original purpose. The oldest cathedral west of the Mississippi, the building was the only structure in the area not razed to make room for the Jefferson Memorial.

Old Cathedral.

A plaque at the church commemorates the founding of the first U.S. chapter of the St. Vincent de Paul Society. The museum in the basement includes an eight-hundred-year-old Spanish crucifix, paintings from the late 1700s, and the original 1772 church bell, whose rich tone is probably due to the two hundred silver dollars cast into the molten bronze.

St. Stanislaus Kostka Church (1413 N. 20th St., 314-421-5948) was St. Louis's first Polish parish, founded in 1880. Prior to that, non-English speaking Poles attended German and Irish parishes, which could do little to satisfy their needs. The present church was erected in 1891, but a fire on February 3, 1928, completely destroyed the sanctuary. Steadfast parishioners continued to attend Mass, even though the windows were broken and the heating did not work.

The renovation included the installation of a copy of the world's largest painting of the crucifixion, *Golgotha,* complete with two thousand figures, by Polish artist Jan Styka for the St. Louis World's Fair of 1904. Artists who assisted Styka on the original helped execute the copy. Surviving the fire was a late-eighteenth-century replica of the famous icon of the Black Madonna of Czestochowa, a powerful symbol of Polish nationalism and religious freedom. When created, the copy was one of only two in the world.

In 1969 Cardinal Karol Wojtyla (now Pope John Paul II) led a service at the church and spent a few hours in the rectory.

St. Vincent de Paul Church (1408 S. 10th St., 314-231-9328) was designed by Meriwether Lewis Clark, whose famous father, explorer William Clark, named him for his comrade, Meriwether Lewis. The Romanesque-style edifice was built in 1844 partly with stones from Holy Trinity Church, one of the city's first Catholic churches. Vincentians founded the parish to serve German immigrants. A fine painting of Saint Vincent by French artist Detroy Pinxit dates from the 1890s. The building of the Third Street Highway in 1952 resulted in the demolition of a couple of parish buildings, and today the rumbling interstate, which replaced the highway, looms just beyond the church's front door.

Near St. Louis

Near the confluence of the Mississippi, Missouri, and Illinois rivers is a 27-foot, 3,000-pound statue of Our Lady, erected by the people of Portage des Sioux in 1957 after being spared from flooding. **Our Lady of the River Shrine** is lighted and used as a navigation aid at night.

Creve Coeur

The **Priory of St. Mary and St. Louis** (500 S. Mason Rd., 314-434-2557) includes a superb chapel, dedicated in 1962, that won many architectural awards. The white circular church has forty lower-level arches with fiberglass windows that let in a delicate light.

Eureka

The inspirational **Shrine of the Black Madonna** (100 St. Joseph's Hill Rd., 314-938-5361) was a twenty-two-year labor of love by Franciscan Fr. Bronislaus Luszcz, a Pole who came to the United States to help run an infirmary for poor, elderly men. Starting in 1938, Father Luszcz created the multicolored, intricate rock grottoes by hauling barrels of water up the hill to mix with concrete, breaking boulders into small pieces, clearing the trees, and leveling the land. Ingenuity was the order of Luszcz's day. He fashioned statues of lambs and rabbits from large cake molds. He embedded in the concrete donations of jewelry and trinkets. The end result is an artistic and spiritual triumph.

Hazelwood

St. Stanislaus Rock Building (700 Howdershell Rd., 314-361-5122), opened in 1823, housed the Jesuit novices in the Midwest. Begun the following year was St. Regis Indian Seminary, the first government-sponsored Native American school west of the Mississippi. The complex became a museum in 1971. The Museum of

Western Jesuit Missions contains a Louis XIV silver monstrance used by Father Marquette.

St. Charles

St. Philippine Duchesne Shrine (619 N. Second St., 314-946-6127) memorializes a frontier-era nun who persevered with good works despite great frustrations. Born in Grenoble, France, in 1769, she was the daughter of a prominent lawyer. Despite her father's objections, she joined a Society of the Sacred Heart convent and eventually volunteered to be a missionary in America. Mother Duchesne believed she was to realize a cherished dream—to bring God to Native Americans. Instead, she was assigned to reestablish the Church among settlers, who were often without priests.

Yet Mother Duchesne, persistent and even stubborn, proved to be visionary. In 1817 she opened in St. Charles the first free school for girls west of the Mississippi. She also began schools in Louisiana and St. Louis. In her sixties, she oversaw six schools in two states. Finally, at the age of seventy-two, she was allowed to travel by boat up the Mississippi to minister to Native Americans in Sugar Creek, Kansas. In only a year she helped found six convents and accepted sixty-four young women into her congregation. The Native American children called her "Quah-kah-ka-num-ad," the woman who prays always. Despite her success, she was told to return to St. Charles. She died in 1852.

Mother Duchesne is entombed at the shrine. Memorabilia related to her is displayed.

Ste. Genevieve

The oldest settlement of Europeans in Missouri is Ste. Genevieve, where in 1732 French miners discovered lead. In 1852 they built a Catholic church. The present **Church of Ste. Genevieve** (9 DuBourg Pl., 573-883-2731), built in 1880, is the third church on the site. The interior has religious paintings that date from 1663, carefully carried here by the French. **Ste. Genevieve Museum** (Merchant St.

and Dubourg Pl.) displays Catholic documents and ecclesiastic objects.

Central Missouri

Fulton

The only twelfth-century English church in America sits at Westminster College (501 Westminster Ave., 573-642-3361). The **Church of Saint Mary the Virgin, Aldermanbury**, originally stood at the corner of Love Lane and Aldermanbury Road in London. After the Great Fire of 1666, the brilliant English architect Christopher Wren rebuilt it. The church remained a house of worship until World War II when a German air raid gutted the interior. In 1965 what was left was packed up and shipped to Westminster College, where the church was reassembled. The college reconstructed the church as a tribute to Winston Churchill, who in 1946 gave his famous "Iron Curtain" speech at the school. Originally Catholic, the church today is nondenominational.

Westphalia

St. Joseph Church (573-455-2320), a stone building, has a commanding bell tower and steeple. The church is the most prominent building in the pleasant hilltop town.

Northern Missouri

Chillicothe

The German Gothic **St. Columban Church** (1111 Trenton St., 816-646-0190) recalls the glories of pre-Vatican II churches.

Conception

Conception Abbey (660-944-2211), founded in 1873, has an impressive Romanesque-style Basilica of the Immaculate Conception. In 1940 it was made a major basilica to honor the monastery's efforts in furthering liturgical worship and Gregorian chant in the United States.

Kansas City

The strikingly unusual **St. Francis Xavier Church** (1001 E. 52nd St., 816-523-5115) was built in the 1950s in a radical minimalist style. The concrete edifice is in the shape of a fish, an ancient Christian symbol. The stained glass is a uniform sea of blue.

The **Cathedral of the Immaculate Conception** (416 W. 12th St., 816-842-0416) was built in 1882, though the parish began in 1835. The cupola was covered with gold leaf in the 1960s. The Stations of the Cross, originally in pastel colors, are from France, and the gorgeous stained-glass windows were made in Germany and England.

Our Lady of Perpetual Help Church (3333 Broadway, 816-561-3771) has glistening white marble altars and shrines. Locals proudly consider the Gothic structure as the quintessential Catholic church.

Our Lady of Sorrows Church (2552 Gillham Rd., 816-421-2112) was the second church in the city for Germans. The church is fondly known as Our Lady of Hallmark: the card giant's headquarters is behind the church. Homilists must resist the urge to point out how gospel messages run a little deeper than those of a greeting card.

St. Patrick Church (1357 N.E. 42nd Terrace, 816-453-5510), dedicated in 1996, is an interesting modern church spiced with old-fashioned Celtic touches.

Near Kansas City

Independence

St. Mary Church (611 N. Liberty St., 816-252-0121) dates from 1822, when Fr. Charles de la Croix began a French and Native American mission. The rear of the church has historical exhibits.

Weston

The Gothic-style **Holy Trinity Church** (407 Cherry St., 816-640-2206) is a true gem. Situated on a hill that overlooks the town, the twin-spired church was built with limestone in 1912. A grand marshal on a coal black horse headed the joyous dedication parade, followed by the village band, flower girls, and people on foot and in carriage.

Fr. Francis Rutkowski, a native of Poland who came from a noble family, founded the parish in 1842. His first quarters were a horse shed, and he took his meals at the Cody home, the uncle and aunt of "Buffalo Bill." The large picture of the Holy Trinity behind the altar, secured by Rutkowski, was a gift from the Queen of Belgium.

Holy Trinity Church.

NEW MEXICO

Northern New Mexico

Abiquiu

Christ found the desert to be spiritually fruitful, and visitors to the **Monastery of Christ in the Desert** (off Rte. 84, 505-470-4515) also renew their spirituality. The isolated Benedictine monastery is located 13 miles down a dirt road off the highway in the starkly beautiful Chama Canyon wilderness. Founded in 1964 by three monks from the Mount Saviour Monastery in New York, the community has two dozen monks from England, Mexico, the Philippines, Vietnam, and, of course, the United States. The solitude and quiet of this monastery is a sure thing.

Albuquerque

The **Church of San Felipe de Neri** (2005 N. Plaza NW, 505-243-4628) has high windows and thick walls, protection against Native American attacks. The church dates from 1706. In 1895 the pueblo architecture was given a Victorian decor. Interestingly, choir members reach their posts by climbing stairs that wind around a spruce tree.

Franciscan Fr. Richard Rohr, a well-known writer and retreat leader, founded the **Center for Action and Contemplation** (1705 Five Points Rd., S.W., 505-242-9588) in the mid 1980s. Rohr combines contemplative prayer and social-justice actions. Residents of the center typically spend the day praying, working with the poor, and taking part in contemplative workshops. The center is located in the former motherhouse of the Franciscan province of Our Lady of Guadalupe.

Near Albuquerque
Bernalillo

No benches are found in the **Mission of Santa Ana Pueblo** (2 Dove Rd., 505-867-3301): the Native Americans, who worshiped as austerely as they lived, knelt on the smooth adobe floor. The mission was founded about 1600. The church's interior has some excellent early religious paintings and an impressive altar screen with large pictures of Jesus and John the Baptist.

Isleta

Built between 1613 and 1621, **St. Augustine Church** at the Isleta Pueblo (off NM 47, 505-869-3398) was severely damaged in the 1680 Pueblo Revolt. Fr. Juan de Padilla, who accompanied Coronado on his expedition, is buried under the altar. Legend has it that his coffin springs out of the ground periodically and his body is shown to be perfectly preserved.

San Felipe

The Franciscans Christianized the **Pueblo of San Felipe** (on Rte. 66) very early in the Spanish conquest of New Mexico. The present church, built between 1700 and 1725, is an adobe building with a fine open-work balcony and attractive towers.

Zia

The **Mission of Zia Pueblo** on Zia Indian Reservation (on Rte. 44, 505-867-3304) has a massive adobe church, unadorned except for a bright coat of whitewash on its fortresslike front. A slightly lopsided bell tower holds one bell. The church's interior, dim and cool, has a small image of Our Lady of the Assumption over the altar. The mission was founded in the early seventeenth century.

Northern New Mexico

Las Trampas

Legend has it that the **Church of the Twelve Apostles** was entrusted to twelve native builders who were expected to live in saintlike fashion. Completed in 1776, the church took a dozen years to build. Near the church is a "death cart," a ghastly wooden statue of the death angel, Dona Sebastiana, with bow drawn.

Picuris

Saint Laurence Church of the Picuris Pueblo (Hwy. 75, 505-587-2957) was rebuilt after the rebellion of 1680. The church is dark inside, like most churches constructed beneath the blazing skies of the Southwest. Beautifully carved beams in the musicians' gallery and in the roof show the patience and artistry of the Native Americans.

Ranchos de Taos

The splendid **Mission of St. Francis of Assisi** (on Rte. 68, 505-758-2754) has been a favorite subject of many Taos artists, including Georgia O'Keeffe. Built in 1710, the adobe church is sometimes referred to as "a symphony in mud."

The rectory displays Henry Ault's mysterious painting *The Shadow of the Cross.* When seen in dim light, a cross not visible in daylight appears over the shoulder of Christ, and the sea and sky glow. The painting was shown at the St. Louis World's Fair of 1904 and given to the parish in 1948.

Sante Fe

Sante Fe means "Holy Faith," and a small downtown stretch has some of the most historic Catholic structures in the country. Start with **San Miguel Mission** (401 Old Santa Fe Trail, 505-983-3974), the oldest church in continuous use in the United States. The simple, earth-hued adobe church was built in 1636 for use of the Tlaxcalans of Mexico, servants of the Spanish colonists. The church was severely damaged in the 1680 Pueblo Revolt and rebuilt in 1710. On display are several paintings on buffalo and deer hides done by the missionaries to teach Bible stories to the Native Americans. Also here is the 800-pound San Jose Bell, cast in Spain in 1356 and brought to the church in the 1800s. The Christian Brothers have run the church since the mid nineteenth century.

Down the street is **Loretto Chapel** (211 Old Santa Fe Trail, 505-984-7971), modeled after the famous Sainte Chapelle in Paris. Built in 1873, the chapel is known for its miraculous staircase, which has two complete 360-degree turns with no central support. No nails were used in its construction. Legend has it that the chapel was nearly finished when it became obvious that there was not enough room for a staircase to the choir loft. In an apparent answer to the prayers of the nuns, an old, bearded man arrived on a donkey and built the staircase, using only a square, a saw, and a tub of water to season the wood. Many believe it was Saint Joseph himself.

The Romanesque-style **Saint Francis Cathedral** (231 Cathedral Pl., 505-982-5619) is made of brown sandstone, a distinct departure from the city's usual pueblo architecture. Jean Baptiste Lamy, the inspiration for Willa Cather's *Death Comes for the Archbishop,* built the church in 1869. He's buried in the crypt beneath the high altar, and a statue of him stands outside the entrance. Lamy made many enemies when he tried to reform the clergy.

America's oldest Madonna, a small wooden statue, rests on the altar in the Conquistador Chapel. It accompanied Don Diego de Vargas on his reconquest of Santa Fe in 1692.

The massive **Cristo Rey Church** (1120 Canyon Rd., 505-983-8528) is the largest adobe structure in the country. It was built in 1940 to commemorate the 400th anniversary of Coronado's exploration of the Southwest. Demonstrating their devotion, parishioners themselves mixed 200 thousand mud-and-straw adobe bricks and lifted them into place. The church has a superb 225-ton stone *reredos* (altar screen).

Built in 1765, **Sanctuario de Guadalupe** (100 Guadalupe, 505-988-2027) is the oldest shrine in the country dedicated to Our Lady of Guadalupe, the patron saint of Mexico. The structure is one of the most attractive churches in the state. It contains a 16th-century masterpiece by a Venetian painter showing Jesus driving the money changers from the temple. The garden has plants from the Holy Land.

Near Sante Fe

Chimayo

El Sanctuario de Chimayo (one mile south of the intersection of Highways 76 and 520, 505-351-4889) is often referred to as the "Lourdes of America." Many miraculous healings have been reported here since 1810. That year Don Bernado Abeyta recovered from a serious illness and had a vision to dig in the earth at a certain spot. He found a crucifix in the sand and built a chapel on the site. The crucifix still sits on the chapel altar. Behind the altar is the sacred sand pit where it was found.

Cordova

Cordova is a hotbed for woodcarving, and small but impressive **St. Anthony of Padua Chapel** (off Hwy. 76) has beautiful handcrafted statues.

Domingo

The **Pueblo of Saint Dominic** (Hwy. 22, 505-465-2214) has one of the state's most unusual churches. The dazzling, white-coated stucco church was built in the late 1800s after a flood destroyed its predecessor. The adobe structure has a sky-blue balcony and a facade painted with figures of two horses facing each other, signifying that the pueblo was a farming community. The collection of

Native American art on display exhibits true joy in creation, despite an obvious lack of knowledge about classical rules of painting.

Jemez Springs

The **Jemez State Monument** (on Hwy. 44 just north of Jemez Springs, 505-829-3530) commemorates the San José de los Jemez Mission and the Guisewa Pueblo ruins. The Franciscans founded the mission in 1622. The museum has reproductions of murals painted on the church walls.

La Cienega

El Ranchos de las Golondrinas (off I-25, 505-471-2261) is a restoration of an early eighteenth-century Spanish colonial ranch. The *capilla,* or chapel, was the worship space for the owners of the ranch. Since priests were few in number, families often conducted their own services. The altar features handmade wooden crosses and carved wooden statues of saints, called *santos.* The floor is made of planks and the ceiling of log beams.

Also here is a *morada,* a chapel used by the Penitentes, a religious fraternity developed when priests were scarce. The Penitentes used their own religious rituals, which emphasized mortification and penance. During Holy Week, some practiced self-flagellation, a practice not sanctioned by the Church.

Pecos

Located in the scenic seclusion of the gorgeous Pecos River Valley is the **Pecos Benedictine Abbey** (505-757-6415). The Benedictines of Benet Lake, Wisconsin, purchased the 1,000-acre property in 1955. Two monasteries are here: Our Lady of Guadalupe Abbey and Mother of Mercy and Peace Monastery. The Spanish-style adobe buildings are the site of many retreats. The first Cursillo in the country was held here. But the abbey is best known for being a charismatic monastery.

Santa Cruz

Built in 1733, the **Church of the Holy Cross** (505-753-3345) has many fine paintings, rare books, and ancient parish registers and letters, including a letter from Charles IV of Spain on the administration of Native American affairs in New Spain. The collection of artifacts provides insight into the romance and danger of missionary work.

Northern New Mexico

Taos

The **Church of San Geronimo** (off Rte. 68 two miles north of Taos, 505-758-8626) was the site of a horrible battle in 1847 in which 150 Native Americans died. They had taken refuge in the church after revolting against U.S. rule. The U.S. Army's artillery destroyed the church and forced the people inside to surrender. A new church was built in 1850. The Native Americans are buried in the adjoining cemetery.

Central New Mexico

Abo

The **Mission of San Gregorio de Abo** (off Rte. 60 nine miles west of Mountainair) is mostly in ruins, but its grandeur can be imagined. A U.S. soldier who viewed the ruins in 1853 wrote, "Abo belongs to the region of romance and fancy, and it will be for the poet and painter to restore to its original beauty this venerable temple."

Mountainair

The large **Mission Church of the Immaculate Conception** (off Rte. 55, eight miles north of Mountainair) has a 100-foot-long, 50-foot-wide interior. It was built about 1620. Years later, Fr. Estevan de Perea was assigned here while he headed the powerful and dreaded Holy Office of the Inquisition.

Socorro

Old San Miguel Mission (403 Camino Real, 505-835-0424), dating from 1615, has been restored several times. The parish church looks quite different from its original appearance, but worshipers know they are on ground that has been holy for nearly four hundred years.

Western New Mexico

Acoma

The impossibly situated **San Estaven del Rey Mission** is part of the Acoma Pueblo (off I-40 on BIA Rd. 22, 505-470-4966), known as the "Sky City." The church sits on a massive sandstone mesa that rises 367 feet above the valley. The Native Americans who built the church in 1629 had either to carry the materials up the steep slopes of the mesa or to hoist them with grass ropes. The church's ceiling logs were cut from trees on Mount Taylor, located more than 15 miles away, and carried on the builders' shoulders without ever touching the ground. The immense church has walls 9 feet thick and 60 feet high. In one of the twin bell towers, which rise 50 feet off the mesa, is a bell given to the pueblo in 1710 by the king of Spain.

The church's large painting of Saint Joseph and the Christ Child was once the subject of a legal case that went all the way to the U.S. Supreme Court. In 1800 Laguna Pueblo, suffering from a prolonged drought, borrowed and then failed to return the painting to Acoma Pueblo. The painting supposedly had miraculous powers. The court ruled in favor of Acoma. When the people from Acoma went to get it, they found it leaning against a tree halfway between the two pueblos. Some believe that Saint Joseph, knowing of the decision, had started the journey home.

The Spaniards conquered the Acomas in 1599 after a bloody battle. The Native Americans later barred Whites from entering their lands. Legend has it that Fr. Juan Ramirez gained entry and began the mission in 1629 after a miraculous rescue. A young girl who was in the crowd at the rim of the pueblo to jeer him slipped and fell. He caught her in the folds of his billowing robes.

Laguna

The **San José Mission**, part of Laguna Pueblo (off Rte. I-40, 505-552-6654), has a brilliant white facade. The church, built in 1699, offers excellent interior artwork.

OKLAHOMA

Eastern Oklahoma

Tulsa

The 250-foot spire of **Holy Family Cathedral** (122 W. Eighth St., 918-582-6247) was once the tallest structure in the city. The cathedral was built in 1914.

The parish was founded in 1899 as an adjunct to a school for Creek girls built by Mother Katharine Drexel, who dedicated her considerable fortune and her life to Blacks and Native Americans.

Katie Drexel was born in 1858 to a very rich and devout family in Philadelphia. She knew by the age of fourteen that she wanted not only to be a nun but to serve America's most disadvantaged people. When she was a child she saw in a book a picture of Columbus with a Native American standing near him and realized that the explorer discovered America so that the Native Americans could learn about God's love for them.

She made her novitiate with the Sisters of Mercy in 1889 and then began her own community, called the Sisters of the Blessed Sacrament for Indians and Colored People. Using money inherited from her parents, she paid for schools and churches. She lived simply, riding in rickety wagons over bumpy country roads and contented herself with outdoor plumbing.

For a time she gave away $1,000 a day. Despite her generosity, income taxes ate into her fortune, and Congress passed a tax-exemption law chiefly for her benefit. The 1932 law gave a tax break to those who had given 90 percent of their net income to charity for the previous ten years. Mother Katharine had met that standard for forty years. When she died in 1955, *Newsweek* hailed her by noting that "she gave her $360 thousand annual income to her order and lived on an allowance of 41 cents a day."

Christ the King Church (1520 S. Rockford Ave., 918-584-4788) regards itself as the first church dedicated under this name; the papal decree establishing the feast was issued in 1925 while the church was under construction. It is one of the nation's finest examples of the early Art Deco style. Among its many outstanding features are the stained-glass windows that show the kings of the Old and New Testaments paying homage to Christ the King.

Sts. Peter and Paul Church (1436 N. 67th E Ave., 918-836-2596), located in a blue-collar neighborhood, was richly conceived and designed. Its International style owes a debt to Mies van der Rohe. The classic sanctuary was strongly influenced by the Bauhaus Movement. Famed liturgical designer Frank Kacmarcik was responsible for the splendid windows splashing light and color across the plain wall behind the altar.

Pawhuska

Immaculate Conception Church (1314 Lynn Ave., 918-287-1414) is located in Osage County, formerly the last reservation of the Osage tribe. The church is known as the "Cathedral of the Osage." The glorious stained-glass windows, crafted in Munich, depicted living tribal members; the Vatican had to grant the church special permission for this. One window shows Columbus meeting a party of Native Americans, and another portrays prominent Osage of that time gathered around a Jesuit missionary. Mother Katharine Drexel built two of her mission schools for the Osages, but they are long gone.

Central Oklahoma
Oklahoma City

Old St. Joseph Cathedral (301 N.W. Fourth St., 405-235-4565), located across the street from where the Federal Building once stood, was heavily damaged in the horrible April 19, 1995, terrorist bombing. The Federal Building destroyed by the blast was built on the site of old St. Joseph School and the former Catholic Charities offices. The church reopened late in 1996.

Our Lady of Mt. Carmel and St. Thérèse Little Flower Church (1125 S. Walker Ave., 405-235-2037) features a soaring campanile visible for miles, ten stained-glass windows depicting the saints of the Carmelite Order, including St. Thérèse of Lisieux, and the first statue of the Saint of the Little Way to be venerated in the United States. The church, built in 1927, adjoins the monastery and headquarters of the St. Thérèse of Oklahoma Province of the Discalced Carmelites.

Near Oklahoma City
Konawa

"Boomer Sooner" is the rallying cry of Oklahomans, but Catholics were late in arriving to the state. The Catholic presence became rooted when the first permanent missionaries, French Benedictine monks exiled by secularization laws, came to Pottawatomie in 1875. Two years later they built **Sacred Heart** in Konawa (Rte. 39), a primitive monastery. Later, they constructed **St. Gregory's Abbey** in Shawnee (1900 W. MacArthur Dr., 405-878-5490).

Piedmont

"Let them prefer nothing whatever to Christ," reads the Rule of Benedict, and the Benedictine Sisters of the **Red Plains Monastery** (728 Richland Rd. SW, 405-528-7965) are committed to seeking God in a communal life of prayer, work, and hospitality. Guests are welcome at the morning, midday, and evening Liturgies of the Hours.

Western Oklahoma

Canute

The rustic **Catholic cemetery** (Rte. 66) has a hillside sepulcher and a bronze life-size figure of the crucified Christ looking down at the two kneeling Mary's below.

TEXAS

Northern Texas
Dallas

St. Peter the Apostle Church (Allen and Cochrane Streets, 214-855-1384) is the city's oldest African American parish. It began in 1905 with twelve members, some of them former slaves. Their church was a hand-me-down, frame church that was dismantled and moved into their neighborhood. St. Peter's Academy, financed by Mother Katharine Drexel, opened in 1908 and served African Americans for eighty years. In the mid 1980s parish membership dwindled. The Dallas Diocese decided to let the parish serve Polish immigrants as well as African Americans. The church contains an image of the Black Madonna of Czestochowa.

The **Cathedral-Santuario de Guadalupe** (2215 Ross Ave., 214-871-1362), built in 1902, is the oldest church in the city. The church's name was changed in 1977 from the Cathedral of the Sacred Heart to the Shrine of Our Lady of Guadalupe as Hispanic parishioners grew in number.

Umbarger

In 1945 an Italian prisoner of war who was interned in an area camp did many of the interior decorations of **St. Mary Church** (218 W. 13th St., 806-499-3531), built in 1929.

Westphalia

The **Church of the Visitation** (817-584-4983) is the largest wooden church in Texas and one of the oldest in continuous use in the country. Parishioners built the rural church in 1895. The stained-glass windows are from Westphalia, Germany. The parish has produced fourteen priests and thirty-eight religious sisters. Locals say the only two roads out of town lead to the seminary and the convent.

Eastern Texas

Austin

Fr. Edward Sorin, the founder of Notre Dame University, established **St. Edward's University** (3001 S. Congress Ave., 512-448-8400) in 1885. The Main Building, designed by famed architect Nicholas Clayton in 1887, has a soaring red steeple. On the third floor is the former school chapel, the Maloney Room, notable for its splendid rose-patterned stained-glass windows. Built as an auditorium, Our Lady Queen of Peace Chapel honors students who lost their lives in war.

Beaumont

St. Anthony Cathedral (Jefferson and Wall Streets) was built with oil money. A 1901 gusher uncovered the richest oil field of the time and led to the founding of oil giants like Texaco, Gulf, Mobil, and Exxon.

Brownsville

Texas is famous for its cowboys. That goes for its priests, too. The Oblate Fathers, who ministered to rancheros spread out over a large area, spent most of their time in the saddle. The order became known as the Calvary of Christ. **Immaculate Conception Cathedral** (1218 E. Jefferson, 210-546-3178) was designed in 1859 by such a priest. Fr. Pierre Yves Keralum studied architecture in France before becoming an equestrian-priest on the plains of Texas.

Corpus Christi

Corpus Christi Cathedral (505 N. Upper Broadway, 512-883-

4213) features two glazed terra cotta domes. The Spanish Colonial Revival-style structure was dedicated in 1940. The apse (the curved part behind the altar) has first-rate art.

Holy Cross Church (1109 N. Staples, 512-888-4012) was once the sole church in the city for Black Catholics. The Gothic-style, stucco structure was built in 1903 as Our Lady of Guadalupe for Hispanics. It was moved twice since then. The wooden sanctuary is cleverly painted to give the appearance of marble. A painting, *The Ugandan Martyrs,* depicts an event from the late 1800s.

Richard Colley, a well-known local architect, designed **Sacred Heart Church** (1308 Comanche, 512-883-6082) in 1942. Colley, who lived for a time in Mexico, copied the Mexican simplicity of construction and ingenuous use of available materials.

Fredericksburg

In 1863 German immigrants built the simple **Marien Kirche** (306 W. San Antonio St., 210-997-9523). The aisles have soapstone floors, but sand sits beneath the pews. In 1906 the congregation built another **St. Mary's Church,** where they currently worship.

Galveston

The city's oldest church is **St. Mary's Cathedral** (2011 Church St., 409-762-9611). It was built in 1848, thanks to a gift of 500,000 bricks from Belgium. The Battle of Galveston during the Civil War left the cathedral riddled with bullets. Before he repaired the damage, Bishop Claude Dubuis observed, "Only on dry days can we say Mass within its walls."

The sumptuous **Bishop's Palace** in Galveston (1402 Broadway, 409-762-2475) was named for Bishop Christopher Byrne, who lived here from 1923 to 1950 after the diocese purchased it for him. The twenty-four-room mansion was built in 1886 for Colonel Walter Gresham, a Virginia native who surrendered with Lee at Appomattox and became a railroad baron in Galveston. The exterior is red sandstone, white limestone, and pink granite. Inside are fourteen fireplaces, two of which were purchased at world's fairs, and archways of black walnut burl. Don't miss the stunning spiral staircase, put together by sixty-one craftsmen over three years. The residence is valued at $5.5 million. Still owned by the Church, it is open to the public.

The gleaming white **Sacred Heart Church** (1302 Broadway, 409-762-6374), designed in Moresque style by one of its priests, is the only U.S. Catholic church built in Islamic style. Its predecessor, a beautiful French Romanesque-style structure, was leveled by the terrible 1900 hurricane. Catholics from all over the country donated money to rebuild the churches in Galveston. Nicholas Clayton, a preeminent Galveston architect, designed the dome atop the church.

Founded in 1888, **Holy Rosary Church** (1420 31st St., 409-762-2478) was the first church built for Black Catholics in Texas. The Dominican Sisters, who staffed the school that preceded the parish by a year, faced bitter opposition from the community for educating blacks. In 1898 the Sisters of Holy Family, a Black order, replaced the Dominicans, staying for eighty-one years. In the 1930s the parish band was extremely popular throughout the city. Today, the Gospel Mass Choir has more than one hundred members. Additionally, the parish is believed to be the only one in the United States with a weekly jazz Mass.

St. Mary's Hospital (404 St. Mary's Blvd., 409-763-5301) was the first Catholic hospital in Texas. In 1866 three Sisters of Charity began Charity Hospital, its original name. The timing was providential: a virulent yellow-fever epidemic hit the city a short time later.

Goliad

Mission Espiritu Santo in Goliad State Historical Park (on Rte. 183, 512-645-3405) was one of the most important missions in New Spain's province of Texas. At its peak, the prosperous mission, moved to this site in 1749, maintained 40 thousand head of cattle. The beef nourished Spanish settlements as distant as Mexico and

Louisiana. The church, granary, convento, and workshop have been restored and contain period furnishings. A museum presents an audiovisual history.

Presidio de la Bahia (2 miles south of Goliad off US 183, 512-645-3752) was a fort built in 1749 to protect Mission Espiritu Santo. Mexican troops secured the fort in 1835 at the outbreak of the Texas Revolution. A band of Texans, most of them Irish Catholics, seized the fort in October, and two months later at the fort's Our Lady of Loretto chapel, ninety-two Texans signed the historic Declaration of Texas Independence from Mexico. The presidio was restored to its original 1836 appearance in 1967. The chapel still holds Mass on Sunday.

Houston

Houston's oldest Catholic church is **Annunciation Church** (1618 Texas Ave., 713-222-2289), finished in 1871. It was constructed with bricks from the old Harris County courthouse, used during the Civil War to house prisoners of war. In 1881 dangerous cracks were discovered in the church wall: the church towers were shifting. The limestone building was redesigned by adding buttresses and a 175-foot tower. The church was stuccoed as well.

The nondenominational **Rothke Chapel** at the Texas Medical Center (3900 Yupon, 713-524-9839) houses fourteen paintings by abstract expressionist Mark Rothko. The God of Raphael and Michelangelo is also the God of Rothko, though Rothko's modern art requires a more active spiritual imagination. The octagonal sanctuary was dedicated in 1971. Outside is a 26-foot steel obelisk that honors the Rev. Martin Luther King, Jr.

Near Houston

La Porte

St. Mary of the Immaculate Conception Church (816 Park Ave., 281-471-2000) was once part of historic St. Mary's Seminary, the first seminary in the South. In 1950 plans were made to relocate the seminary to Houston, and the parish was established. For three years, until the seminary was built, seminarians and parishioners shared St. Mary's.

Wallis

Guardian Angels Church (5610 Demel St., 409-478-6532) is one of the state's "painted churches," lavishly decorated to make its immigrant parishioners feel at home. Czechs founded the parish in 1892. Completed in 1915, the present church is a large solid-wood structure in the Gothic style. Its pillars are painted to simulate marble.

New Braunfels

Hitler hated the Hummel images, denouncing the depiction of German children with "hydrocephalic heads," and the Nazis banned the German distribution of the art of Franciscan Sister Maria Innocentia, better known as Berta Hummel. Hummels are freely and amply displayed at the **Hummel Museum** (1900 Main Plaza, 937-456-4151). The museum has more than 350 pieces of

Hummel Museum.

original Hummel paintings, drawings, and sketches, on which the figurines are based, and more than 1,500 figurines. The museum's video room shows the life of Sister Hummel.

Born in 1909 in Bavaria, Hummel was a star student at the prestigious Academy of Applied Arts in Munich before deciding to join the Franciscans in Siessen. She loved children and taught art at the convent school. As a reward for good work she gave her students original picture cards, which brought her talent to the attention of her superiors. To raise money for the community, they allowed her to publish a collection of her drawings titled simply *Das Hummel-Buch*. Fortuitously, a craftsman at a porcelain factory on the verge of closing bought the book and convinced the owner to recreate her drawings as porcelain figurines. Hummels became immensely popular following World War II when returning soldiers carried them home as gifts. Hummel died in 1946, having contracted tuberculosis during the war, when religious communities were persecuted and suffered from miserable living conditions.

Why are her figurines so appealing? Hummel, still in touch with the innocence of her own childhood, captured children in carefree moments of play. Her art gloried in the wonder and the freshness of youthful experience. She also drew madonnas, angels, and wayside shrines.

Incidentally, the special project director at the museum is the "living Hummel," Sieglinde Schoen Smith, who was the subject of at least two of Hummel's works when she was a young child.

Panna Maria

A big Northern city was not the initial port of entry for Polish immigrants in the nineteenth century: it was the small town of Panna Maria, named after the Virgin Mary. One hundred Polish families, seeking refuge from political oppression, came in 1854. Two years earlier, Franciscan Fr. Leopold Moczygemba had settled here. The immigrants arrived on Christmas Eve after a 200-mile walk from Galveston. They built the **Immaculate Conception of the Blessed Virgin Mary Church** (210-780-2748), the nation's oldest Polish parish. The Gothic Revival-style structure, rebuilt in 1877, contains a mosaic of the Black Madonna, given to the town by President Johnson in 1966. The Panna Maria grade school is the successor to the original school and is run by Felician Sisters.

San Antonio

The **Alamo** (Alamo Plaza at Alamo and Houston Streets, 210-225-1391), revered as a symbol of courageous patriotism, was actually a mission church until 1793. Mission San Antonio de Valero, begun in 1718, was named after the Marquis de Valero, a powerful Spanish official in Mexico. The famous Alamo building, the one seen on innumerable postcards, is the former mission church.

The Alamo.

Mission San Antonio was one of thirty-six missions founded by Spain in Texas between 1680 and 1793. Five of the missions are in San Antonio along the San Antonio River. The Franciscans came to convert Native Americans. The soldiers and settlers accompanying them were sent by Spanish rulers to expand their nation's empire.

Mission San Antonio flourished for several decades before its ineffectiveness led to its secularization in 1793. The site then became a fortress. The mission church, constructed in 1744, has been restored. A museum has a slide show on the battle and another one on the history of the mission.

Mission Concepción (807 Mission Rd., 210-229-5732) is a huge structure with twin bell towers. Begun in 1731, it is the oldest unrestored stone Catholic church in the country. One reason it has endured is because it was built on bedrock and is impervious to shifts of the earth. Jim Bowie and other Texas volunteers once camped here after the mission was secularized.

Mission Espada (10040 Espada Rd., 210-627-2021), founded in 1731, is the most remote of the San Antonio missions. In 1760 Fr. Bartolome Garcia of Espada helped break down tribal divisions and enhanced the teaching of religion and the arts by preparing a grammar in the most common Native American language. The mission was noted for its green pasture lands that supported four thousand head of cattle. Relentless Apache raids on the livestock discouraged Native Americans at the mission and led some of them to leave.

The current church was built in the late 1800s. Double-tiered Moorish arches support three bells over the church's simple stone facade. The statue of Saint Francis inside dates from 1780.

The "Queen of the Missions" is **Mission San José** (6539 San José, 210-229-4770), the best restored of the missions. The superb chapel, one of the finest examples of the Spanish Renaissance style, has wonderful carved-stone ornamentation. A Spanish Franciscan who toured U.S. missions in 1777 had this to say: "San José is in truth the first mission in America, not in point of time, but in point of beauty, plan and strength, so that there is not a presidio along the entire frontier that can compare with it." Especially notable is "Rosa's window," bordered by scrolls and foliage, in the sacristy. The name came about because either the sculptor was mourning the death of his wife, Rose, or the window was associated with Saint Rose's Day.

The founder of the mission was the wise and warm Fr. Antonio Margil de Jesus, learned, cultured, and ascetically handsome. Nowhere in New Spain did the Native Americans flourish more than under Father Margil. The fields bore rich crops of corn, sweet and Irish potatoes, brown beans, cantaloupes, watermelons, olives, and peaches, and the Native Americans' living quarters were unusually clean and comfortable.

Mission San Juan (9101 Graf Rd., 210-534-3161) is located in a quiet, semirural area. Established in 1731, the mission was originally just a friary and a granary. The ruins of a large church, begun in 1760 but not finished, can be seen. The convento has been converted into a small museum.

The **Chapel of Miracles** (113 Ruiz St.) is a deep expression of one family's enduring faith. Don Juan Ximenes built the tiny chapel in the 1870s. His descendants, who live across the street, take care of it. Inside the chapel is an 8-foot-high wooden crucifix that hung in the Alamo mission. In the chapel are small tin *milagros* left by those who prayed for miracles.

San Fernando Cathedral (115 Main Plaza, 210-227-1297) was begun by a group of intrepid settlers from the Canary Islands who came to the missions at the request of the Franciscans, who wanted the settlers to serve as models of practicing Catholics to the Native Americans. After an arduous year's journey, fifteen bedraggled families arrived in 1731. Seven years later they laid the cornerstone for the original church, making it the nation's oldest cathedral. Much of the original church was replaced stone by stone and brick by brick in 1872, without an interruption of services.

Alamo defenders are interred in the church. Above a votive altar is a Black Christ, a replica of a famous 1595 figure in Esquipulas, Guatemala. Flanking the altar are photos of people whose prayers were answered.

The Gothic church has a massive dome, which marks the precise city center and from which all distances to the city are measured.

St. Joseph Church (623 E. Commerce, 210-227-0126) is affectionately referred to as "St. Joske's" because adjoining it was Joske's department store (now Dillard's). Germans built the church in 1868. In an unexpected cultural twist in a city with many Latinos, a male choir group sings in German during Mass on the last Sunday of the month.

Carmelite Fr. Raymond Gomez was so moved by a trip to France in which he met with the blood sisters of Thérèse of Lisieux that he vowed to build a shrine in honor of her. The **Little Flower Shrine** (906 Kentucky Ave., 210-735-9126) was dedicated in 1931. The Romanesque-style church, made of Indiana limestone, has a tall bell tower that houses six great bells that regularly strike the opening chords of the Gloria and the Te Deum. Inside the church is the

Tomb Chapel, containing a life-size image of the body of the Little Flower.

San Juan

Near the Mexican border is the solemn **Virgen de San Juan del Valle Shrine** (400 N. Nebraska, 210-787-0033). The shrine holds a replica of a statue of the Immaculate Conception brought to Mexico by the first Spanish missionaries. The original statue was held over the body of a young girl who came back to life. A modern miracle occurred in 1970 when a deranged pilot, who detested Catholics, crashed into the chapel while fifty priests were concelebrating Mass. The worshipers were uninjured, and the church was rebuilt.

Near Schulenburg

Dubina

Sts. Cyril and Methodius Church (512-594-3836) is one of Texas's several "painted churches," featuring ornate ceilings and walls. Settlers from Europe founded these churches, all located

Sts. Cyril and Methodius Church. *(Earl Nottingham)*

near Schulenburg, and decorated them fancifully to remind them of their heritage. Czech immigrants built Sts. Cyril and Methodius around the turn of the century. A host of brightly colored angels and flowers embellish the church's interior.

Ammannsville

St. John the Baptist Church offers elaborate stenciling, infill, freehand, and marbling. Pre-Vatican II statues of Jesus and John the Baptist sit atop the high altar. The stained-glass windows depict women saints on one side and male saints on the other, a sign of long ago when the sexes sat on opposite sides.

High Hill

The brick **St. Mary's Church** (409-561-8455), built by Austrians in 1905, has golden floral decorations painted on the blue background of the lofty ceiling.

Praha

The little town of Praha was named after Prague, and the **Church of the Assumption of the Blessed Virgin Mary** (512-865-3560) is a Czech-type church. The vaulted ceiling, painted by a Swiss-born artist when the church was built in the 1890s, has not been repainted since.

Warrenton

Not everything is big in Texas. One of the world's smallest Catholic churches is **Saint Martin Church** (409-378-2277). Measuring 16 feet by 20 feet, the church has twelve pews. Mass is offered once a year on All Souls' Day. The chapel, a mission of St. John Church in Fayetteville, dates from 1886. The pastor then, building a new school, ran out of lumber and tore down the church in Warrenton. He had enough lumber to build a chapel.

Western Texas

El Paso

Just a few feet from the Mexican border is **Sierra de Christo Rey**, a 33-foot-high statue of Christ the King. Perched atop a 4,756-foot peak, the statue is visible from I-10. The figure was carved from Cordova cream limestone in 1938. A winding footpath to the shrine is lined with the fourteen Stations of the Cross. Thousands make the climb on the last Sunday of October, the feast of Christ the King.

Socorro Mission (on FM 258 two miles east of Ysleta, 915-859-7718) was founded in 1681 for the now-extinct Piros. The shape of the chapel facade represents the Piro rainstorm deity. Next to the altar is a hand-carved statue of San Miguel. Legend has it that it was being moved by cart from a church in Mexico to New Mexico when the cart miraculously became too heavy to push as it passed Socorro. So the church claimed it.

Ysleta Mission (131 S. Zaragoza, 915-859-7913) is the oldest mission in Texas's oldest town. Franciscans founded the mission in 1681 to convert the Tiguas. Much of the mission was destroyed by a flooded Rio Grande in 1740 and again by a fire in 1907. It was rebuilt and its name changed to Our Lady of Mount Carmel. Near the altar is a Christ-in-a-coffin, dating from 1722 and used in Easter processions. The white-washed adobe buildings have blue doors and window trim, a color the Native Americans believed protected against evil.

WEST

ARIZONA

Northern Arizona

Sedona

The Oak Creek Canyon is famous for its towering red cliffs and the red-hued **Chapel of the Holy Cross** (Hwy. 179, 520-634-4805). The chapel, erected as a memorial to parents of sculptor Margaret Staude, rises out of the rock face of Twin Buttes. A 90-foot cross stands against the panoramic view. Above the chapel is the Shrine of the Red Rocks, where a hand-hewn wooden cross marks an outdoor altar.

Window Rock

The Franciscans began **St. Michael's Mission** (AZ 264 near Window Rock, 520-871-4171) in 1898 to serve the Navajo. Unlike earlier Franciscans, criticized for not learning the native language, the friars mastered the difficult Navajo language and quickly composed and printed a catechism, bible history, and dictionary. The large stone church dates from 1937. A historical museum occupies the original mission building.

Southern Arizona

Bisbee

St. Patrick's Church (Higgins Hill, 520-432-5753), perched 200 feet above the floor of Tombstone Canyon, boasts forty-one world-class stained-glass windows and a colorful past.

Bisbee became a boomtown at the turn of the century with the discovery of copper, and droves of Irish and Welsh fortune-seekers arrived. On Sundays at the original St. Patrick's they spilled out the door and kneeled in the weeds. In 1913 Fr. Constant Mandin approached wealthy mine owner Thomas Higgins about donating land for a new church. Sure, Higgins said, as long as the church faces the mountain peaks and his mine. By 1917 Mandin, who often donned work clothes and lent a hand to parishioners, had himself a glorious new church, a copy of St. Mary's Church in an Irish enclave in Whitehaven, England.

Emil Frei, who studied at the famed Munich Academy of Art before immigrating to the United States in the late 1800s, designed the magnificent windows. His windows won the grand prize at the 1904 Louisiana Purchase Exposition. The ten largest windows on both sides of St. Patrick's show the life of Christ, including two 25-foot-high windows depicting his birth and Ascension. In the choir loft at the rear of the church is a large window showing the Assumption of the Blessed Virgin Mary.

Frei created his masterpieces from lead crystal glass that was painted, detailed, and fired to create vibrant colors with subtle textures. Some visitors to the church train binoculars on the windows to explore Frei's fine, delicate strokes and his exacting attention to detail. His faces show a rich emotional expression uncommon in stained glass.

St. David

Located in Apache country, **Holy Trinity Monastery** (602-720-4642) is an interesting mix of people and animals. The Benedictine monks keep peacocks and farm animals, also tending a pecan tree orchard. Community members include laypeople and even married couples. Some retreatants, taking advantage of sixteen power hook-ups in the back, park their RVs or vans and stay for months on end.

The founding of the monastery in the 1970s was a fluke of sorts. A Benedictine was asked to convert the former Wilderness Ranch for Boys into a retreat center. Reluctant to commit himself, he agreed to do so only if his Benedictine community approved. To his surprise, they did.

Behind the chapel is an outdoor Stations of the Cross made from weathered wood and old ranch tools.

Scottsdale

The Franciscans helped spread the faith in Arizona, and at the **Franciscan Renewal Center** (5802 E. Lincoln Dr., 602-948-7460) they stoke the flames of faith. Begun in 1951, the center is housed in an attractive Spanish-style white-walled building with a red-tiled roof. A former resort, the center still has the charms of a place of leisure, including palm trees, well-kept courtyards, and meticulous landscaping. The peaceful chapel seats nearly three hundred. The Prayer of Saint Francis is prominently displayed in copper letters on a wall near the entrance: "Where there is hatred, let me sow love; where there is injury, pardon; where there is doubt, faith."

Tucson

St. Augustine's Cathedral (192 S. Stone Ave., 520-623-6351) is an outstanding example of Mexican Baroque architecture. Its magnificent stone facade, completed in 1928, was inspired by the Cathedral of Querataro in Mexico. With the exception of the facade and towers, the cathedral was demolished and rebuilt in the late 1960s.

The Tucson area has a long association with the name of Saint Augustine, owing to the Spanish military and mission presence in the 1700s. Two villages named San Augustin del Tucson once existed, and both towns had churches named St. Augustine. A third St. Augustine Church was built in the mid 1800s. A historical marker in a small park downtown at Church and Broadway marks the location of that adobe and stone structure. The church's arched portal decorates the entrance to the **Arizona Historical Society Museum** (949 E. 2nd St.).

One of the most beautiful Spanish missions is **Mission San Xavier del Bac** (near I-19 and Mission Rd., 9 miles southwest of Tucson, 602-294-2624). Known as the "White Dove of the Desert," its domes, arches, and carvings, covered with white stucco, shimmer in the desert light. Its elaborate interior is far superior to that of most Spanish mission churches.

Mission San Xavier del Bac. *(Steve Gibson)*

The legendary horseback priest Fr. Eusebio Francisco Kino established the mission in 1700. In the spring of 1687 Kino, a Jesuit from Italy, entered southern Arizona and began spreading the faith among the highly civilized Pimas. Kino was devout, resourceful, and rugged. He could ride 800 miles in 25 days, exploring, baptizing, and building. He used his saddle as a pillow.

He established a string of missions from Mexico through Arizona. In typically modest fashion, he wrote about San Xavier del Bac, "Anybody might have [founded] it. But His whisper came to me." Kino died eleven years later, and his church was destroyed in a revolt by the Native Americans in 1751. Franciscans and Native Americans built the current church from 1782 to 1797. Since that time it has faithfully served the Papagos.

The church was recently restored for the third time in this century. Left untouched once again was the unfinished bell tower. The reason the Franciscans never completed the tower is a mystery. A popular legend is that a Native American worker fell to his death from the tower during construction, and Native Americans refused to climb up to finish the job. Another explanation is that the unfinished tower suggests that the preaching of the Gospel is never-ending. After sifting through documents, a local historian discovered a less fanciful theory for the incomplete tower: the mission was broke.

Tumacacori

Most of the churches founded by Father Kino exist only as crumbling adobe walls. But one of the oldest and best-preserved structures is at **Tumacacori** (Tumacacori National Historical Park, 1891 E. Frontage Rd., 520-398-2341).

The Pima invited Kino to visit Tumacacori in 1691. The priest wrote at the time that "very good beginnings were made in spiritual and temporal matters." A more elaborate structure, begun in 1800 by a Spanish Franciscan and completed in 1822, supplanted Kino's simple church. The imposing adobe church is an impressive example of Spanish Colonial Baroque architecture. To the right of its entrance is the baptistry, whose adobe walls are 9-feet thick and support a three-story bell tower. The mission's cemetery includes an unusual mortuary chapel. An arched door serves as the entrance, and two holes above provide ventilation.

A museum offers several exciting dioramas on the mission's past. A 14-minute video revisits the early days of the mission.

CALIFORNIA

San Diego

On July 1, 1769, a band of 119 sick and ragged men led by an indomitable Franciscan priest arrived in what was to become San Diego. One hundred men had died on their two-month journey from further north in California. Provisions were growing ever more scarce. Fr. Junipero Serra stood but 5 feet 2 inches and suffered from a painful leg malady. Yet he and his men founded the first mission in California, **San Diego de Alcala** (10818 San Diego Mission Rd., 619-281-8449). Over time, twenty-one missions would stretch like a necklace down the coast of California. Serra, the "apostle of California," brought Christianity and Western civilization to the Native Americans.

The original mission was a simple, thatched-roof hut on Presidio Hill. It was later moved to its current site in what is now central San Diego.

The Native Americans resisted the evangelization efforts. In 1774 tensions mounted, and Native Americans attacked the mission, burning the church and killing Fr. Luis Jayme, California's first martyr. Serra, making sure the culprits were not slain in return, was able to broker a peace. Before long the mission began to flourish. Evangelization took root, and Mission San Diego became a viable economic entity.

At its height in the first two decades of the nineteenth century the mission was grazing 20 thousand sheep and 10 thousand head of cattle. Its wines were famous, and its olive trees were to form the mother orchard for the state's olive industry.

Mission San Diego and the other missions came to halt in the

1830s when the Mexican government secularized the missions and their lands were absorbed into private ranches. (The United States did not take possession of California until 1848.) Mission buildings fell into disrepair. They became taverns, stables, and hog barns.

The white Spanish-style church of the San Diego Mission, completed in 1813 and redolent with age, is a 1941 reconstruction. Visitors can see the primitive conditions of the missionaries' lives. A restored bedroom contains a bed whose mattress is a loose web of leather strips. The **Father Luis Jayme Museum** on the grounds includes a collection of Native American arts, mission documents, relics, and ecclesiastical art.

The twenty-one missions were strung along the El Camino Real, a dirt road in the 1700s. The road eventually became a stagecoach route, and today roughly parallels U.S. Highway 101. The missions remain vital today. Eighteen of the twenty-one are, or are attached to, parishes.

Several of the missions recently celebrated their bicentennial, and the glory of the missionaries' preaching the Gospel and converting untold numbers were recalled. Yet some Native Americans and other also remembered the tragedies of those times. Living conditions were often harsh. European diseases like measles, flu, and syphilis ravaged the Native American population. In 1805, for instance, an epidemic at Mission San Francisco killed every child under the age of five.

Not only lives were lost but a distinct culture. The Spaniards often exploited the Native Americans as cheap labor and forced them to adopt Western ways. The missions rightfully ought to be celebrated for bringing the light of Christ to California, but an unintended consequence was suffering and death.

St. Agnes Church (1140 Evergreen, 619-223-2200) opened in 1908 to serve Portuguese fishermen living along San Diego Bay. Some Sunday Masses are said in Portuguese, and the parish celebrates the Festa at Pentecost in honor of Isabella of Portugal.

St. Brigid Church (4735 Cass St., 619-483-3030) features life-size Stations of the Cross that run the entire length of both sides of the nave. Dom Gregory de Wit, O.S.B., a renowned liturgical artist, created the murals in 1948. Outside the church is a rose garden adorned with murals of Mary.

The **Church of the Immaculata** (5998 Alcala Park, at the University of San Diego, 619-574-5700), the proto-cathedral of San Diego, features striking Spanish Mediterranean architecture. The church, built in 1959 on a grand scale, is 200 feet long and 148 feet wide. Atop a blue-tiled dome is a statue of Our Lady of the Immaculate Conception, standing nearly 11 feet high and weighing 8,500 pounds. The 300-pound cross atop the bell tower soars 167 feet above the ground. Originally intended to serve as the main chapel of the university, the church today is a separate parish.

St. Jude Shrine of the West (1129 S. 38th St., 619-264-2195) is a lively parish that serves Hispanics. Close by is the house and hermitage of the Missionaries of Charity. A two-day fiesta, including a neighborhood procession, is held annually on Saint Jude's feast.

The **Junipero Serra Museum** (2727 Presidio Dr., 619-297-3258), a stately mission-style building, is perched on a hill that overlooks the original site of Mission San Diego, where the settlement of California began. On display are belongings of the Native Americans, Spaniards, and Mexicans who formed this diverse community. Included is one of the first paintings brought to California; it was damaged in a Native American attack but was salvaged. The museum is located in **Presidio Park**, which features an unusual cross made from the floor tile ruins. Statues of Father Serra, the founder of the missions, and a Native American evoke the distant past. Inspiration Point up the hill is a popular place for weddings. It's also an apt place to reflect and pray.

Near San Diego

Coronado

Sacred Heart Church (672 B. Ave., 619-435-3167) is a Romanesque-style structure built in 1920. During World War II it was the parish for sailors stationed at the naval base on Coronado. The parish was established in 1897 when the Hotel del Coronado, a famous seafront resort, was opened.

La Jolla

Near the ocean is the striking **Mary, Star of the Sea Church** (7727 Girard Ave., 619-454-2631), built in 1937 in mission style.

On the back wall of the sanctuary is a magnificent mural by John Henry de Rosen, a celebrated ecclesiastical artist who decorated the pope's private chapel at Castel Gandolfo. The painting shows a tall, ivory-colored Madonna amid a gold-and-silver-leaf background that complements the church's simple and austere white interior.

Mary, Star of the Sea Church. *(John Durant)*

San Luis Rey

Mission San Luis Rey De Francia (4050 Mission Ave., 760-757-3651), the eighteenth mission, was the most successful. The "King of the Missions" counted 3,000 converts. By 1831 the mission boasted a harvest of 2,500 barrels of wine and 395,000 bushels of grain, as well as 12,150 horses, 26,000 cattle, and 25,500 sheep. Much of its success was due to Fr. Antonio Peyri, loved by the Native Americans. For 23 years he ran the mission with firm mildness.

Some visitors called the elaborate church, featuring a dramatic bell tower, a "palace." The interior is a happy arrangement of arches and huge pilasters painted to resemble black marble. To the right of the sanctuary is a famous Mortuary Chapel, an architectural delight. In the courtyard is the first pepper tree planted in the West.

The historical collection here includes vestments, chalices, furnishings, and books used by the Franciscans. Also in the museum is a facsimile of the deed signed by President Lincoln, restoring the mission property to the church following the secularization era. Like the other missions in the mid-1800s after Mexico secularized the missions, the Native Americans left and the property decayed. The "King of the Missions" was no more.

Los Angeles

Built in 1969, **St. Basil Church** (637 S. Kingsley Dr., 213-381-6191) is an imposing skyscraper-like church, a bold, modern structure built with reinforced concrete that can withstand a powerful earthquake. The church's seven massive towers are symbolic of the twelve apostles and the twelve tribes of Israel. Lacing the towers together are contemporary stained-glass windows. The *baldachino* above the altar consists of forty-five twisted metal strips that suggest the shape of a great angel. The strips serve as a frame for a magnificent fourteenth-century Tuscan crucifix. Outside, looking out over the busy traffic on Wilshire Boulevard, is an ivory-colored statue of Our Lady of the Angels.

On September 4, 2000, if all goes according to plan, a magnificent new cathedral that is expected to stand for five hundred years will be dedicated in downtown Los Angeles. The $50 million **Cathedral of Our Lady of the Angels** will occupy a 5.8-acre plot bounded by Grand Avenue, Temple and Hill Streets, and 101 Freeway. The new church replaces the earthquake-damaged **Cathedral of St. Vibiana** (Second and Main Streets, 213-624-3941). The Archdiocese of Los Angeles wanted to build the cathedral on the site of St. Vibiana's, but its demolition was blocked by a suit brought by preservationists.

The 48,000-square-foot cathedral will combine 2,000 years of tradition with the demands of serving a modern diverse church. The style will be California Hispanic, along with a strong mission flavor. Prominent features will include a computerized bell tower, 160 feet tall with 38 bells, a meditation garden, a small museum, and a mission-style colonnade. The most outstanding feature will be light. Windows and light shafts will diffuse daylight into the alabaster walls of the cathedral. At night the alabaster will be back-lighted, so the cathedral will glow.

Our Lady Queen of the Angels, also known as **Plaza Church** (535 N. Main St., 213-629-3101), is the city's oldest church. Native Americans built the original part of the adobe building in 1822. It was rebuilt mission-style in 1862. The distinctive bell tower was erected in 1875, and the church was restored and enlarged in 1912.

It is surely the only church in the world whose construction was supervised by a former pirate and financed through seven barrels of brandy and one thousand head of cattle. Joseph Chapman was a happy-go-lucky sailor in Honolulu who in 1818 was shanghaied into the service of a notorious French pirate. Chapman was captured on a raid of Rancho de Refugio, the home of fabulously wealthy Don José Maria Ortega. Instead of having Chapman hanged, Ortega put him to work on his land. Chapman proved to be a highly skilled tradesman. One night over a fine bottle of wine from Mission Santa Ines, the mayor of Los Angeles complained to Ortega that he had no one to build a much-needed church. Chapman was put in charge.

The Franciscans had no money. But they did have seven barrels of brandy. Chapman convinced owners of ranchos to donate cattle. He bartered the cattle for lumber and sold the wine to pay for labor. The end of the story is the best part. Chapman was married to Ortega's daughter in the church. She had fallen for his rugged good looks the moment she saw him and was the one who had intervened so that he wasn't hanged.

Loyola Law School (1441 W. Olympia Blvd., 213-736-1000) has a fine Romanesque chapel.

Our Lady of the Bright Mount Church (3424 W. Adams Blvd., 213-734-5249) contains an exceptional mosaic of Our Lady of Czestochowa.

St. Vincent de Paul Church (621 W. Adams Blvd., 213-749-8950) was designed in 1925 in the ornate Spanish style known as

Churrigueresque. A wealthy oilman, Edward Doheny, donated the funds to pay for the church. The interior is decorated in brightly colored tiles.

Near Los Angeles

Glendale

Forest Lawn Memorial Park (1712 S. Glendale Ave., 800-204-3131) has the largest religious painting in the world. Celebrated Polish artist Jan Styka executed the epic *Golgotha* in 1951 after its conception by Ignacy Jan Paderewski, a Polish statesman. Nearly 20 million people have viewed the painting, 195 feet long and 45 feet high. Viewers are ushered into an 800-seat hall and treated to a 20-minute recorded lecture and a light beam that moves across the painting.

Mission Hills

Mission San Fernando, Rey de Espana (15151 San Fernando Mission Blvd., 818-361-0186) was one of the most prosperous missions. Founded in 1797, the mission taught Native Americans cattle ranching and farming. Here stood the largest freestanding adobe structure in California, a guest house for visitors. Its nineteen semi-circular arches give the building an air of dominance. Don't miss the great wine vat, with its ingenious system of pipes, and a clever foot-washing basin for the grape-trodding Native Americans.

Also on the grounds are a museum, a Native American craft room, and gardens with plants from the other twenty missions. Here, too, is a bronze statue of Father Serra, though he did not found this mission. He stands looking out over the valley, a walking stick in his right hand and his left arm resting on the shoulder of a Native American boy.

Adjacent to the mission is **Queen of the Angels Seminary**, where modern neophytes are trained to evangelize, as did the Franciscans long ago. Also adjoining the mission is the new **San Fernando**

Mission Cemetery, which includes a moving **Shrine to the Unborn**. A marble sculpture of Madonna and child stands nearly 6 feet high on a black base. The monument to the unborn is one of more than five hundred placed in cemeteries across the country by the Knights of Columbus. Pause and pray at the marble memorial bench, sculpted with an image of a flame at one end as a reminder of the slaughter of innocents.

San Gabriel

One of the most prosperous missions, due to its location at a crossroads between Mexico and the United States, was **Mission San Gabriel** (537 W. Mission Dr., 626-457-3035). More than two thousand Native Americans worked the mission lands and tended 40 thousand head of cattle. The mission once controlled an astounding 1.5 million acres, including the San Gabriel Valley.

Built in 1806, the church has narrow windows and Moorish features. The original walls are 4 feet thick, giving the mission a fortress-like appearance. Behind the altar are six exquisitely painted Mexican statues. The cemetery is the oldest in Los Angeles County and contains a tall cross that is a memorial to the six thousand Native Americans buried here.

On the grounds are paintings of the Stations of the Cross, probably the oldest Native American sacred pictorial art in California. The paint base was olive oil, and wildflowers provided the colors.

Santa Monica

God sheds his grace on thee from sea to shining sea. On a grassy knoll overlooking the vast Pacific Ocean is a **Statue of Saint Monica**, gazing prayerfully at Wilshire Boulevard with her back to the ocean.

Ventura

Father Serra's ninth and last mission was **Mission San Buenaventura** (225 E. Main St., 805-643-4318). An aging and ailing Serra traveled here on Easter Sunday, 1782, to officiate at the ceremonial opening. He died two years later, after having spent thirty-four years as a missionary in the New World, including fourteen in California.

The mission was one of the most durable ones. Except for one month in 1818 when pirates ravaged the area, San Buenaventura has offered uninterrupted religious services.

The mission was known for its fine gardens and vast grazing lands. The flamboyant altar and hand-hammered, copper baptismal font of the church, built in 1809, are original, as is the statue of Saint Bonaventure. The Spanish crucifix is believed to be four hundred years old.

In the museum are a wooden bell (the mission was the only one to use them), an elegant confessional carved by Native Americans, and baptismal and death records signed by Serra.

Orange County

Orange

Holy Family Cathedral (566 S. Glassell St., 714-639-2900) is worth a look, especially because of what's growing just in front of it. It's a Moreton Bay fig tree, more than 80 feet tall and 150 feet wide. Planted in 1875, it's one of four trees in Orange County to be designated as historical landmarks. The city had to rebuild the sidewalk to accommodate the root system. Homilists inside the cathedral have been known to use the tree as a symbol of the deep roots of the Catholic Church.

San Juan Capistrano

Founded in 1776 as the seventh mission, **Mission San Juan Capistrano** (Camino Capistrano and Ortega Hwy., 714-248-2048) is the most popular of the missions. It accounts for more than one-fourth of the two million people who visit the missions each year. The magnificent church, featuring an arched roof of seven domes, was the most ambitious architectural achievement of the missionaries. The gilded cock atop the soaring sandstone tower could be seen 9 miles away in Los Angeles. The church stood just six years when a great earthquake leveled it on the Feast of the Immaculate Conception in 1812. Forty Native Americans at Mass perished amid the tumbling stones.

A replica church has been built not far from the ruins. Also here is the unpretentious **Serra Chapel**, built in 1778, making it the oldest church in California. It is the only church still in existence where Serra is known to have said Mass. Worth seeing, too, are period rooms and exhibits.

The mission is famous for its celebrated swallows that congregate in the church ruins. The gentle birds are as identifiable with Capistrano as cats are with the Coliseum in Rome. Each year, late in the fall, the swallows take wing into the blue sky, and each spring, on or near Saint Joseph's Day, they return, building their nests in the peaceful eaves of the mission.

Yorba Linda

The **John Paul II Polish Center** (3999 Rose Dr., 714-996-8161), filled with artifacts related to the Polish religious heritage, was established to serve Polish Americans.

Southern California

Bakersfield

Father Francisco Garces Monument.

The **Father Francisco Garces Monument** (on a traffic circle on N. Chester Ave.) honors an eighteenth-century pioneer priest. Garces was the first White man to enter Nevada and Tulare County. Though a benefactor to Native Americans, they clubbed him to death in 1781 during an uprising at the Mission La Purisima Concepción.

Fresno

The lovely **St. Anne's Chapel** (1550 N. Fresno St., 209-488-7400), part of a diocesan conference center, is the site of weekly Masses in English and Portuguese that are broadcast to audiences worldwide. The chapel was built in 1952 for Ryan Preparatory Seminary, now closed. Carl Huneke, a San Franciscan artist who learned his craft in his native Germany, created the two dozen superb stained-glass windows.

St. Helen Church in Fresno (4870 E. Belmont Ave., 209-255-3871) boasts a triumph in glass—a brilliant rose window of the church's namesake. Carl Huneke of San Francisco, who created stained-glass windows for eighty churches in Northern California from 1942 until his death in 1972, made the window. St. Helen's began in 1955 on what had been a 10-acre pumpkin patch.

Visalia

St. Mary's Church (608 Church St., 559-734-9522) was established in 1861, when it was the only church for a vast stretch of California. Eighty-six churches and several missions trace their ancestry to it.

St. Mary's Church.

Central Coast

Carmel

The second mission founded by Serra was **Mission San Carlos Borromeo** (3080 Rio Rd., 408-624-1271). The mission, where Serra was headquartered, is the hands-down choice as the most beautiful. The waiting list for weddings is more than a year and a half.

An unknown professional stonemason from Mexico designed the sandstone church, which was completed in 1797. The church has a neoclassical facade and a square bell tower with a pyramidal roof. Over the front door is a chalkrock Virgin of Guadalupe, the oldest piece of European art in California. The statue of Mary to the left of the altar dates from the eighteenth century and may have been brought from Mexico by Father Serra.

The church deteriorated in the mid 1800s. In 1879 the writer Robert Louis Stevenson helped spur the restoration of the church when he wrote, "The United States mint can coin many millions more dollar pieces, but not a single Native American, and when the Carmel church is in the dust, not all the wealth of the states and territories can replace what has been lost."

Recreated rooms include Serra's own ascetic cell, a no-frills kitchen, and the first library in California. Serra is buried at the foot of the altar. Also laid to rest here was his efficient successor, Fr. Fermin Lasuen.

Jolon

In the aptly named Valley of the Oaks, Father Serra celebrated Mass on July 14, 1771, near a small stream. With him were several companions and one Native American. That day he established his third mission, **San Antonio de Padua** (1 Mission Creek Rd., 408-385-4478). The mission became known for its cattle, flour, and fine horses. The clever priests initiated a remarkable system of irrigation. They dammed the river 3 miles above the mission, and pipes carried the water to the buildings and fields.

The best restored of all the missions, San Antonio looks as it did in its heyday. Inside the picturesque church, completed in 1813, is the same statue of Saint Anthony before which the Native Americans prayed more than two hundred years ago. A bell at the mission, rung by Serra, called Native Americans to the site the day the mission was founded.

Lompoc

A furious Native American revolt in 1823 jolted **Mission La Purisima Concepción** (2295 Purisima Rd., 805-733-3713). The Native Americans held the mission for more than a month. When the mission was retaken, at least seven of the Native American leaders were executed. Once prosperous, the mission never recovered.

Founded on the Feast of the Immaculate Conception in 1787 as the eleventh mission, La Purisima was demolished by an earthquake in 1812 and doggedly rebuilt the next year. The mission has been faithfully recreated. The gracious church features a long, gabled roof. The nearby state historical park has exact copies of carved mission furniture.

San Juan Bautista

Mission San Juan Bautista (408 S. 2nd St., 408-623-2127) is recognizable to any film buff. Kim Novak fell for James Stewart in Hitchcock's *Vertigo* at the mission's quirky bell tower. Actually, the studio built the tower seen in the film, based on the mission's tower, and superimposed it onto the mission.

Founded in 1797, San Juan Bautista was noted for its music. The Franciscans organized Native American boy choirs. The sheet music can be found in the museum, along with a rare barrel organ. Turning the handle of the organ produced an odd but pleasing sound. Supposedly, marauding Tulares Native Americans were halted in their tracks by the unusual music, thus saving the mission.

The mission was blessed with the presence of Father de la Cuesta, a first-rate scientist and linguist who spoke twelve Native American dialects. His gentle manner endeared him to the Native Americans. Terribly crippled by arthritis in his later years, he fulfilled his pastoral duties with the aid of loyal Native Americans who carried him from pueblo to village in a rawhide litter slung between two poles.

The church, built in 1812, was a miracle of construction. Its great arch, flanked by two lower naves, rose to a height of 55 feet. A central nave with two ambulatories is common in European churches but was rare in the mission world, which depended on baked adobe brick and strong timbers lashed with rawhide. The priests later had to reinforce the roof by bricking up five of the arches.

San Luis Obispo

Founded in 1772, **Mission San Luis Obispo** (751 Palm St., 805-781-8220) was the fifth of Father Serra's missions. The expedition's diarist, Fr. Juan Crespi, described the region as a broad valley where the ground was literally plowed up by bears, hence the area became known as the Valley of the Bears. Those same bears proved to be crucial. On the verge of starvation that year, the mission was saved by a productive bear hunt.

The mission ministered to the Chumashes, experts in basket-making and building canoes. Another Native American tribe, envious of the mission's prosperity, set fire to the church's thatched roof with flaming arrows. The mission resorted to red roof tiles, which became a standard feature of the missions.

Fr. Luis Martinez, a burly, two-fisted man of great generosity and eccentric humor, expertly and justly ran the mission for thirty-four years. Martinez withstood every challenge. When the feared pirate Bouchard terrorized the California coast in 1818, Martinez formed a band of warriors to keep the pirate at bay.

The altar of the church has four wooden statues clustered about the central carved figure of Saint Louis, bishop of Toulouse. The original copper baptismal font has a hinged cover and a wooden pedestal decorated with colorful, childlike Native American paintings.

A museum offers a number of interesting exhibits, including the original altar. Also on display is an extensive picture collection that details mission life.

San Miguel

Though located adjacent to busy Highway 101, **Mission San**

Miguel Arcangel (775 Mission St., 805-467-3256) is one of the lesser known missions. Yet it offers the most authentic experience. The church, completed in 1821, is the only one whose paintings and decorative elements have never been retouched by subsequent artists. The art, done with colors drawn from flowers, is amazingly complex. Native Americans did the painting following the design of a Spanish artist. The six-foot statue of Saint Michael behind the altar is brilliantly carved. Other highlights are a lovely bell-canopied pulpit, statues of Saint Anthony and Saint Francis, and an interesting confessional. With arches of different types and sizes, the vaulted corridors of the outbuildings are surreal.

The mission, the sixteenth, began in 1797 and suffered one tragedy after the next. Two priests went insane, and another died because of food poisoning, perhaps intentional. In the mid nineteenth century, after the last priest had left the mission, a notorious mass murder occurred on the mission grounds. A man named William Reed lived with his family in one of the buildings. While providing hospitality to five discharged U.S. soldiers, he made the mistake of bragging about his wealth. The soldiers left but returned later that night. Ten people, the entire Reed family and several others, were slaughtered.

Santa Barbara

Mission Santa Barbara (2201 Laguna St., 805-682-4713), the tenth mission, was the first founded by Fr. Fermin Lasuen, Serra's successor. Begun on Saint Barbara's feast on December 4, 1786, it is the only mission that has been continuously occupied from its founding to the present. The second most visited mission in the chain, it possesses a wealth of historical material on Father Serra, and it is the headquarters of those advocating his sainthood.

Santa Barbara is known as the "Queen of the Missions." Its marvelous stone church, built in 1820, stands on a hill overlooking the town. The twin-towered, tile-roofed church is one of the best-preserved mission churches. The interior is a gracious rectangle broken with two side altars and two chapels in the rear. In the plaza is a lovely octagonal fountain.

The missionaries planted orange and olive trees and built a dam two miles upstream and then an aqueduct to carry water to its groves. A museum displays Native American artifacts, tools, and relics.

Soledad

Mission Soledad (36641 Ft. Army Rd., 805-686-1211), the thirteenth mission, began inauspiciously in 1791, failed to attract many converts, and ended tragically. The mission was named, appropriately enough as it turned out, in honor of Our Lady of Solitude. The idea may have come from an expedition that stopped here in 1769. A priest noted that the spot was a good place for a mission. A Native American visiting the camp then uttered a word that sounded like *soledad,* Spanish for loneliness.

No more than seven hundred Native Americans were ever associated with Soledad. Sickness was rampant, and food was scarce. In 1835 the emaciated body of Fr. Vicente de Sarria, who apparently starved to death, was found near the altar. Loyal Native Americans carried his body over the hills for burial at Mission San Antonio, leaving behind a deserted mission.

Solvang

Disasters and misfortunes plagued **Mission Santa Ines** (1760 Mission Dr., 805-688-4815). Founded as the nineteenth mission in 1804, Santa Ines suffered an earthquake in 1812 and an attack by rebel Native Americans in 1821.

Notwithstanding its sorry history, the mission has a raw, unpretentious beauty. The church has a beautiful altar screen with a wonderful carved figure of Saint Agnes gazing down on the altar from a shell-like niche. The short passage from the altar to the sacristy offers bright, joyful Native American decoctions. The ceiling beams display fine examples of Native American painting.

San Francisco

The **Convent of Sacred Heart High School** (2222 Broadway, 415-563-2900) was originally the grand private mansion of James Leary Flood. Built in 1913 with nearly an unlimited budget, the residence was more on the scale of a great hotel. Constructed with pink Tennessee marble, the mansion features a fabulous facade whose intricate stonework is unmatched in the city. The mammoth, 140-foot-long entrance hall is paved with marble and ends in a bay window that overlooks the Golden Gate.

Next door to the convent is the **School of the Sacred Heart** (2200 Broadway), built for Joseph Donohoe Grant, the heir to a dry-goods fortune. The red brick and limestone home became the property of the sisters in 1948.

A Dominican described **St. Dominic's Church** (2390 Bush St., 415-567-7824) as "a sermon in stone" when it was being built in 1926. The English Gothic church is one of the city's most beautiful.

The church decorations were an international effort. The high altar was carved of botticino marble in Italy and shipped to the United States in seventy-six crates. The front of the altar carries a relief carving of Fra Angelico's famous painting of Saint Dominic at the foot of the Cross. A woodcarving studio in Oberammergau, Germany, carved the oak altars and confessionals. An accomplished Belgian artist designed the statues of the Blessed Mother and Saint Rose of Lima in the Lady Chapel, the angels under the roof beam, the numerous saints around the sanctuary, and Saints Francis and Dominic at the main interior doors.

The church's **Shrine to Saint Jude Thaddeus**, begun in 1935, is a popular draw for the devout. Seven novenas are held each year; the most popular, in October, ends on the feast of Saint Jude.

After the 1989 earthquake damaged the church, the parish turned to a medieval concept to make it safe. Nearly $7 million was raised from far and wide to construct nine flying buttresses that rise from concrete piers deep underground and soar to connect at a beam that girdles the church at the roofline.

The best California garden in Japantown surrounds **St. Francis Xavier Church** (1801 Octavia St., 415-567-9855) on three sides. The neatly trimmed shrubbery and lone pine tree offer a peaceful setting for quiet prayer. Completed in 1939, the modest stucco church with a green tile roof still serves Japanese Americans. Its stained-glass windows depict Saint Francis Xavier and other missionaries to Asia. The church, true to its purpose, includes a Japanese-style gatelike entrance porch and a square tower with a pagoda roof topped by a wrought-iron cross. During World War II the pastor, true to his purpose, accompanied his parishioners into detention camps.

The **Cathedral of St. Mary of the Assumption** (1111 Gough St., 415-567-2020) was the first cathedral built after the liturgical reforms of Vatican II. The church proves that splendid structures belong to modern times as well as ancient days. The gleaming white cathedral rises from a square base to become an equal-armed Greek cross topped by a thin silver cross. The interior is graced with beautiful sculptures of the Blessed Lady by Enrico Manfrini of Milan. Above the simple but luxurious stone altar is a gold cross. The cathedral's glory is its *baldachino,* silver threads of thin sparkling rods that glisten like heavenly rain above the altar.

Mission Dolores (320 Dolores St., 415-621-8203) is San Francisco's oldest intact building and perhaps its greatest treasure. The adobe church, completed in 1791, was built so solidly that it withstood the mighty 1906 earthquake. The church's dedication was marked with a joyous parade and fiesta culminating with fireworks and the boom of cannons. The three original bronze bells carried overland from Mexico in the 1820s still hang in their niches. Fr. Francisco Palou, who is buried in the adjacent cemetery, designed the mission.

The stunning ceiling of the chapel is done in earth tones in a chevronlike design. It is patterned after the basket designs of the extinct Costanoan people—the only remaining artwork connected to them. The hand-carved altars and statues came from Mexico in 1780.

The mission, the sixth of the twenty-one, was founded in 1776. It was one of the least successful of the missions. The climate was not favorable to either agriculture or the health of the Native Americans who lived here.

The cemetery includes an unusual monument to Charles Cora, who hanged himself while awaiting trial by a vigilante's committee in 1856. A large brown sandstone marker is decorated with firemen's helmets and upside-down torches.

Sts. Peter and Paul Church (666 Filbert St., 415-421-0809), the "Italian cathedral" of San Francisco, is simply spectacular. Testament to its grandeur is its place in Hollywood lore. When it was being built in 1922, the legendary filmmaker Cecil B. DeMille showed up to film its construction for a scene in the silent movie classic *The Ten Commandments.* The church's twin spires, illuminated at night, rise with quiet dignity over the neighborhood. The church was founded as San Francisco's Italian-language parish, and at its dedication it was saluted as "a monument which glorifies God and reflects honor upon our city, our colony and our far away Italy."

The interior, crowded with statues and images, calls to mind churches in Italy. The altar area is a busy wonder, an abundance of extravagant marble spires and life-size angels.

The 130-foot high **Mount Davidson Cross** that towers over the city has withstood a flurry of litigation. Atheists opposing the city landmark went to court over it, and the courts ruled in 1996 that city ownership of the structure violates the constitution's ban on government preference in religion. The latest plan was for the city to preserve the cross by selling the public land to the highest bidder.

The **National Shrine of St. Francis of Assisi** (Vallejo St. and Columbus Ave.) was the site of the city's first parish, founded in 1849 after gold was discovered near Sacramento. The state's first ordination of a priest took place at the original church. The current church, built in 1860, was closed in 1994 because of stricter building codes in the wake of the 1989 earthquake. It was reopened as a shrine in 1998.

Old St. Mary's Cathedral (660 California St., 415-288-3800) has survived numerous earthquakes and fires as well as neighborhood changes since it was dedicated in 1854. Its red bricks and ironwork were shipped around Cape Horn. Originally named the Cathedral of St. Mary of the Immaculate Conception, it was the first U.S. church so named, as its plans were drawn up just weeks after Pope Pius IX proclaimed the dogma of the Immaculate Conception in 1854.

Two large clocks in the church's 90-foot-high Gothic tower were the community timepieces for early San Franciscans. Beneath one of the clocks, meant as a caution to revelers at nearby night spots, is the inscription, "Son, observe the time and fly from evil."

During World War II its basement hosted innumerable social affairs for members of the armed forces. An estimated 450 thousand men and women in uniform passed through the basement doors.

Across from the Dolores Mission was the site of the first girls' school in San Francisco. **Old Notre Dame School** (347 Dolores St.), a high school, was founded in 1868. Also here was the Convent of the Sisters of Notre Dame de Namur. Both closed in 1981. The original building was dynamited in 1906 to save the Dolores Mission from the fires spreading in the wake of the great earthquake. The present mansard-roofed building was constructed the following year on the old foundation.

Irish eyes smile when beholding **St. Patrick Church** (756 Mission St., 415-421-3730), built to be the church of the Irish on the West Coast. Founded in 1851 as one of the city's first churches, St. Patrick's was rebuilt following the earthquake of 1906. Msgr. John Rogers, the pastor who was a native of Ireland, saw to it that the Irish national colors—green, white, and gold—appeared throughout the church in the marble work. The clerestory windows portray the pre-Christian beliefs and traditions of the Irish. Four stained-glass windows depict the life of Saint Patrick. Other windows show the country's patron saints, seen in alphabetical order by county. The main altar carries the coat of arms of the four provinces of Ireland. The artistry throughout the church is outstanding.

St. Paul's Church (221 Valley St., 415-648-7538) features exquisite stained-glass windows and interior painting. The church was transformed into St. Katherine's convent for the movie *Sister Act* starring Whoopi Goldberg.

Near San Francisco

Fremont

Mission San José (43300 Mission Blvd., 510-657-1797) became the fourteenth California mission when it was founded in 1797. The mission's best-known figure by far is Fr. Narciso Duran, an accomplished musician who arrived in 1806. He began a Native American orchestra with instruments the musicians made themselves.

During the Gold Rush the mission, already declining, was converted into a trading post for miners. A powerful earthquake in 1868 destroyed the mission buildings. A replica was constructed in 1985. A museum displays artifacts of the mission era.

Oakland

Sacred Heart Church (4025 Martin Luther King Jr. Way, 510-655-9209) is notable for the spirited effort it took to erect it in 1997. The 1989 earthquake had severely damaged the previous church. Parishioners, many elderly and not affluent, dug deep to pay the $1.4 million tab. With its stucco walls, the church calls to mind a California mission. The roof is topped by a copper cross salvaged from the old church.

San José

St. Joseph Cathedral (80 S. Market St., 408-283-8100) dates from 1803 when a small adobe church was erected, making it the first parish in California. The current church is the fifth one to be built; earthquakes and fire claimed the others. Its Odell Organ is one of only four of its kind in the United States. A tracker organ, it operates mechanically without the aid of electricity. The organ was restored and reinstalled when the cathedral underwent a $17 million renovation in 1990.

San Rafael

Mission San Rafael Arcangel (1104 5th Ave., 415-454-8141), the twentieth mission, began as a hospital auxiliary for Mission Dolores in 1817. Eventually, Native Americans sickened by European diseases also were taken here from other missions. The mission's Fr. Luis Gil was the only Franciscan in California who had medical training.

The modest mission deteriorated quickly after 1840, and tiles and bells, orchards and bushes vanished until a lone pear tree remained. Today a replica church building stands here.

Santa Clara

Father Serra founded **Mission Santa Clara** (on the campus of Santa Clara University, 408-554-4023), the eighth mission, only three months before he died in 1777. Heavy rains in 1779 forced the mission to move to its current site from its original site in what became San José. The mission was withering away under Mexican secularization in 1851 when it was assigned to the care of the Jesuits. Santa Clara University dates from that year.

Fr. José Viader, one of the legendary mission priests, lived at Mission Santa Clara. A rough-and-tumble man who was also kind and just, Viader was once attacked by three pagan Native Americans on his way back from a sick call. The priest fought them off. The next day the brawniest of the three Native Americans appeared at the mission and asked to be baptized. He was given the name Marcelo and some land of his own. Marcelo lived to be one hundred years old, and his picture can be seen at the museum.

In front of the restored church is the Serra Cross, made of old mission rafters. Behind a small glass pane are fragments of the original mission cross. The site is rich in relics and archival materials, consisting of paintings, furniture, vestments, and a crucifix that belonged to the saintly Fr. Magin Catala of the mission.

Santa Cruz

Mission Santa Cruz (126 High St., 408-426-5686), the twelfth mission, was founded in 1791. The mission counted only five hundred converts within five years and less than half that remained by 1800. The Native Americans were content with hunting and fishing and had little use for the mission. A town that was founded nearby was also problematic. The settlers and Native Americans fought and roistered, and the Spanish men pursued the Native American women. The priests angered the Native Americans by punishing only the women.

Little is left of the twenty original buildings. The present brick church, completed in 1891, was built thanks to a woman, lame from a childhood injury, who was cured at Lourdes. A reconstruction of an adobe church built in 1794 is nearby.

Sonoma

Mission San Francisco Solano (100 E. Spain St., 707-938-1519) was the twenty-first and final mission of California. Founded in 1823, the mission was plagued by the cruel leadership of Fr. José Altimira, who flogged the Native Americans for little reason and was repaid in kind with hatred, theft, and desertion.

The mission was the site of the American revolt against Mexican authority in 1846. California was proclaimed an independent republic, and the California Bear Flag was first raised within the shadow of the mission. Within a month, events elsewhere brought California under U.S. control. The simple adobe mission church has been beautifully restored.

Northern California

Mariposa

A Gold Rush church is **St. Joseph** (Bullion St., 209-966-2522). The owners of the Mariposa Mine, which was operating directly beneath the church, donated the land. Dedicated in 1863, the church is still in use today. Its elegant design and typical New England steeple makes it one of the area's most photographed landmarks.

Sacramento

The **Abbey of New Clairvaux** (Seventh and C streets, Vina, 916-839-2161) is a Trappist monastery founded by the monks from Gethsemani, Kentucky, where Thomas Merton lived. In fact, Merton's spiritual director helped establish the abbey in 1955.

Located in the fertile valley of the Sacramento River, the abbey was once the largest winery in the country. The monks continue to put the land to good use. The income from the prune and walnut orchards is their main source of support.

The abbey is arranged like a small village with open, connecting cloisters. A creek flows through the abbey's 600 acres, and a mile away is the Sacramento River.

Patrick Manogue, the first bishop of Sacramento, is probably the subject of more stories than any other bishop or priest in California. He built the elegant **Cathedral of the Blessed Sacrament** (1017 11th St., 916-444-3071), patterned after a Paris church, the L'eglise de Sainte Trinité.

Born in Kilkenny County, Ireland, in 1832, he lost both of his parents to sickness. In 1848 he came to the United States, attended college, and then quit school to raise money to bring his brothers and sisters over. Manogue found work as a miner in California. Six feet three inches, powerfully built, and trusted by his fellow miners, he settled innumerable disputes, many of which might have turned violent.

Determined to be a priest, he saved his wages and financed his education at a distinguished seminary in Paris. After ordination he was assigned to Virginia City, Nevada, a rough frontier town. Manogue was up to the task. Once, discovering that one of his parishioners was dying, he rode on horse at night to a lonely cabin. When he arrived, the woman's husband stormed out the door, waving a pistol and threatening to shoot him if he came any nearer. Manogue leveled him with one punch. He prayed with the woman. As he left, he returned the gun to the husband, who was sitting quietly on the porch.

Manogue became bishop of Sacramento in 1886, and the money used to build the cathedral came from four men who made their fortune from the Comstock silver lode in Virginia City. One of them was John Mackay, an ordinary miner who became the richest man in the world but never forgot his old miner friend. In 1895 Manogue died in the cathedral he built.

Yosemite National Park

Postcard-pretty **Our Lady of the Snows** (209-372-4729), an interdenominational chapel, graces the wilderness of Yosemite Valley at Yosemite National Park.

NEVADA

Las Vegas

Sin City's most popular spiritual destination is **Guardian Angel Cathedral** (336 Cathedral Way, 702-735-5241), known as the "cathedral on the strip." More than eight thousand worshipers, most of them tourists, crowd into this modern church every weekend. Redefining the concept of the Saturday evening Mass, the 2:30 P.M. Saturday afternoon Mass draws the most worshipers.

Everything in Las Vegas is on a grand scale, and so is the cathedral. The sanctuary has a 70-foot-tall painting of the risen Christ. The facade features a 23-foot-high mosaic mural of a guardian angel. The late Paul R. Williams, a distinguished African-American architect who studied with Frank Lloyd Wright, designed the church, built in 1963. He angled the interior's ceiling to form angel wings.

One of the church's stained-glass windows, titled *The Mask of Reality,* depicts the Hilton, Stardust, Desert Inn, Sands, and Landmark hotels. The casinos signify recreation. Also represented in the window are science, industry, agriculture, and culture.

Isabel Piczek designed *The Mask of Reality,* and her sister Edith created the mural of the guardian angel. The Hungarian-born sisters were the first women—as well as the first teenagers—to work inside the Vatican. In 1954 they won a competition to paint a fresco mural in the Pontifical Biblical Institute. Ordered by communist authorities to study art in Moscow after winning the competition, they fled Hungary and made their way to Rome. Today the sisters work together in Los Angeles. Their sacred art is displayed in about five hundred buildings in seven countries.

Guardian Angel collects nearly $700 in casino chips every weekend. They are cashed in at Caesar's Palace. (Give to Caesar what is Caesar's!) The priest assigned this duty is known, of course, as the chip-monk.

A block from the MGM Grand, Excalibur, and Tropicana, the **Shrine of the Most Holy Redeemer** (55 E. Reno Ave., 702-891-8600) was built in 1992 to serve the millions of Las Vegas tourists. Donations from MGM Grand, Caesar's World, and Palace Station helped to build the shrine. The 2,200-seat church has bronze statues of the Nativity, the Last Supper, and the Crucifixion.

Reno

The contemporary **St. Thérèse, Church of the Little Flower** (875 E. Plumb Lane, 702-322-2255) hosts a popular devotion to Saint Jude.

Near Reno

Virginia City

St. Mary in the Mountain (Taylor and E Streets, 702-847-9099) owes its existence to a mine owner's promise. A fire in 1875 was raging out of control when John Mackay, one of the richest men in the world, vowed to rebuild the church if parishioners saved his mine instead. They did, and he did. The Gothic-revival structure has a bell in its belfry that survived the conflagration.

UTAH

Northern Utah

Hunstville

Trappist monks from Gethsemani in Kentucky began the **Abbey of Our Lady of the Holy Trinity** (1250 S. 9500 East, 801-745-3784) in 1947. The abbey, set in a gentle plain ringed by mountains, was constructed of interconnected Quonset-type buildings. The monks offer honey, cheese, and stone-ground flour for sale. The retreat house, open to adult men, has room for twelve.

Salt Lake City

The superb **Cathedral of the Madeleine** (331 E. S. Temple St., 801-328-8941) was built in 1909 with funds donated by wealthy Catholic mining families. Over the main entrance are impressive carvings of Christ and the twelve apostles. The Gothic Revival–style interior is adorned with excellent paintings and carvings. The church's intricate stained-glass windows were made in Munich.

Near Salt Lake City

Park City

Devastating fires mark the history of **St. Mary of the Assumption Church** (121 Park Ave., 801-649-9676). The first church burned down in 1884. The successor survived the fire in 1898 that destroyed much of the city but was severely damaged by a fire in 1950 that began when the incense burner was emptied into a wastebasket. The lovely stone church was carefully restored.

Central Utah

Price

Notre Dame de Lourdes Church (200 N. Carbon Ave., 801-637-1846) is an interesting prairie-style building with a peaked roof. Fr. Alfredo Giovannoni, who ministered mostly to Italians, built the church in 1923, but the church's name came about because French and French Basques contributed funds.

St. Mary's of the Assumption Church in Park City (121 Park Ave., 801-649-9676) was built in 1884 for the Irish miners who flocked here after silver was discovered.

ALASKA

Anchorage

Alaska has snow, ice, and a strong Catholic presence. Anchor down in Anchorage, come in from the cold, and visit **Holy Family Cathedral** (818 W. Fifth Ave., 907-276-3455). The first church at this site was moved from the town of Knik in the 1920s using horse and sleigh. Pope John Paul II visited the cathedral in 1981.

Dillingham

Holy Rosary Church (907-842-5581), one of the nation's most remote parishes, serves twenty small, priestless communities in the Alaskan "bush." The parish is one of many rural parishes financially assisted by the Chicago-based Catholic Church Extension Society, founded in 1905. The society was instrumental in fueling the growth of the Church in areas with few Catholics, especially in the South and the West. It once funded three chapel cars, "churches on wheels," that rode the rails from town to town.

Fairbanks

Immaculate Conception Church (115 N. Cushman St., 907-452-3533) originally stood on the opposite side of the Chena River. In 1911 Fr. Francis Moore decided the church should be closer to the hospital on the north side of the river. When the river froze over, parishioners removed the church from its foundation and rolled it across the ice on logs pulled by horses. Notable in the church are the stained-glass windows and pressed-tin ceiling.

Juneau

The rugged beauty of the Alaskan wilderness surrounds the **Shrine of St. Thérèse** (21425 Glacier Hwy., north of Juneau, 907-789-9815), located on a tiny island just offshore. The quaint stone chapel and retreat house are reached from the mainland by a 400-foot causeway. As literature from the shrine says, many come here "to let the majesty of God and the nature he created wash over them like a healing balm."

Construction of the shrine began in 1933 under Jesuit Bishop Crimont, who was from St. Thérèse's native France and knew members of her family. He died in 1945 and is buried in the crypt of the chapel.

The $3,000 construction cost was raised through appeal letters from the editor of the *Alaska Catholic* newspaper. Most donations were 25 cents or a dollar. A post office was set up on Crow Island (later renamed Shrine Island) for eight years, and the requests for financial help bore the cancellation stamp of St. Thérèse, Alaska.

Yukon Territory

Tens of thousands swarmed to **Dawson** in 1897 when gold was discovered. There to help them was the "Saint of Dawson," Jesuit Fr. William Judge, one of the true heroes of his time.

Almost overnight Dawson became a tent city as prospectors poured in. Sanitation was poor. Miners ran out of money, food, and hope. A Baltimore native, Judge built **St. Mary's Church** and hospital for them and tended to their physical needs as much as their spiritual wants. Writer Jack London was one of many patients treated for scurvy at the hospital. Judge worked nonstop, even running up stairs to save time. He rebuilt the church after it burned down. An exhausted Judge dropped dead from pneumonia at the age of forty-nine in 1899. Every business shut down until after his funeral.

The second St. Mary's burned down, too, but a new St. Mary's is going strong. A monument marks Judge's grave at the north end of town, near the spot of the original church. The hospital is long gone, but in town is the **Father Judge Memorial Medical Clinic**.

HAWAII

Oahu

Following the arrival of Protestant missionaries, French priests disembarked in Honolulu in 1827. Queen Kaahumanu, who had been converted by the Congregationalists, was not pleased. For a decade Catholic priests and converts were persecuted. The turning point came when a young convert was tied to a tree and scourged. The incident convinced people of goodwill to come together to put a stop to the persecution.

The first church built by the French missionaries was the **Cathedral of Our Lady of Peace** in Honolulu (1184 Bishop St., 808-536-7036). The church, made of native coral blocks, dates from 1843. The island's first pipe organ played here in 1846. Father Damien, the leper priest, was ordained in 1864 in the church. No pews were installed until late in the nineteenth century as worshipers brought grass mats on which to kneel.

In the courtyard is a gold-leaf painted statue of Our Lady of Peace, erected in 1893, that is a copy of a more ancient image venerated in France. Nearby is the stump of the first non-native tree planted in Hawaii. In the 1820s the French priests planted several seeds of mesquite, brought from the king's garden in Paris. Seeds from the single *kiawe,* as the tree is called in Hawaiian, spread rapidly throughout the islands.

Waikiki Beach is a great place for a tan—and a prayer. Directly across from the beach is **St. Augustine Church** (130 Ohua Ave., 808-923-7024), a modern building surrounded by a sea of high rises. Stroll inside for a break from the sun and bask in the serene light that filters gently through the stained-glass windows.

A controversial **Sculpture of Father Damien** stands on Beretanai Street close to the State Capitol in Honolulu. The bronze statue, dedicated in 1969, was based on a photo of the priest taken shortly before he died of Hansen's disease, and his features are bloated.

Hawaii

A hidden gem is **St. Benedict's Painted Church** in Honaunau (808-328-2227). Its Gothic belfry makes the small church look like a miniature castle. But the real treasures are inside. The walls show biblical scenes, and the masterful painted illusion behind the altar makes it seem you are in the famous Spanish cathedral in Burgos. The painter was the pastor, Fr. John Berchman Velghe. A Belgian, Velghe used ordinary house paint for the church. He was pastor from 1899 to 1904. His artistry is also found in many churches in Polynesia.

The oldest Catholic church on Hawaii is **St. Michael the Archangel** in Holualoa (75 5769 Alii Dr., Kailua-Kona). The church began as a grass chapel after Picpus priests established a mission in 1839. The current church, built in 1850, was restored in 1935. The Coral Grotto was built over a defunct water well in 1940. Parishioners and orphans cared for by a local priest dived off the Kona coast to retrieve the 2,500 pieces of coral for the grotto.

Capped by a blue tin roof, **St. Peter's Chapel** in Kona is affectionately known as the Little Blue Church. The interior has starkly plain bare wooden walls and a simple crucifix. The only splash of color comes from the fresh flowers inevitably on the altar. Behind the blue church are the blue waters of the ocean. Tidal waves twice pushed the church off its foundation; parishioners determinedly moved it back.

Star of the Sea Church in Kalapana, a small town south of Hilo on Hawaii, is known as the Painted Church. In the 1920s Fr. Evarist Gielen of Belgium, working mostly at night by oil lamp, painted vividly colored murals on the church ceiling. Using bright blues, oranges, and purples, he depicted Christ, the angel Gabriel, and scenes from the Nativity and interspersed a host of colorful symbols.

Kauai

The eight-sided **St. Sylvester Church** in Kilauea (808-822-4804) was constructed of lava and wood. A stream runs by the church, which is nearly engulfed by lobster claw plants, crotons, and mango and avocado trees.

Maui

Tiny **St. Gabriel's Church** in Keanae (655 Haiku Rd., 808-248-8369) is a beautiful red-and-white structure.

Holy Ghost Church in Kula (9 Lawler Rd., 808-878-1091) takes its octagonal shape from legend and the faith of a Portuguese queen. In the fifteenth century a withering drought devastated Portugal. Queen Isabella offered her eight-sided crown in prayer to the Holy Ghost in return for an end to the drought. When the rains came, she gave her crown to the Catholic Church in Lisbon. Holy Ghost Church serves Portuguese, and each year the parish holds a free luau on Pentecost Sunday to commemorate the miracle. A girl from the parish is chosen to portray Queen Isabella in a procession around the church grounds. The church keeps a replica of the crown.

An inspiring sculpture of Father Damien is at **Holy Rosary Church** in Paia (954 Baldwin Ave., 808-579-9551). The heroic priest stands with a leper, whose face conveys suffering but also dignity and hope.

Hawaii is awash with tiny chapels and shrines, like the **Miracle of Fatima Shrine** in Wailua. Its name relates to its providential founding. A freak storm in the 1860s washed up just enough coral onto Wailua Beach to construct a chapel.

Molokai

Fr. Damien, the leper priest who arrived on the island in 1873, put together **St. Philomena Church** in Kalawao on Molokai that year. The church was actually built in Honolulu by another priest and shipped in small pieces to Molokai. Always acutely aware of the needs of those with leprosy, Father Damien cut squares in the floor through which worshipers could spit. Those with severe leprosy could not control their mouths and were ashamed to soil the church floor.

Born in Belgium in 1840, Father Damien came to Hawaii as a last-minute replacement for his brother-priest, who had become ill. After ministering on Hawaii for eight years, he bravely volunteered his services at the leper colony. Fearful of the spread of the disease, King Kamehameha V established the colony in 1865 on the Makanalua peninsula, the most remote part of his kingdom. Banished were those with leprosy and even those with a skin disease or bad sunburn who were mistaken for having leprosy. They were rounded up, transported on a boat while locked in a cage, and then tossed overboard near the shore.

Before Father Damien arrived, the eight hundred residents of the colony lived under unspeakable conditions, in the most primitive huts or simply on the beach. Many died of starvation. Hungry wild dogs and pigs prowled the shallow graves of the burying ground.

One of the first residents visited by Father Damien lay on a mat soaked with his own waste. The man was near death, and Father Damien gave him the last rites. To his horror, when he went to anoint the man's paralyzed legs, he discovered that the man's legs moved. An army of worms were chewing away his feet.

Father Damien, bolstered by the courage of his convictions, saw those with leprosy as children of God. He built them shelters, tended to their wounds, blessed and embraced them. He restored their dignity. He tirelessly fought government and church authorities for more aid. He was so relentless in his appeals that the government ordered him not to travel anywhere else on Molokai.

Father Damien contracted leprosy and died at the age of forty-nine in 1889. Inspired by his example, Franciscan sisters and others had come to the colony to carry on his work.

Today leprosy, now called Hansen's disease, is noncontagious. Those with the disease, thanks to sulfa drugs, can lead close to normal lives.

The cemetery that adjoins St. Philomena's has a monument to Father Damien that marks his original burial spot; his remains were returned to Belgium in 1936.

Molokai has two other churches built by Father Damien. Built in 1876, **St. Joseph Church** in Kamalo (808-553-5220) is a compact, white, wood-frame structure. Its small wooden altar is usually adorned with a jar of flowers. A picture of Father Damien decorates a wall, and outside is a black metal sculpture of him.

Our Lady of Sorrows Church in Kalua'aha has a pretty pen-and-ink drawing of the Stations of the Cross. Constructed in 1874 by Father Damien, the church was rebuilt in 1966. A wooden statue of the priest is on the grounds.

BIBLIOGRAPHY

Armstrong, Cara, Foster Armstrong, and Richard Klein. *A Guide to Cleveland's Sacred Land-marks.* Kent, Ohio: Kent State University Press, 1992.

Avella, Steven, Edward Kantowicz, and Ellen Skerrett. *Catholicism, Chicago Style.* Chicago: Loyola University Press, 1993.

Bearse, Ray, ed. *Maine: A Guide to the Vacation State.* Boston: Houghton, Mifflin Co., 1969.

Benton, Christine. *Country Roads and Scenic Drives in the Middle Atlantic States.* Chicago: Contemporary Books, 1979.

Bisignani, J. D. *Hawaii Handbook.* Chico, Calif.: Moon Publications, 1995.

Carper, Alison. "Was Pierre Toussaint a Saint?" *Catholic Digest* (June 1991): 53.

Colbert, Judy. *Maryland and Delaware Off the Beaten Path.* Old Saybrook, Conn.: Globe Pequot Press, 1990.

Copp, Jay. "Chicago Remembers Mother Cabrini." *St. Anthony Messenger* (July 1995): 28.

———. "Ethnic Clashes in U.S. Led to Polish National Catholic Church." *Catholic Heritage* (July/August 1997): 14.

———. "Inspired by a Martyr." *Catholic Digest* (March 1995): 103.

———. "Where Prayer Prevails." *Catholic Digest* (March 1996): 64.

Curtis, Wayne. *Maine Off the Beaten Path.* Old Saybrook, Conn.: Globe Pequot Press, 1992.

Davenport, Don. *Country Roads of Wisconsin.* Oaks, Pa.: Country Roads Press, 1996.

Deedy, John. "The Legacy of Dorothy Day." *Catholic Digest* (February 1990): 90.

DeLano, Patti, and Cathy Johnson. *Kansas Off the Beaten Path.* Old Saybrook, Conn.: Globe Pequot Press, 1996.

Delehanty, Randolph. *The Ultimate Guide to San Francisco.* San Francisco: Chronicle Books, 1989.

Demeter, Richard. *Irish America: The Historical Travel Guide.* Pasadena, Calif.: Cranford Press, 1995.

Dunn, Jerry Camarillo Jr. *The Smithsonian Guide to Historic America: The Rocky Mountain States.* New York: Stewart, Tabori and Chang, 1989.

Dunn, Jerry Camarillo Jr., Alice Gordon, and Mel White. *The Smithsonian Guide to Historic America: Texas and the Arkansas River Valley.* New York: Stewart, Tabori and Chang, 1990.

Durham, Michael. *The Smithsonian Guide to Historic America: The Desert States.* New York: Stewart, Tabori and Chang, 1990.

———. *The Smithsonian Guide to Historic America: The Mid-Atlantic States.* New York: Stewart, Tabori and Chang, 1989.

DuRocher, Julie Dale. "Our Lady of the Battle of New Orleans." *Catholic Digest* (January 1991): 70.

Erickson, Lori. *Iowa Off the Beaten Path.* Old Saybrook, Conn.: Globe Pequot Press, 1993.

Fanselow, Julie. *Idaho Off the Beaten Path.* Old Saybrook, Conn.: Globe Pequot Press, 1995.

Fifield, Barringer. *Seeing Pittsburgh.* Pittsburgh: University of Pittsburgh, 1996.

Freely, John. *Blue Guide: Boston and Cambridge.* New York: W. W. Norton and Company, 1994.

Friedman, Ralph. *In Search of Western Oregon.* Caldwell, Idaho: Caxton Printers, 1990.

Galazka, Jacek, and Albert Juszczak. *Polish Heritage Travel Guide to USA and Canada.* Cornwall Bridge, Conn.: Polish Heritage Publications, 1992.

Gerow, Rev. Richard Oliver. *Catholicity in Mississippi.* Natchez, Miss.: Hope Haven Press, 1939.

Giglio, Msgr. Charles, ed. *Building God's Kingdom: A History of the Diocese of Camden.* Palmyra, N.J.: DeVece and Shaffer Inc., 1987.

Gutek, Gerald, and Patricia Gutek. *Experiencing America's Past: A Travel Guide to Museum Villages.* Columbia, S.C.: University of South Carolina Press, 1994.

Guthrie, Rev. Milton, Josephine King, and Brother Joel William McGraw, F.S.C. *Between the Rivers: The Catholic Heritage of West Tennessee.* Memphis: J. S. Sanders and Company, 1996.

Holmes, Robert. *Rhode Island, Boston and New England.* Lincolnwood, Ill.: Passport Books, 1994.

Hudson, Patricia. *The Smithsonian Guide to Historic America: Carolinas and the Appalachian States.* New York: Stewart, Tabori and Chang, 1989.

Jennison, Peter, and Christina Tree. *Vermont: An Explorer's Guide.* Woodstock, Vt.: Countryman Press, 1992.

Kazlow, Gertrude, and Pamela Nonken. *Milwaukee and More.* West Bloomfield, Mich.: A and M, 1993.

Koenig, Harry. *A History of the Parishes of the Archdiocese of Chicago.* Chicago: Archdiocese of Chicago, 1980.

Leeds, Mark. *Ethnic New York.* Lincolnwood, Ill.: Passport Books, 1991.

Lewis, Norma. "Father William H. Judge, Klondike Priest." *Catholic Heritage* (July/August 1997): 18.

Logan, William Bryant. *The Smithsonian Guide to Historic America: The Deep South.* New York: Stewart, Tabori and Chang, 1989.

Logan, William Bryant, and Susan Ochshorn. *The Smithsonian Guide to Historic America: The Pacific States.* New York: Stewart, Tabori and Chang, 1989.

Malone, Russ. *Hippocrene USA Guide to Irish America.* New York: Hippocrene Books, 1994.

Marshall, Alex. *Let's Travel: Pathways through Iowa.* St. Paul, Minn.: Clark and Miles, 1995.

Martin, Gay. *Louisiana Off the Beaten Path.* Old Saybrook, Conn.: Globe Pequot Press, 1990.

McCoy, Michael. *Montana Off the Beaten Path.* Old Saybrook, Conn.: Globe Pequot Press, 1993.

McGaw, Sister Martha Mary. "The Nun Who Spent $1,000 a Day." *Catholic Digest* (December 1980): 53.

McGowan, Cecilia. "The Faith of Flannery O'Connor." *Catholic Digest* (February 1983): 74.

McPhee, Mary. "Since Lilies of the Field." *Catholic Digest* (December 1974): 21.

Messinger, Jean, and Mary Jane Rust. *Faith in High Places: Historic Country Churches of Colorado.* Boulder, Colo.: R. Rinehart, 1995.

Moran, Anthony. *Pilgrim's Guide to America.* Huntington, Ind.: Our Sunday Visitor, 1992.

Muse, Vance. *The Smithsonian Guide to Historic America: Northern New England.* New York: Stewart, Tabori and Chang, 1989.

Noel, Tom. *Colorado Catholicism.* Denver: University Press of Colorado, 1989.

Oakley, Myrna. *Oregon Off the Beaten Path.* Old Saybrook, Conn.: Globe Pequot Press, 1994.

Picher, Don. *Washington Handbook.* Chico, Calif.: Moon Publications, 1997.

Rancilio, Charlotte. "America's Newest Saint." *Catholic Digest* (October 1988): 105.

Rogak, Lisa. *Vermont Off the Beaten Path.* Old Saybrook, Conn.: Globe Pequot Press, 1992.

Rummel, O. Praem., Rev. Leo. *History of the Catholic Church in Wisconsin.* Madison, Wis.: Wisconsin State Council of the Knights of Columbus, 1976.

Shelgran, Margaret. "Father Damien of Molokai." *Catholic Digest* (April 1987): 79.

Stamwitz, Alicia Von. "Philadelphia's Reluctant Bishop." *Catholic Digest* (May 1990): 68.

Stevens, Clifford. "Father Flanagan of Boys Town." *Catholic Digest* (July 1987): 49.

Strecker, Zoe. *Kentucky Off the Beaten Path.* Old Saybrook, Conn.: Globe Pequot Press, 1992.

Sullivan, Kay. *The Catholic Tourist Guide.* New York: Meredith Press, 1967.

Svensson, Robert. "The Pirate Who Built a Church." *Catholic Digest* (March 1979): 90.

Swain, Liz. "Las Vegas Church." *St. Anthony Messenger* (January 1996): 37.

Thomas, Phyllis. *Indiana Off the Beaten Path.* Old Saybrook, Conn.: Globe Pequot Press, 1992.

Thornton, Rev. Francis Beauchesne. *Catholic Shrines in the United States and Canada.* New York: Wilfred Funk, Inc., 1954.

Tree, Christina. *Massachusetts: An Explorer's Guide.* Taftsville, Vt.: Countryman Press, 1979.

U.S. Federal Writers' Project. *Florida: A Guide to the Southernmost State.* New York: Oxford University Press, 1939.

Vanderholt, Rev. James. *Lone Star Catholicism: A Measure of Faith.* Beaumont, Texas, 1997.

Vuilleumier, Marion Rawson. *America's Religious Treasures.* New York: Harper and Row, 1976.

Weber, Msgr. Francis J. "The California Mission Series." Gates, Kingsley and Gates Mortuary.

Weldon, Shawn. "Babe Ruth's Biggest Double." *Catholic Digest* (August 1994): 113.

Wiencek, Henry. *The Smithsonian Guide to Historic America: Southern New England.* New York: Stewart, Tabori and Chang, 1989.

———. *The Smithsonian Guide to Historic America: Virginia and the Capital Region.* New York: Stewart, Tabori and Chang, 1989.

Wilson, Ray D. *Missouri Historical Tour Guide.* Carpentersville, Ill.: Crossroads Communications, 1988.

———. *Nebraska Historical Tour Guide.* Carpentersville, Ill.: Crossroads Communications, 1988.

Winckler, Suzanne. *The Smithsonian Guide to Historic America: The Great Lakes States.* New York: Stewart, Tabori and Chang, 1989.

———. *The Smithsonian Guide to Historic America: The Plains States.* New York: Stewart, Tabori and Chang, 1990.

Wright Pressentin, Carol Von. *Blue Guide: New York.* New York: W. W. Norton and Company, 1991.

Wurman, Richard Saul. *Boston Access.* New York: Harper Perennial, 1991.

———. *Los Angeles Access.* New York: Access Press, 1996.

———. *New York City Access.* New York: Access Press, 1994.

INDEX OF PLACES

ABOUT THE AUTHOR

Jay Copp has worked as a reporter for *The New World,* the newspaper of the Archdiocese of Chicago. He currently writes for DePaul University. His articles have appeared in *U.S. Catholic, St. Anthony Messenger, Catholic Digest, America, Our Sunday Visitor, Columbia, Ohio*, and *Kiwanis,* and he is a longtime contributor to Catholic News Service. He has a master's degree from the Medill School of Journalism at Northwestern University. He lives in La Grange Park, Illinois, with his wife, Laura, and their two children, Kevin and Andrew.